Edited by Alexander Gorlin and Victoria Newhouse

Housing the Nation

Social Equity, Architecture, and the Future of Affordable Housing

RIZZOLI
NEW YORK

New York · Paris · London · Milan

Contents

Introduction

The need for affordable housing has never been more urgent. The United Nations Universal Declaration of Human Rights, written in 1948 by a commission chaired by Eleanor Roosevelt, states that housing is a human right. The role of a well-functioning society is to provide, at the very least, the basic human needs that allow each member of a community to thrive and live in a manner beneficial to all. But in many areas, predominantly urban areas, the cost of housing has become a barrier for low- and middle-income families, preventing them from accessing the same opportunities and resources as their more affluent peers. This situation creates a cycle of poverty and inequality that is difficult to break. Because the poverty rates of Blacks and Hispanics are at least twice those of non-Hispanic Whites,[1] housing affordability is not just an economic challenge, it is also a matter of social justice.

What is affordable housing? One common metric, defined by government agencies such as the New York City Housing Authority, is based simply on the percentage of income devoted to rent. To be affordable, housing cannot be more than 30 percent of household income. Another metric for measuring income in relation to housing is based on Area Median Income—the midpoint of income distribution in a particular area—as established by the US Department of Housing and Urban Development. How income relates to AMI determines which category the household fits into: extremely low income (0–30 percent of AMI), very low (31–50 percent), low (51–80 percent), moderate (81–120 percent), or middle (121–65 percent). Households in the very low AMI bracket have the greatest need for affordable housing. However, in many cases, a higher percentage of

1
John Creamer, "Inequalities Persist Despite Decline in Poverty for All Major Race and Hispanic Origin Groups," US Census Bureau, Sept. 15, 2020, https://www .census.gov/library /stories/2020/09 /poverty-rates -for-blacks-and -hispanics -reached-historic -lows-in-2019.html.

housing is set aside for income brackets above this level, which results in a paucity of housing for those most in need. AMI as a metric is often abused by cities and developers to make housing appear affordable, when in reality they are focusing on the higher income brackets.

As of December 2022, more than 40 percent of the US population was considered rent burdened, that is, spending more than 30 percent of income on rent.[2] Rents have doubled and tripled in cities such as Miami and Nashville, areas that until recently have been affordable places to live. Homelessness, the most dire result of the affordability crisis, has become more prevalent in many cities, such as Austin and Portland, Oregon. This disruption to the housing market gives rise to social dislocation, pain, and economic instability in people who cannot afford to live reasonably close to their jobs. Simply put, there is not enough affordable housing either existing, under construction, or planned for the future, and what is under construction is not built fast enough to make a dent in the enormous demand.

The insufficiency of affordable housing, combined with long-standing income inequality coinciding with race, means that this wealthy country, built on principles of equality and fundamental rights, has become unjust and dysfunctional. A nation that denies fair housing to its people, especially its people of color, is on the road to a breakdown. This calamitous state of affairs was our catalyst for creation of this book.

What distinguishes *Housing the Nation* from other volumes is its holistic, clear-sighted, pragmatic view of the affordable housing crisis in the United States. The collected essays analyze the complex root causes of the present situation; explore various perspectives on the issue; and propose potential solutions. The writers—expert economists, community organizers, housing advocates, land-use lawyers, government officials, architects, planners, thinkers, and academics—are actively engaged in the many aspects of building affordable housing.

We have divided the book into five sections. The first, "The Big Picture," takes a sweeping look at the current housing landscape: economic policy, income inequality, gentrification, and homelessness:

Economist **Dean Baker** argues that unprecedented levels of income inequality in the United States have exacerbated the problem of affordable housing. In recent decades, an increasingly disproportionate share of the country's wealth has gone to the top 10 percent and especially the top 1 percent of households. As the wealthy use more land, less land is left for others, and it becomes more expensive. In addition, the uses allowed on that limited supply of land are restricted by zoning, often racist in nature, and political opposition, among many other reasons.

Richard Florida, an urban studies theorist, discusses the economic success and urban revitalization that have benefited great cities like New York and San Francisco but that have also sent housing prices and gentrification sky-high, pricing out middle-class residents and service workers. While these problems were once limited to global metropoles, thanks to the COVID-19 pandemic, they now affect US metropolitan areas large and small.

Scholar and co-founder of progressive policy magazine the *American Prospect*, **Robert Kuttner** champions a true social housing sector sponsored by government, one that is removed from the vicissitudes of the real estate industry. He offers as examples Vienna, which has built well-designed affordable housing since the 1920s, resulting in

2
"More Than 19 Million Renters Burdened by Housing Costs," press release, US Census Bureau, Dec. 8, 2022, https://www.census.gov/newsroom/press-releases/2022/renters-burdened-by-housing-costs.html.

myriad benefits, including job creation; and the Netherlands, where approximately 75 percent of rental housing is subsidized by the state. In both cases, housing is permanently affordable and never enters the for-profit sector.

Community organizer **Michael Gecan** contends that citizens' groups are the key to jump-starting affordable housing. He recalls the critical role labor unions played in producing hundreds of thousands of starter co-ops in New York City as well as the success of the citizen organizers of East Brooklyn Congregations, who shepherded the building of 5,000 single-family ownership homes for the Nehemiah Plan despite the lack of involvement from traditional affordable housing advocates. Only an organized base of people can make improvement happen, he notes, because only local leaders and residents can provide the critical social knowledge essential to housing development.

Rosanne Haggerty, founder and director of two organizations that develop strategies to end homelessness, demonstrates that the complexities of providing affordable housing constitute what systems theorists call a system: a set of interconnected components. Without intention and accountability toward a common goal, systems will fail. She offers the Built for Zero movement (based on the Vision Zero initiative for improving road safety in Sweden) as a way to eliminate homelessness, severe housing cost-burden, unsafe living conditions, and discrimination.

The second group of essays, "Racial Injustice and Housing," uncovers the tawdry and immoral laws that have underpinned racist segregation of cities and suburbs for over a century:

J. Phillip Thompson, professor of planning and politics, paints a horrifying picture of the racial inequities suffered by African Americans since the early 20th century: exclusion from the economic reforms instituted in response to the Great Depression, omission from the benefits of the GI Bill, racism in the real estate industry, redlining in the financial system, and, more recently, climate change, job displacement incurred by automation, and racial demographic shifts.

Land-use lawyer and architect **Margery Perlmutter** considers neighborhood degradation due to private and public neglect, public policy, and inattentive urban planning, which results in dangerous, insalubrious slums without supporting services. Queensbridge Houses in Queens, New York, the largest public housing project in the country, was poorly served at the time of its construction—a site zoned for manufacturing, a bare-bones budget—and continues to be so. While nearby areas have been upzoned, fostering thriving mixed-use districts, Queensbridge is hemmed in by manufacturing and frustrated in any attempt to improve amenities.

David Dante Troutt, a professor of law, shows how Newark, New Jersey, his longtime professional home, has seen its poorest, Black wards invaded by large institutional investors who profit from low entry costs (often the result of foreclosure) and then impose high rates on stable renters. How to achieve economic autonomy and regulatory protection? How to do away with systemic disqualification and information deficits?

Professor **Justin Steil** explains how low-income populations and communities of color are especially vulnerable to the impact of climate disasters—hurricanes, floods, and wildfires. Federal disaster relief programs often help the well-to-do rather than those most affected by these calamities. Legal actions brought by fair-housing, racial-equity, and other advocacy groups have the potential to reduce inequality based on race and foster environmental justice.

"Points of View," the third section, presents case studies in affordable housing in New York and Los Angeles, two cities that have devoted enormous energy and funding to their housing crises:

Christopher Hawthorne, who has been involved with affordable housing from the outside, as the architecture critic for the *Los Angeles Times*, and inside, as the chief design officer for Los Angeles under Mayor Eric Garcetti, shares firsthand experience with the complexities of building publicly funded affordable housing in that city and other major cities. While some progress has been made—with, for instance, the construction of 10,000 accessory dwelling units in single-family neighborhoods—many initiatives are stalled or stopped by public opposition. Hawthorne maintains that architecture has a place in affordable housing and zoning reform but that the role of politics has proven more powerful.

Architect **David Burney**, former head of the Design Excellence program at the New York City Housing Authority, outlines the history of public housing in the United States as well as the current lack of any cogent federal policy on housing. NYCHA, established in 1934 during the Great Depression, is the largest housing authority in the country. In its early years, it benefited from Public Works Administration funding and public and governmental support for housing for returning veterans; more recently, it has been diminished by a "quiet war of attrition" on the part of the federal government. Turning NYCHA around will require capital investment in both building new units and sustaining/maintaining existing units.

For-profit real estate developer **Jon McMillan** offers a snapshot of set-asides—that is, including affordable housing in new, market-rate rental housing—in New York. The cost of construction in New York—the highest in the country—means that affordable housing cannot be built without subsidies or other funding mechanisms. His itemization of the costs and revenues associated with an affordable apartment goes a long way toward answering the question of why rents are high and affordable housing is limited.

Professors **Viren Brahmbhatt** and **Richard Plunz** highlight two landmark housing moments in New York City—the 1879 Tenement House Competition and the 2013 adAPT NYC Design Competition—to trace changing needs for, attitudes toward, and innovative strategies in affordable housing over more than a century. Micro-living, the subject of the second competition, is a useful model to meet the needs of the many single-individual households of the 21st century. At the same time, this typology demonstrates that city regulation of housing lags behind the demographics of those who seek housing today.

Kenneth Frampton, an architect far better known as a professor and historian of modern architecture, and **Mark Ginsberg**, a principal of his own architecture firm, offer an explanation and a long-overdue evaluation of Marcus Garvey Village, a low-rise, high-density development of 625 units in the Brownsville section of Brooklyn. Frampton, one of the team of original architects, recalls that the project was designed according to respected theories of the time, as offered by Jane Jacobs in *Death and Life of Great American Cities* and Oscar Newman in *Defensible Space: Crime Prevention through Urban Design*. When completed, the development was hailed as an innovative model for low-cost housing. Nevertheless, it became crime-ridden and dangerous. Renovation architect Ginsberg critiques the original design and describes various improvements that have rendered Marcus Garvey Village a more viable community.

The fourth series of essays, "In Search of Solutions," puts forward several initiatives aimed at solving aspects of the affordable housing crisis:

Architect, planner, and New Urbanism founder **Andrés Duany** and writer and project manager **Fernando Pagés Ruiz** offer work in manufactured residences (mobile homes rebranded) by DPZ CoDesign (formerly Duany Plater-Zyberk & Co.) as one way to provide affordable housing. DPZ CoDesign's Modern House uses design to counter the negative associations and poor quality of much manufactured housing. Other improvements include sensitive community planning and hybrid financing models.

Rural Studio, an undergraduate design/build program founded at Auburn University by Samuel Mockbee and D. K. Ruth, has created a legacy of more than 200 single-family houses and community-focused projects, all built with extensive client engagement. Auburn research manager **Jessica Holmes** and current Rural Studio associate director **Rusty Smith** describe the related Front Porch Initiative, which extends house designs along with institutional knowledge and proven product recommendations to a growing group of external housing providers across eight southeastern states.

Architects **Alan Organschi** and **Elizabeth Gray** and research director **Andrew Ruff** draw attention to the environmental externalities—consumption of raw material, energy use, degradation of the environment—that contribute to the true cost of any building project. A consideration of these factors offers a broader range of options in making homeownership or rental truly affordable. Mass timber is one cost-effective and sustainable alternative to traditional building materials. Cross-laminated timber, for instance, reduces the overall number of building materials, limiting construction and related costs; improves energy efficiency and air quality in the finished structure; and sequesters carbon permanently rather than releasing greenhouse gases into the atmosphere.

The fifth and final section of the book is a portfolio of well-designed affordable housing projects across the United States. Until recently, affordable housing was not known for high-quality design. Instead, housing developments were unattractive, cheaply built, and poorly maintained, often because funding for upkeep and repair was not a priority for state or local government. Many affordable housing projects were abandoned; some were demolished outright, including Pruitt-Igoe in St. Louis. This state of affairs is especially ironic considering that one of the main goals of early modern architecture was to create better places for people to live. Fortunately, there has been a resurgence of worthy design within restricted budgets as demonstrated in buildings by Alexander Gorlin Architects, Bernheimer Architecture, Body Lawson Associates, Brooks+Scarpa, DPZ CoDesign, Koning Eizenberg Architecture, Leddy Maytum Stacy Architects, Michael Hsu Office of Architecture, Michael Maltzan Architecture, Paulett Taggart Architects (in collaboration with Studio Vara on one project), Christine Pierron and Mark Weinke, Rural Studio, Studio Gang, and Studio Twenty Seven Architecture and Leo A. Daly.

As the housing crisis in the United States has grown ever more dire—over half a million people experience homelessness every night—the focus on solutions grows ever more intense. Among reasons for measured optimism are new legislation on zoning and land use; newly developed building materials and methods; new models for supportive programming; and new attitudes.

Several states, including Massachusetts, Utah, New York, and Florida, have passed or are in the process of passing zoning legislation that will allow multifamily housing;

efforts to sanction low-cost residential uses near transit corridors are also underway. Utah has made certain policy regulations—such as those for height and strip mall conversion—more amenable to construction of affordable homes. California has passed legislation that allows accessory dwelling units to be built on properties zoned for single-family residential use, which may result in nearly a million new, low-cost housing units. Also in California, state legislators require every community to plan for more housing.

One innovative construction process is 3-D printing, a computer-based method that can be used for exterior walls, interior walls, and fittings all at once, producing housing units more cheaply and more quickly than conventional construction. In some cases, the material is concrete; a plant-based, recyclable material has also been used.[3] Developers in Austin, Texas, and Rancho Mirage, California, have built housing with this method.

The building regulations that have limited the use of mass timber, generally put into effect for traditional wood construction, are being modified, albeit slowly. Some US jurisdictions have approved mass timber for buildings of up to eight stories; Europe permits even taller structures. As with most other materials and methods, increased use is likely to reduce cost.

Shipping containers, generally 20 or 40 feet long, have been retrofitted to provide inexpensive shelters. In Newark, New Jersey, Hope Village offers 24 units of housing in 7 shipping containers. A second Hope Village was under construction as of May 2023. A demonstration project in Phoenix, Arizona, consists of 5 solar-powered housing units.

LIFTbuild is a system of vertical construction that keeps ground space clear, permitting construction on unusually tight properties. Each component is fabricated on site and installed floor by floor in a kind of modular construction, making the building site safer and more efficient.[4] Under construction in March 2023 was the Exchange, a 16-story, 165-unit residential building in Detroit.

Houston has been unusually successful in dealing with the unhoused, implementing the kind of united effort that Rosanne Haggerty describes in her essay. Since 2011, the city has reduced homelessness by 63 percent thanks to teamwork led by Houston's Coalition for the Homeless. The organization brings together county and city officials, local service providers, corporations, and charitable nonprofits in a model that could serve other communities.

And we are learning from our mistakes. Modern developments completed in the 1970s—Marcus Garvey Village in Brooklyn, Lambert Houses in the Bronx, and Twin Parks in the Bronx—were recognized as models of low-cost residential construction. Yet flaws emerged quickly, and the projects became characterized by crime and disrepair. Rehabilitation efforts in the 2010s and 2020s have improved the prospects of Marcus Garvey and Lambert.

Combining various innovations—increasing the number of levers available to promote affordable housing—results in an array of original and unconventional approaches to the housing crisis. Land-use, tax, and financing restrictions can be overcome with increased density limits, allowance of multifamily homes in suburban downtowns, an end to warehousing of vacant land, greater availability of mixed-use development, and easing of restrictions on the conversion of office buildings to residential.

Ultimately, the goal of *Housing the Nation* is to provide a comprehensive and accessible guide to affordable housing, equipping policymakers, community leaders, developers, and local residents with the knowledge and tools they need to address this

3
Debra Kamin, "The Potential of Printed Housing," *New York Times*, Sept. 29, 2021, B5.

4
Shane Reiner-Roth, "Not Skipping Leg Day," *Architect's Newspaper*, Mar./ Apr. 2023, 19.

critical problem. By exploring the causes of housing unaffordability, examining the barriers that prevent low- and middle-income families from attaining affordable housing, and highlighting potential solutions and innovations, this book will serve as an important resource.

It is essential to note that the political obstacles to funding and building affordable housing, often rooted in systemic racism, cannot be overcome by materials and methods alone. Confronting bigotry and self-interest is an ongoing challenge in innumerable areas of activity, not just affordable housing. But confronted they must be, for all deserve to live in a secure place of dignity that they are proud to call home. **— AG and VN**

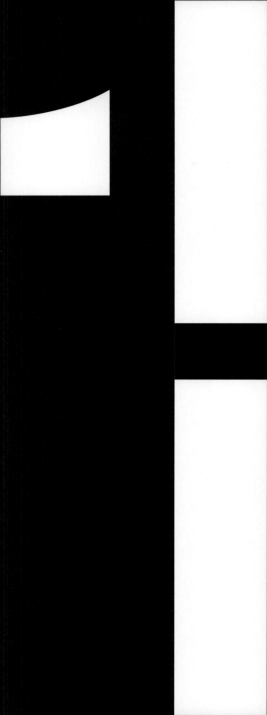

The Big Picture

Income Inequality and Affordable Housing

Dean Baker

is senior economist and co-founder of the Center for Economic and Policy Research in Washington, DC. His most recent book is *Rigged: How Globalization and the Rules of the Modern Economy Were Structured to Make the Rich Richer*.

The decades of the 1980s through the 2010s have seen a sharp increase in income inequality. In the quarter century following World War II, the United States experienced extraordinarily fast productivity growth, which was relatively evenly shared among workers and businesses. Profits rose roughly in step with the economy, as did wages, for workers at both the bottom and the top.

The path taken by the economy changed in the 1980s. The growth in productivity was slower than in the boom years following World War II and also diverged from the growth in wages for typical workers. The gains that *were* realized went disproportionately to the population in the top 10 percent of the income distribution, and especially to the top 1 percent. Other factors that have been responsible for the rise in inequality over this period are anti-inflationary macroeconomic policy; selective free trade; the decline of unions; the weakening of labor market regulations that protect workers; the strengthening of patent and copyright monopolies; the growth in the size of the financial sector; and the corruption of the corporate governance structure.

The rise in inequality matters more for housing than for items like cars and clothes. The supply of land is inherently limited; in the short term, the supply of housing is limited as well. More housing available to those at the top means less for everyone else. The problem is compounded by how the winners in the upward redistribution since the 1980s have chosen to use their political power: they have acted to limit the construction of housing in order to protect aesthetic features of their neighborhoods and exclude more moderate-income people.

The Basics of Upward Redistribution

The period since the end of World War II can be divided into two parts. In the first period, roughly the quarter century from the end of the war until 1973, the economy grew rapidly and the benefits of growth were broadly shared. Productivity—the amount of goods and services produced in an hour of work—increased at an annual rate of 2.5 percent. Wages increased at roughly the same pace. Both individuals and companies were doing well: workers saw substantial improvements in living standards over time, and corporate profits grew in step with the economy.

After 1973, the story changed. The rate of productivity growth slowed sharply to roughly 1 percent annually. Economists have not reached consensus on the reason for the slowdown. Surges in the price of oil and other commodities in the 1970s were clearly a factor, though the slower pace of productivity growth has continued to the present. The exception was the period between 1995 and 2005, when productivity growth accelerated to roughly its pre-1973 pace before slowing once again.

The slower productivity growth was accompanied by a sharply upward redistribution of income. The top 10 percent of households had income growth that far outpaced the overall average, with the top 5 percent doing even better, and the top 1 percent doing better still (fig. 1). Given the pronounced decrease in productivity growth, this upward redistribution meant that households in the middle and bottom of the income distribution saw only small gains in income, and over long periods saw income that did not even keep pace with inflation.

1. Income Shares

Source
Thomas Piketty and Emmanuel Saez, *Income Inequality in the United States, 1913–1998, Quarterly Journal of Economics* 118, no. 1 (Feb. 2003); updated tables, Emmanuel Saez website, UC Berkeley, https:// eml.berkeley .edu/~saez /TabFig2017.xls.

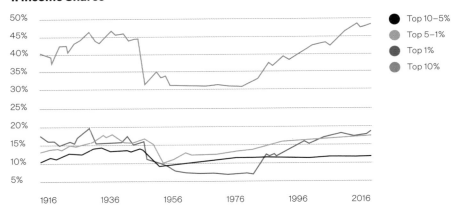

Once wage is adjusted according to changes in prices over this period, the median worker (the person in the middle of the wage distribution, i.e., half of all workers earn more and half earn less) actually lost ground (fig. 2). Although there were periods of sustained real wage growth—most notably in the late 1990s and the years just before the pandemic hit—they have been the exception since 1980.

Since most people get most of their income from working, the story of wages is roughly equivalent to the story of income. The years since 1980 have been characterized by both slow growth and upward redistribution, meaning that those at the middle and bottom have benefited little from the economy over this period.

2. Median Wage and Productivity Growth

Source
Bureau of Labor Statistics, Economic Policy Institute, and author's calculations.

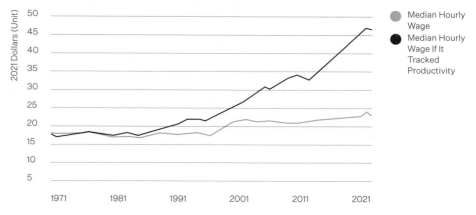

Legend:
- Median Hourly Wage
- Median Hourly Wage If It Tracked Productivity

The Causes of Upward Redistribution

The factors responsible for the upward redistribution of the last four decades fed on each other in many ways. For example, it is more difficult for workers to organize and sustain a union in a period of high unemployment, since the threat of firing the organizers has far greater consequences. So high unemployment and lower rates of unionization are to some extent part of the same narrative.

High unemployment was probably the single most important factor in the upward redistribution over this period. The unemployment rate averaged 5.1 percent between 1947 and 1979 and 6.2 percent between 1980 and 2019 (before the pandemic).[1] The main culprit here is the Federal Reserve Board. The Fed has a dual mandate: to support policies that promote price stability—that is, policies that promote low inflation—and to advance high levels of employment.

In the decades immediately after World War II, the Fed took its commitment to high levels of employment seriously, trying to keep the unemployment rate as low as possible. But in the years since 1980, the central bank quite explicitly made low inflation its primary, if not its only, goal. At the start of the 1980s, then Fed chair Paul Volcker decided that he would push the unemployment rate as high as necessary to bring inflation down from the double-digit rate reached in the 1970s. His actions toward this end led to the worst recession since the Great Depression, with the unemployment rate peaking at 10.8 percent in 1982.

The unemployment rate did come down as the economy recovered post-1982, but it never fell back to the levels of the 1950s and 1960s. Volcker's successors, most notably Alan Greenspan, continued Volcker's focus on low inflation. Only the current Fed chair, Jerome Powell, has reaffirmed the Fed's commitment to high employment. As a result of the Fed's disproportionate concern with inflation, the unemployment rate has been considerably higher since 1980 than it was before 1980.

The difference in unemployment rates matters to those without jobs, but it also affects the ability of tens of millions of workers to secure wage gains. In periods of low unemployment, workers at the middle and bottom of the pay ladder have the bargaining power they need to secure real wage gains—even in low-paying sectors like restaurants and retail. In periods of high unemployment, generally only more highly educated workers are in a position to get pay increases.[2]

1
Data from the Current Population Survey, Bureau of Labor Statistics.

2
See Dean Baker and Jared Bernstein, *Getting Back to Full Employment: A Better Bargain for Working People* (Washington, DC: Center for Economic and Policy Research, 2013).

3
A discussion of the shrinking manufacturing wage premium can be found in Dean Baker, "Is Intellectual Property the Root of All Evil?," in *The Great Polarization: How Ideas, Power and Policy Drive Inequality*, ed. Rudiger L. von Arnim and Joseph E. Stiglitz (New York: Columbia University Press, 2022). See also Baker, "A Cold War with China, Global Warming, and Why We Can't Have Nice Things," Center for Economic and Policy Research, June 23, 2022, https://www.cepr.net/a-cold-war-with-china-global-warming-and-why-we-cant-have-nice-things/.

4
Larry Mishel, *The Enormous Impact of Eroded Collective Bargaining on Wages* (Washington, DC: Economic Policy Institute, 2021).

It is evident that the Fed's decision to focus on fighting inflation had huge consequences for less-educated workers and those who are disadvantaged in the labor market more generally. The unemployment rate for Blacks is typically twice the unemployment rate for Whites, while for Hispanics, the unemployment rate is typically one and a half times as high as for Whites. These and other disadvantaged groups paid the biggest price, in terms of both employment and wages, for the Fed's anti-inflation policy.

It is common to claim that the United States has sought to promote free trade over the last four decades. In fact, most of our trade deals are actually called "free trade" agreements. But this term is misleading. Removing barriers to trade in manufactured goods has been a major focus of trade policy since the 1980s. **Selective free trade**—deals that eliminate tariffs, quotas, and other trade barriers—has made it easier to import clothes, cars, and a wide range of other manufactured goods.

Fewer trade barriers have also made it less stringent for companies to take advantage of lower-cost labor by moving manufacturing operations to developing countries like China and Mexico. The lower costs in these countries have lowered the prices of manufactured goods in the United States. However, transferring manufacturing operations offshore also led to massive job loss, with the number of manufacturing jobs in the United States plummeting as the trade deficit soared.

The loss of millions of manufacturing jobs put downward pressure on the pay of the workers who retained their jobs. Pre-1980, manufacturing was a relatively high-paying industry, offering a substantial wage premium, especially for workers without college degrees. In this way, manufacturing wages helped to raise the pay of non-college-educated workers more generally. But by 2021, the wage premium in manufacturing had largely disappeared.[3]

It is important to realize that the loss of jobs and the decrease in wages for less-educated workers were not inevitable results of globalization. While exposing manufacturing workers to competition with low-paid workers in developing countries had the predictable result of lowering the pay in the United States, there was no effort to expose the most highly paid workers here, like doctors and dentists, to the same sort of competition.

Additionally, trade agreements that made it easier for foreign professionals to train to US standards and then practice in the United States could have been implemented, but the administration of both parties chose not to go this route. In fact, in many cases, increased regulations protected US professionals from competition. For example, the number of foreign-educated doctors accepted into US residency programs was reduced. As a result of protectionist barriers, the most highly educated professionals in the United States earn far more than their counterparts in other wealthy countries.

The policy of selective free trade exposes only less wealthy and less politically powerful workers to foreign competition. The result of selective free trade—predicted and actual—has been greater inequality in the labor market.

In 1980, more than 20 percent of the private sector workforce was unionized. By 2021, unionization in the private sector was just over 6 percent.[4] This **decline in the unionization rate** was largely intentional. The Reagan administration substantially weakened the National Labor Relations Board, the main government agency responsible for protecting workers' rights to organize.

Reductions in the NLRB's budget under Reagan led to a severe staffing shortage, which in turn generated long delays in hearing complaints of violations against the

National Labor Relations Act. These delays often made filing a complaint pointless. If workers trying to organize a union get fired—a clear violation of the law—but it takes more than two years for their case to be heard, the issue will likely be largely moot. The penalty for an employer in this case is some back pay and the requirement that workers be offered their jobs back. However, if a decision is reached two years after the complaint, the organizing drive will likely have been killed.

In addition to delays, the members appointed to the NLRB by Reagan and subsequent Republican presidents were far more hostile to unions than had been the case with board members appointed by prior Republican presidents. NLRB members appointed by Eisenhower or Nixon did not vote very differently from members appointed by Democratic presidents.

With little to fear from the NLRB, employers became far more aggressive in trying to block union drives. They also acted more aggressively against unions that already existed. It became standard practice to threaten to fire and replace striking workers. While this practice was always legal, companies rarely exercised it until March 1981, when Reagan fired striking air traffic controllers.

Because of the increased difficulty in organizing unions, and the more aggressive policies of employers toward the unions that do exist, organized labor is today a far less important factor in the economy than it was in the quarter century after World War II. As a result, tens of millions of workers are less able to secure their share of the benefits of economic growth.

Another factor that has diminished the bargaining power of ordinary workers and in turn upward distribution is the **weakening of labor market regulations** designed to protect workers. The most obvious example, though there are numerous others, is the minimum wage. Between 1938, when the national minimum wage was created, and 1968, it largely kept pace with productivity growth. This parallel progression meant that as the country grew richer, even the lowest-paid workers shared in the gains and saw their living standards rise.

After 1968, this set of circumstances was no longer true. The minimum wage not only did not keep pace with productivity, it did not even keep pace with inflation. A worker earning the current national minimum wage of $7.25 an hour would be able to buy substantially less with their paycheck than a minimum wage worker in 1968. If the minimum wage had continued to keep pace with productivity growth, it would currently be over $23 an hour.[5]

Other labor market regulations were weakened along with the minimum wage. The Fair Labor Standards Act, which created the national minimum wage in 1938, also required that employees who work more than 40 hours a week receive an overtime premium equal to 150 percent of their normal wage. But employers have been able to circumvent this law by paying workers weekly rather than hourly.

A further effort to avoid employer obligations altogether is to have workers classified as independent contractors rather than employees. The most visible examples are the ride-sharing services Uber and Lyft, but the practice is common in other sectors. If a worker is classified as an independent contractor, the employer is not bound by minimum wage or overtime rules, nor does the employer have to pay unemployment insurance or workers' compensation for workers who are injured on the job.

Since the 1980s, the federal government has enacted **stronger rules on patents, copyrights, and other forms of intellectual property**. As a result, the companies and

5
See Dean Baker, "The $23 an Hour Minimum Wage," Center for Economic and Policy Research, Aug. 19, 2021, https://cepr.net /the-26-an-hour -minimum-wage/.

workers who are in a position to benefit from these protections have seen their income rise at the expense of everyone else's.

These circumstances can be seen most clearly in the case of prescription drugs. Before 1980, the United States had been spending roughly 0.4 percent of GDP on prescription drugs, with no clear upward trend. After 1980, spending on prescription drugs skyrocketed. It now stands at more than $500 billion annually, more than 2.2 percent of GDP.[6]

6
See Baker, "Is Intellectual Property."

The biggest factor in this increase in spending was the strengthening of prescription drug patents and related protections, most notably the 1980 Bayh-Dole Act. The bipartisan bill allowed drug companies to secure patents on research that was largely funded by the government. Subsequent legislation and court rulings further empowered patent holders.

The increased spending on prescription drugs is money out of the pockets of ordinary workers. Patents and related protections add more than $400 billion to the annual prescription drug bill in the United States. The effect of these higher drug prices is comparable to a tax of the same amount. Once other sectors where intellectual property accounts for a large share of the price of the product—medical equipment, computers, and software, for instance—are added, spending can easily rise to more than $1 trillion annually. Again, this money is drawn from the wallets of ordinary workers and paid to the small segment of the population that gains from government-granted monopolies.

The years since 1980 have seen an **explosion in the size of the financial sector** relative to the size of the economy as a whole. The financial sector plays an essential role in a capitalist economy: it allocates capital to firms that want to invest and to individuals who need to borrow to pay for a home, an education, or a business start-up. However, finance is an intermediate good (like trucking, for instance). It does not directly provide anything of value to consumers, as health care and housing do.

For this reason, an efficient financial sector is a small financial sector. Just as the trucking industry should be as small as possible—just large enough to move goods to where they are needed—the financial sector should be able to meet the economy's needs using as few resources as possible. The expansion of the financial sector has decreased its efficiency. To take the most extreme example, the narrow financial sector involving securities and commodities trading and investment banking expanded from 0.4 percent of GDP in the mid-1970s to over 2 percent of GDP in the current economy.[7]

7
Data from the Bureau of Economic Analysis, National Income and Product Accounts, Tables 6.2B and 6.2D.

As is the case with prescription drugs, the additional money going into the financial sector comes out of the pockets of everyone else. This may be directly, in the form of costs to administer a retirement account or fees to banks and other financial institutions, or indirectly, through higher costs that businesses are forced to bear because of the bloated financial sector.

And the financial sector makes some people very rich. Many of the richest people in the country get their income as hedge fund or private equity partners.

The ratio of the pay of top corporate executives to the pay of ordinary workers has escalated dramatically since the 1970s, a result of the **corrupt corporate governance structure**. In the 1960s, the pay of CEOs averaged a bit more than 20 times the pay of ordinary workers. This ratio rose to more than 200 to 1 by the end of the 1990s and has continued to edge higher since 2000.

If CEOs actually added this much value to the companies they run, there would be an argument for CEO salaries of $20 to $30 million a year, or even more. However, there is considerable evidence that CEOs do *not* add value of that magnitude. For example, a comparison between returns to shareholders and CEO pay between 2006 and 2015 shows that higher CEO pay is actually associated with lower returns to shareholders.[8]

Note that the issue here is not a moral one, despite arguments that people should not get such exorbitant salaries. The issue is purely an economic one: the CEOs do not earn their paychecks. If this is indeed the case, why do companies pay CEOs more than they are worth?

The answer to this question lies in the structure of corporate governance. CEO pay is most directly determined by a company's board of directors. While corporate boards ostensibly represent shareholders, they tend in fact to owe their allegiance primarily to CEOs and other executives.

Top management usually plays a large role in selecting board members. Once selected, directors are on the board to stay. The reelection rate for directors nominated by their fellow board members is over 99 percent. The best way to ensure reelection, then, and to keep a lucrative part-time job, is to stay on good terms with the rest of the board. These particulars discourage questions like "Can we pay our CEO less?" or "Can we get someone as good for half the salary?" Interestingly, a recent survey of corporate directors found that the vast majority did not see restraining the pay of top management as one of their job responsibilities.[9]

Like the explosion in the financial sector, CEO pay is important not only in regard to the relatively small number of very highly paid CEOs but in regard to its impact on pay structures in the economy more generally. If the CEO is paid $20 million, then the CFO may be salaried at $10 to $12 million; even third-tier executives may have salaries in the $2 to $3 million range.

In addition, high salaries for top executives in the corporate world push up executive pay at universities, foundations, and other nonprofit organizations. It is common for presidents of major universities to be paid more than $1 million a year, and sometimes more than $2 million. And once again, more pay going to the top means less pay for everyone else. The excessive salaries of CEOs, and top management more generally, create more demand on the resources of the economy, limiting its ability to meet the needs of ordinary workers.

Income Inequality and Housing

While the rise in inequality since the 1980s has had consequences in just about every area of economic and social life, its impact on the availability of housing for those with low and moderate incomes is especially notable. There are few limits on producing most of the items that people consume. An increase in demand for clothes or cars means that manufacturing will produce more clothes and cars.

Housing, however, is subject to significant limits, at least in the short term. Major cities like New York, Los Angeles, and San Francisco have a limited amount of land available for construction. If wealthy people take up more of this land because they are building bigger houses, or second residences, or they want to join or establish country clubs in metropolitan areas, then less land, and more expensive land, is left for everyone else. In effect, the upward redistribution of the last four decades has priced millions of low- and moderate-income people out of housing in many desirable cities.

The impact of limited land resources is magnified when the winners in this upward redistribution themselves act to restrict the supply of housing. Restraints can take the

8
See Ric Marshall and Linda-Eling Lee, *Are CEOs Paid for Performance? Evaluating the Effectiveness of Equity Incentives* (New York: MSCI, 2016).

9
Steven Boivie et al., "Corporate Directors' Implicit Theories of the Roles and Duties of Boards," *Strategic Management Journal* 42, no. 9 (Sept. 2021), https://onlinelibrary.wiley.com/doi/10.1002/smj.3320.

form of zoning restrictions that severely limit the construction of multifamily units or political opposition that restricts the use of public funds to support the construction of more housing for low- and moderate-income families.

Thus it is unquestionable that the upward redistribution of income over the last four decades is directly related to the shortage of affordable housing. Changing zoning laws and securing more government funding for affordable housing will help to ease the shortage, but the struggle will be an uphill one if most of the gains from economic growth continue to go to those at the top.

America's Expanding Housing Crisis

Richard Florida
is an urbanist and university professor at the University of Toronto's Rotman School of Management and distinguished scholar-in-residence at the university's School of Cities. Florida is the author of several books including *The Rise of the Creative Class* and *The New Urban Crisis*.

Not so long ago, America's housing crisis was limited by and large to expensive superstar cities like New York and leading tech hubs like the San Francisco Bay Area, Boston, and Seattle. One effect of the COVID-19 pandemic was to spread that crisis clear across the country. For years, Steve Case, the entrepreneur and venture capitalist who founded AOL, has argued that the United States would benefit if highly innovative technology companies and start-ups shifted their locations from the East and West Coasts to the neglected heartlands—what he calls the "rise of the rest."[1] But thanks in part to the explosion of remote work, the nation has witnessed the "rise of the *rents*" instead. Cities and metropolitan areas from Austin, Nashville, and Miami to Bozeman and Boise have seen their housing prices rocket to unprecedented heights.

In my 2017 book, *The New Urban Crisis*, I argued that the old urban crisis—which took place in the 1960s and 1970s—was a consequence of a loss of urban economic function, due in large part to a combination of deindustrialization and White flight.[2] As manufacturing facilities were transferred from northern and midwestern industrial cities to greenfield locations in the Sunbelt or offshored to other countries, urban unemployment skyrocketed, housing decayed, crime and violence increased, and social problems multiplied and spiraled out of control. The new urban crisis, in contrast, is a product of economic success and urban revitalization. As knowledge-based industries and more educated and affluent workers returned to great cities like New York and San Francisco, housing prices surged, gentrification went into high gear, and middle-class residents and service workers were priced out.

1
Rise of the Rest, *Beyond Silicon Valley: Coastal Dollars and Local Investors Accelerate Early-Stage Startup Funding Across the US*, report, 2002, https://revolution.com/beyond-silicon-valley-report/assets/files/Beyond-Silicon-Valley.pdf.

2
Richard Florida, *The New Urban Crisis* (New York: Basic Books, 2017).

3
Ruth Glass, *London: Aspects of Change* (London: MacGibbon and Kee, 1964).

Generally speaking, gentrification describes the transformation of a neighborhood when higher-income people move in. The term was coined in the early 1960s by Ruth Glass, who used it to describe the transformation of working-class London neighborhoods by an affluent urban gentry. "Once this process of 'gentrification' starts in a district," she wrote, "it goes on rapidly until all or most of the working-class residents are displaced and the whole social character of the district is changed."[3]

In the early days of the urban revival—the late 1970s through the 1990s—gentrification in its classic sense was confined to large global cities such as London, New York, Paris, Boston, Berlin, Washington, DC, and San Francisco. But as urban revitalization accelerated, housing prices in the hottest metros began to outstrip the earning capacities of all but highly paid knowledge workers and, in the most desirable urban districts, all but the very rich. New York, London, and Paris fell victim not just to gentrification but to full-on "plutocratization" as real estate became a new asset class for the global 1 percent. When *The New Urban Crisis* was published in 2017, the three top large US metros on my New Urban Crisis Index—a composite measure of housing unaffordability, economic inequality, and economic segregation—were Los Angeles, New York, and San Francisco.

Then came the COVID-19 pandemic, which spread the new urban crisis and the housing affordability crisis that is its most salient symptom to a whole new set of cities, suburbs, and even rural areas. COVID-19 was not so much a disruption or fundamental break with the past as it was an accelerator of a number of trends already underway. Part of the reason for this was the flexibility of remote work, which allows workers, especially workers with families, to consider a wider range of housing options. Unfettered from the need to be close to their offices and emboldened by unprecedentedly low mortgage rates, members of the creative class began moving to suburbs, smaller Sunbelt metros, satellite cities, and high-amenity rural areas in a quest for affordability and outdoor space.

A new phase—pandemic gentrification—set in as housing prices surged by 50, 60, and even 70-plus percent in once affordable Sunbelt metros and rural Zoom Towns.[4] Between 1992 and the end of 2021, the median sale price of US homes more than tripled, from just under $150,000 to over $500,000 (fig. 1). Within that period were two very sharp spikes in housing prices: the first during the run-up to the 2008 economic and

1. US Housing Prices, 1992—2021

Source
US Census Bureau and US Department of Housing and Urban Development, Median Sales Price of Houses Sold for the United States, FRED, Federal Reserve Bank of St. Louis, accessed June 27, 2022, https://fred.stlouisfed.org/series/MSPUS.

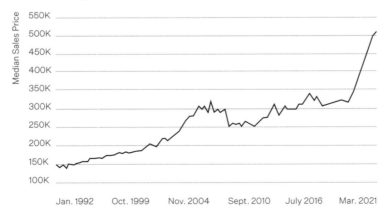

4
Randall Roberts, "Inside the Battle for Control of a Legendary Music Club—And the Soul of a High Desert Town," *Los Angeles Times*, July 21, 2022, https://www .latimes.com /entertainment -arts/music/story /2022-07-21 /pappy-harriets -pioneertown -lawsuit-owners -desert.

financial crisis and the bigger second one after the onset of the pandemic. Since 2020, housing prices have risen by nearly a third (32.4 percent) across the United States as a whole.[5]

But the increase in housing prices has not been evenly distributed. The biggest surges were in "rise of the rest" metros, especially in the Sunbelt (fig. 2). Cape Coral, Florida, experienced the largest percentage increase in median housing prices (72.0 percent) between May 2020 and May 2022. Five additional metros saw 60-plus percent increases: Austin, Texas (68.5%); Boise, Idaho (66.7%); North Port, Florida (66.7%); Provo, Utah (65.7%); and Phoenix, Arizona (62.1%). Lakeland, Florida; Ogden and Salt Lake City, Utah; and Dallas, Texas, which have all seen their housing prices rise by more than 50 percent, round out the top ten. Florida and Utah each have three of the top ten metros for housing inflation; Texas has two. While Miami failed to make the top ten in terms of percentage increases in housing prices, it surged past Los Angeles as the second-least-affordable housing market in the country, thanks to its lower income level. With a median asking price of $589,000 as of February 2022 and a typical median income of just $43,401, the average Miami family would have to spend roughly 80 percent of its income to cover housing costs.[6]

2. Ten Metros with the Largest Percentage Increase in Housing Prices

Source
Dana Anderson, "More Than 40% of Home Sellers Are Dropping Their Prices in Salt Lake City, Boise, Sacramento and Other Pandemic Hot Spots," Redfin, June 21, 2022, https://www.redfin .com/news/price -drops-increase -may-2022/.

Metro	Percent Increase in Median Housing Price, May 2020–May 2022	Median Sale Price, May 2022
Cape Coral, FL	72.0%	$420,000
Austin, TX	68.5%	$556,000
Boise, ID	66.7%	$549,990
North Port, FL	66.7%	$475,000
Provo, UT	65.7%	$550,000
Phoenix, AZ	62.1%	$486,000
Lakeland, FL	57.3%	$334,950
Ogden, UT	57.2%	$500,000
Salt Lake City, UT	56.2%	$556,000
Dallas, TX	55.7%	$467,000

The picture is a little different in the ten metros that saw the biggest absolute change in housing prices between December 2020 and December 2021 (fig. 3). While the "rise of the rest" metros saw the largest percentage increases, leading tech hubs and coastal centers, particularly in California, have seen the largest dollar increases. Housing prices increased by more than $200,000 in San Jose and San Francisco, four times the national average increase. San Diego saw an increase of more than $160,000, more than three times the national average. The rest saw increases in excess of $105,000, at least double the national average.

The rapid rise in housing values is captured in a startling statistic. Over the course of the pandemic, the average home price in America rose by more than the average worker earns. Between December 2020 and December 2021, the nation's median income was $50,000. During that same period, national home values grew by an average of $52,667. That amount is more than the 2021 median annual wage in 25 out of the 38 major

5
Zillow, "Two Years In: Housing Market Transformed by Prices, Lack of Inventory," press release, Mar. 17, 2022, https:// zillow.mediaroom .com/2022-03 -17-Two-years-in -Housing-market -transformed-by -prices,-lack-of -inventory.

3. Ten Metros with the Largest Absolute Increase in Housing Prices

Source
Zillow,
"Skyrocketing
Home Values Out-
Earn Salaries," Mar.
18, 2022, https://
www.zillow
.com/research
/home-value
-appreciation
-incomes-30862/.

Metro	Absolute Growth in Housing Price, December 2020–December 2021
San Jose–Sunnyvale–Santa Clara, CA	$229,277
San Francisco–Oakland–Hayward, CA	$204,914
San Diego–Carlsbad, CA	$160,493
Urban Honolulu, HI	$138,254
Los Angeles–Long Beach–Anaheim, CA	$131,979
Seattle–Tacoma–Bellevue, WA	$131,129
Boise City, ID	$124,979
Salt Lake City, UT	$119,539
Riverside–San Bernardino–Ontario, CA	$111,014
Denver–Aurora-Lakewood, CO	$108,922
US Average	$52,667

6
RealtyHop,
"RealtyHop
Housing
Affordability Index:
February 2022,"
Mar. 4, 2022,
https://www
.realtyhop
.com/blog
/housing
-affordability
-index-february
-2022/.

7
Zillow,
"Skyrocketing
Home Values."

metros. In 11 metros, home price increases surpassed $100,000,[7] and in two metros, San Jose and San Francisco, the increase was more than $200,000.

It is not just home prices that surged. Homeownership is by definition concentrated among more affluent and advantaged Americans. Less advantaged and younger Americans are much likelier to rent, and rents have surged as much as or more than the cost of owning a home (fig. 4). Between May 2021 and May 2022, rents rose by more than 15 percent across the United States, averaging more than $2,000 per month.[8]

Like home prices, rents rose at much steeper rates in many of the "rise of the rest" cities and metro areas (fig. 5). Between May 2021 an May 2022, Miami saw a 45 percent increase in rents, the largest in the nation. Orlando, Providence, San Diego, Tampa, Austin, Boston, Nashville, Las Vegas, and San Jose all experienced rent increases of 20 percent or more.

The great irony of our new age of knowledge-based capitalism and remote work is that many observers believe that we have at last overcome the constraints of land

4. Rise in Rents, 1983–2021

Source
US Bureau of
Labor Statistics,
Consumer Price
Index for All Urban
Consumers:
Rent of Primary
Residence in
US City Average,
FRED, Federal
Reserve Bank of St.
Louis, accessed
June 27, 2022,
https://fred
.stlouisfed
.org/series
/CUUR0000SEHA.

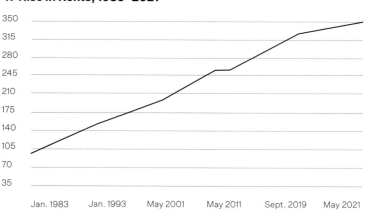

Note
Index 1982–
1984=100,
monthly, not
seasonally
adjusted.

8
Tim Ellis, "Rental Market Tracker: Typical U.S. Asking Rent Surpassed $2,000 for First Time in May," Redfin, June 9, 2022, https://www .redfin.com/news /redfin-rental -report-may-2022/.

and geography. But that is not at all the case. As our economy grows more innovative, land has become even more expensive. In *The New Urban Crisis*, I dubbed this "the land nexus"—a consequence of the cramming of talent and economic activity into smaller and smaller slivers of space. As the advantaged and the affluent stake their claims to the best urban locations, everyone else is pressed into less desirable neighborhoods or pushed out into the suburbs and exurbs. By spurring the dispersal of the advantaged and affluent to smaller cities, suburbs, and rural areas, the pandemic made land and housing more expensive across the board.

5. Ten Metros for Largest Rise in Rents, May 2021–May 2022

Source
Joel Berner and Danielle Hale, "May Rental Report: Rent Continues to Surge Nationwide, but Growth Starts to Slow," Realtor. com, June 22, 2022, https://www .realtor.com /research/may -2022-rent/.

Metro	Percent Increase, May 2021–May 2022	Median Sale Price, May 2022
Miami–Fort Lauderdale–West Palm Beach, FL	72.0%	$420,000
Orlando–Kissimmee–Sanford, FL	68.5%	$556,000
Providence–Warwick, RI–MA	66.7%	$549,990
San Diego–Carlsbad, CA	66.7%	$475,000
Tampa–St. Petersburg–Clearwater, FL	65.7%	$550,000
Austin–Round Rock, TX	62.1%	$486,000
Boston–Cambridge–Newton, MA–NH	57.3%	$334,950
Ogden, UT	57.2%	$500,000
Nashville–Davidson–Murfreesboro–Franklin, TN	56.2%	$556,000
San Jose–Sunnyvale–Santa Clara, CA	55.7%	$467,000

9
McKinsey Global Institute, "The Rise and Rise of the Global Balance Sheet: How Productively Are We Using Our Wealth?" Nov. 15, 2022, https://www .mckinsey.com /industries /financial-services /our-insights /the-rise-and -rise-of-the-global -balance-sheet -how-productively -are-we-using-our -wealth.

A few basic data points help drive this point home. A 2021 study found that real estate comprises as much as two-thirds of the assets of ten advanced countries (United States, United Kingdom, China, Germany, Japan, France, Canada, Sweden, Australia, and Mexico), and more than half of that value is land.[9] Other studies place the value of land in the United States at $30 trillion, roughly double the country's level of annual economic output, or GDP.[10]

Real estate and housing are so central an asset class that they account for most of the gains to capital that Thomas Piketty famously documented in *Capital in the Twenty-First Century*.[11] In an important study, the economist Matthew Rognlie found that rising real estate values, captured mainly by the richest 1 percent, have been the core contributor to rising inequality across the world.[12]

The theorist who best explained this growing crisis of housing affordability was a 19th-century American named Henry George. A contemporary of Karl Marx, George was a political economist and activist who ran for mayor of New York City in 1886. *Progress and Poverty*, his most influential book, was written in 1879 and sold millions of copies. While Marx famously divided the modern world into two great classes, capitalists and workers, George identified a third economic class, real estate owners or landlords. In Marx's view, it was capitalists who made off with the surplus value generated by labor. According to George, it was real estate owners who made off with the surplus generated by *both* capital and labor. As he wrote, "The progress of invention constantly tends to give a larger proportion of the produce to the owners of land, and a smaller and smaller proportion to labor and capital."[13]

10
David Albouy, Gabriel Ehrlich, and Minchul Shin, "Metropolitan Land Values," *Review of Economics and Statistics* 100,

no. 3 (2018):
454–66, https://
doi.org/10.1162
/rest_a_00710.

11
Thomas Piketty,
*Capital in
the Twenty-
First Century*,
trans. Arthur
Goldhammer
(Cambridge, MA:
Harvard University
Press, 2014).

12
Matthew Rognlie,
"Deciphering the
Fall and Rise in the
Net Capital Share:
Accumulation
or Scarcity?,"
Brookings Papers
on Economic
Activity, spring
2015, https://www
.brookings.edu
/wp-content
/uploads/2016
/07/2015a_rognlie
.pdf.

13
Henry George,
*Progress and
Poverty: An
Inquiry into the
Cause of Industrial
Depressions, and
of Increase of Want
with Increase of
Wealth* (New York:
D. Appleton, 1879).

14
Noah Smith,
"Piketty's Three
Big Mistakes,"
Bloomberg View,
Mar. 27, 2015,
https://www
.bloomberg.com
/opinion/articles
/2015-03-27
/piketty-s-three
-big-mistakes-in
-inequality-analysis.

George's analysis captures the essence of America's current housing affordability crisis. Huge shares of the productive bounty of the knowledge economy are being plowed into real estate, forcing working- and middle-class Americans to pay greater and greater shares of their hard-earned money for shelter. As one commentator summed it up in 2015: "It's *landlords*, not corporate overlords, who are sucking up the wealth in the economy."[14]

Even with Joe Biden in the White House, America remains too polarized for anything like a national strategy for housing affordability to be possible. It is even harder to imagine red states like Florida, Texas, and other Sunbelt states doing anything on their own to address the crisis. It is more likely that housing prices will come down as a result of an economic downturn or crash as these cities and metros are more prone to boom-and-bust cycles. Blue states and cities will probably develop initiatives to make housing more affordable, including so-called YIMBY (Yes in My Backyard) strategies to spur more housing construction and inclusionary zoning, in which developers include significant shares of affordable housing units, as much as 25 or 30 percent, in exchange for increased densities or other incentives.

All that said, real estate and land present a fundamental contradiction in the midst of the knowledge economy. They are both a fetter on long-term economic growth and prosperity and a drain on the livelihoods and lifestyles of the American people.

The Case for Permanent Social Housing

Robert Kuttner

is co-founder and co-editor of the *American Prospect* and Meyer and Ida Kirstein Professor at Brandeis University's Heller School for Social Policy and Management. He was a longtime columnist for *Business Week*, the *Boston Globe*, and the *Washington Post* syndicate. Kuttner's most recent book is *Going Big: FDR's Legacy, Biden's New Deal, and the Struggle to Save Democracy*.

America faces a crisis of affordable housing. In most major metropolitan areas, the median rent is several times what a household can afford based on median income. First-time homeownership is becoming ever further out of reach.[1]

The core problem is that we lack a true social housing sector, except at very modest scale. By social housing, I mean housing that is removed in perpetuity from market pricing pressures. The only exceptions are the roughly 1 million remaining public housing units in the United States, built through a program introduced in 1937 as part of the New Deal, plus a small and still experimental sector of limited equity co-ops and community land trusts, neither of which receives significant public funding.

Legislation passed in 1998, the Faircloth Amendment, capped the total number of federally funded public housing units, requiring one unit to be removed from the stock for every unit added. Congress fails to appropriate the funds to maintain the public housing that exists. A backlog in basic maintenance estimated at $70 billion makes public housing the housing of last resort for anyone who is poor and lacks other choices. And since 1998 public housing has been thinned out and turned into mixed-income rentals, further depleting the supply of low-rent units.[2]

The rest of our subsidized housing exists within a market system, where market forces (inadequate supply, rising demand, expensive land) relentlessly bid up the cost of available units and increase the cost of subsidy required to make up the gap between the affordable rent and the owner's costs. The only real solution is to create and gradually

1

Andrew Aurand et al., *Out of Reach: The High Cost of Housing*, report (Washington, DC: National Low Income Housing Coalition, 2021), https://nlihc.org /sites/default/files /oor/2021/Out-of -Reach_2021.pdf.

2

Maggie McCarty, *Introduction to Public Housing*, report (Washington, DC: Congressional Research Service, 2014), https://sgp .fas.org/crs/misc /R41654.pdf.

3

Alexander von Hoffman, *To Preserve Affordable Housing in the United States: A Policy History*, working paper (Cambridge, MA: Harvard Joint Center for Housing Studies, 2016), https://www.jchs .harvard.edu/sites /default/files/von _hoffman_to _preserve _affordable_housing _april16.pdf.

expand a true social housing sector of land and units permanently protected from market forces, on the model of public spaces like the Grand Canyon or Central Park.

Affordable Housing and the Market Sector

Beyond the small remnant of traditional public housing, most of today's subsidized housing piggybacks on market-rate housing. Though reliance on market forces is assumed to enhance efficiency, there are three problems with this approach.

First, as market housing becomes increasingly costly, the government must pay more and more to subsidize any given unit of affordable housing. Second, while some programs, such as the Section 8 Housing Choice Voucher program and the traditional public housing program, are supposed to be entitlements, only about 25 percent of those who qualify based on income actually get the housing. Who receives it and who stays on interminable waiting lists is more random than need-based. Third, with the exception of traditional public housing, many affordable units leave the social housing sector as soon as the landlord or developer finds it expedient to stop taking the subsidy and begin charging market rents. Literally trillions of dollars have gone to subsidize low-rent housing, but for all the taxpayer expense, there is no permanent supply of social housing. Clearly we need a permanent social sector.

Private Developers and the Expiring-Use Problem. As public housing fell into disfavor, the Kennedy administration in 1961 turned to nonprofit developers. Working under Section 221(d)3 of the National Housing Act, these developers built about 160,000 units of housing, some of it excellent. But there were too few competent nonprofit sponsors to take the program to scale, and management problems soon emerged.

In 1968, the Johnson administration and Congress replaced Section 221(d)3 with Section 236. The concept of Section 236 was to use FHA mortgage insurance, mortgage interest subsidies, and tax subsidies to attract private, for-profit developers to build and manage affordable housing. As an additional inducement, the developer was required to retain these units as low-rent housing only until the mortgage was paid off or the original contract with HUD expired, a period that was often as short as 15 years. At the end of that time, the developer or landlord was free to evict low-income tenants and convert the property to ordinary market-rate housing. In HUD jargon, the loss of subsidized units over time is known as "expiring use."

After extensive problems involving mismanagement and loan defaults, Section 236, which subsidized the construction of about 544,000 units, was replaced in 1974 by the Section 8 program. This new approach used rent subsidies to promote new construction or substantial rehabilitation and created another 850,000 units. In the late 1980s and 1990s, as these below-market mortgages were paid off, more than a million units whose developers had benefited from extensive public subsidy were at risk of being lost to the stock of affordable housing.

To counter the expiring-use problem, Congress enacted several laws that attempted to slow the conversion process and protect tenants. But since developers had a contractual right to exit the program, these efforts worked only to the extent that the government offered even more money to the developer, subsidizing the units all over again. By the early 2000s, according to one authoritative study, about half the federal government's financial support for low-income housing, which was supposed to produce more housing, was going to preserve the supply of affordable units that had already been subsidized once.[3]

4
Maggie McCarty,
*An Overview of the
Section 8 Housing
Programs: Housing
Choice Vouchers
and Project-
Based Rental
Assistance*, report
(Washington, DC:
Congressional
Research Service,
2014), https://
crsreports
.congress.gov
/product/pdf/RL
/RL32284/19.

5
Democrats
Appropriations
Committee,
"Appropriations
Committee
Releases Fiscal
Year 2022
Transportation,
and Housing
and Urban
Development, and
Related Agencies
Funding Bill,"
press release, July
11, 2021, https://
democrats
-appropriations
.house.gov/news
/press-releases
/appropriations
-committee
-releases-fiscal
-year-2022
-transportation
-and-housing;
Shelby R. King,
"Universal Housing
Vouchers: A
Promise or a
Pipe Dream?,"
Shelterforce, Aug.
19, 2021, https://
shelterforce
.org/2021/08/19
/universal-housing
-vouchers-a
-promise-or-a
-pipe-dream; Liz
Osborn, "FY23
Omnibus Spending
Bill Mixed Bag for
Affordable Housing,
Enterprise

Because supervision was at once too bureaucratic and too lax, these government-subsidized and privately developed housing projects had high default rates. Developers could qualify for the subsidy almost as an entitlement. It was easy to rig the books by understating maintenance costs, allowing financially dubious projects to be approved. Often developers put in little of their own capital and could make back their investment in a few years, underinvest in maintenance, and be none the worse if the project became insolvent. In Boston, in 1972, federally subsidized developments accounted for some 60 percent of all residential construction. By 1977, two-thirds of them were in default. The government then had the further challenge of figuring out what to do with subsidized developments that came into its possession.

Section 8 and Its Defects. The original Section 8 program, enacted in 1974 as a streamlined alternative to Section 236, was intended to increase the housing supply. Once certified for housing vouchers, a developer could build a new affordable project, knowing that it would readily attract tenants. The vouchers would pay the difference between market rent and what the tenant could afford, typically about 30 percent of the tenant's adjusted gross income. As a system for producing new construction, however, this approach turned out to have many of the same problems as Section 236, and it was transformed by Congress in 1983 into a voucher program to subsidize rents in existing, privately owned rental housing.

Under the current Section 8 system, a renter who qualifies based on income receives a voucher and is free to shop around for housing. A landlord who participates in the program is paid based on HUD's calculation of the unit's fair market rent. The tenant rent covers a portion of that amount, and the government makes up the difference via the voucher.[4]

The more the market value of the property increases, the more the government has to subsidize the landlord. Additionally, if the apartment happens to be located in a gentrifying area, there is nothing to prevent the landlord from quitting the program and charging market rents. In this case, taxpayer money that has been spent, often for decades, on subsidizing a form of social housing has nothing permanent to show for it. The social housing sector gradually shrinks.

Today, Section 8 subsidizes about 2.3 million units, housing some 5 million people, at an annual cost of about $28 billion.[5] Republicans, developers, and landlords support the program, because of both free-market ideology and self-interest; Democrats and affordable housing advocates support it despite its flaws, because it can win funding in a deeply divided Congress. But the basic problem of the landlord being able to quit the program remains, as does the ever-increasing cost of subsidies needed to keep pace with rising market values.

Low-Income Housing Tax Credit. In 1986, frustrated by the myriad problems of housing programs based on subsidizing private developers, both housing advocates and the Reagan administration looked for another approach. By the 1980s, a cohort of financially and technically competent community development corporations had come into being as nonprofit housing developers. What the CDCs lacked was the equity capital to build housing and also ongoing sources of subsidy for affordable rents. The low-income housing tax credit was intended to fill that gap.

Under the LIHTC, the federal government allocates tax credits to state governments, which then award them to developers of affordable rental housing through a competitive process. Nonprofit developers cannot use the credits, since they pay no

The Case for Permanent Social Housing

blog, Dec. 20, 2022, https:// www.enterprise community.org /blog/fy23 -omnibus-spending -bill-mixed-bag -affordable -housing/.

taxes, but they can sell them to investors, who provide equity capital to the project. As legal partners, the investors can use the tax credits, which are good for ten years, to offset taxes owed on their other income or can in turn sell the credit to other passive investors. Since its inception, the LIHTC has subsidized construction of over 2 million units of affordable housing. The annual cost to the Treasury in foregone taxes is about $9.5 billion.

The LIHTC approach is less than ideal on several grounds. One problem is "leakage." A good part of the annual $9.5 billion ends up in the pockets of wealthy investors—both those who buy the tax credits and the middlemen who syndicate the credits to others—rather than subsidizing the housing. It would be far more cost-effective to subsidize the low-income projects directly. A related problem is how to keep the units affordable once the ten-year tax credit expires, since there is no ongoing source of subsidy.

A second challenge is complexity. Even the most competent nonprofit community housing developer spends an inordinate amount of time cobbling together enough subsidy from diverse sources to make the numbers work. Some of the subsidy comes from the tax credit, but community development corporations and kindred nonprofit developers need other subsidy streams from local and federal government sources. The time and effort required to develop relatively few units are excessive.

6
Will Fischer, *Low-Income Housing Tax Credit Could Do More to Expand Opportunity for Poor Families*, report (Washington, DC: Center on Budget and Policy Priorities, 2018), https://www.cbpp .org/research /housing/low -income-housing -tax-credit-could -do-more-to -expand -opportunity -for-poor.

A third criticism is that many state housing authorities tend to approve projects that are in areas of concentrated poverty. According to a study by the Center on Budget and Policy Priorities, just 15 percent of LIHTC units are located in areas with little poverty.[6] The program thus adds to the economic isolation of the poor.

The LIHTC is another instance of a badly flawed second-best—which, in the absence of anything better, enjoys broad political support. It is a case of what economic historians call "path dependence." The reliance on the tax credit and the existence of a large ecosystem of low-income housing developers, syndicators of tax shelter, and advocates of affordable housing reinforce political support for a system that nobody really likes while also precluding alternatives.

Mandatory or Voluntary Inclusionary Housing Agreements. One other approach to affordable housing requires or incentivizes developers of market-priced multifamily housing to set aside some of their units at lower rents.[7] There are three versions of this approach. One, used extensively in New York State, under the 421-a program, offers generous tax credits against property tax to developers or landlords who agree to set aside a percentage of the rental units, typically 20 to 30, as affordable, with "affordable" defined in terms of a fraction of local median income. Some developers of luxury buildings provided access to the reduced-rent apartments only via a separate entrance, so that upper-income tenants did not have to rub elbows with the poor. So-called poor doors were banned in New York State in 2015, but developers find other ways to separate luxury and affordable housing. The entire approach has been widely criticized as inefficient. In recent years, New York State has given away on the order of a billion dollars a year to induce developers to offer these low-rent units. Housing advocates have argued that it would be far more cost-effective for the state to simply build the low-rent housing directly or via nonprofit developers. The 421-a tax credit in New York expired on June 15, 2022, and is not available for new projects, though it can still be used for projects that started before December 22, 2022. It is widely expected to be reinstated.

7
"Reviewing Development Proposals," Inclusionary Housing, accessed Jan. 17, 2023, https:// inclusionary housing.org /making-it-work /supporting -builders/reviewing -development -proposals/.

A second version of this strategy operates at the city level. In New York City, neighborhood organizations or developers can petition city authorities to rezone districts in exchange for setting aside a percentage of housing units as affordable or meeting other social goals. This program, on the books since 2013, has produced only a few thousand units.

A third tactic requires all developers of multifamily housing above a given number of units or a given density to provide a fraction of affordable units. Some cities that use this approach, such as Boston, permit the developer to site the low-rent units elsewhere, or simply to pay into a fund in lieu of providing the units—a literal tax. As of 2019, there were a total of 1,019 such inclusionary housing programs in 734 jurisdictions in 31 states and the District of Columbia, and they had produced about 110,000 affordable units.[8]

Inclusionary housing agreements sometimes reduce spatial segregation by social class. They are arguably better than nothing, but they make production of affordable housing a by-product of development of luxury housing, and the scale is inadequate. During periods when luxury housing markets are saturated and new development slows, production of affordable housing also suffers. And once again, this strategy is captive to market forces and meets only a fraction of the need.

The Continuing Assault on Public Housing. The steady decline of public housing in the United States is deeply intertwined with race and racism. When public housing was first built as part of the New Deal in 1937, it was explicitly segregated, in the North as well as in the South. This was the price that Southern Democrats demanded to allow the program to pass Congress. In its first years, public housing was not intended for the dependent poor but for the well-behaved working class. Public housing complexes enforced standards of good conduct. In 1950, the median public housing tenant made 57 percent of the national median income. By the 1990s, that figure had fallen to just 20 percent.[9]

What happened? The great postwar suburban migration, subsidized by federal highways, tax breaks, and mortgage insurance, drew millions of White families out of cities. Public housing became integrated, then resegregated as Whites moved out. By the 1970s, public housing had lost political support, leaving projects as unattractive and often dangerous housing for extremely poor African Americans. Large towers such as Pruitt-Igoe in St. Louis and Robert Taylor Homes in Chicago were designed and built basically to warehouse the dependent poor, with little thought for how the buildings would function as social communities. While some projects remain viable, they have little political support.

In 1998, the Clinton administration sought to stabilize public housing projects by demolishing some, renovating others, and turning many into mixed-income complexes under the HOPE VI program. The program invested $6.1 billion in rehabilitating and thinning out derelict public housing complexes, resulting in the loss of at least 300,000 public housing units. Some cites lost 30 percent of their public housing. According to *Housing Policy in the United States*, a book by New School professor Alex Schwartz, only 24 percent of the residents displaced by HOPE VI were able to find other subsidized housing.[10]

Rent Control. One further strategy for maintaining affordable housing is rent control. The main arguments against it are, first, that by denying landlords market-rate rentals, rent control causes them to underinvest in maintenance; second, that rent control does nothing to increase the supply of new affordable housing; and third, that the

8
Ruoniu Wang and Sowmya Balachandran, "Inclusionary Housing in the United States: Dynamics of Local Policy and Outcomes in Diverse Markets," *Housing Studies*, June 1, 2021, https://doi.org /10.1080 /02673037.2021 .1929863.

9
Jeff Andrews, "Affordable Housing Is in Crisis: Is Public Housing the Solution?," Curbed, Jan. 13, 2020, https://archive .curbed.com/2020 /1/13/21026108 /public-housing -faircloth -amendment -election-2020.

10
Alex F. Schwartz, *Housing Policy in the United States*, 4th ed. (New York: Routledge, 2021).

beneficiaries of rent control are not those most in need of affordable housing but those who happen to have lived in a rent-controlled building for a long period (or who got lucky when they took over a lease), some of whom are affluent.

Rent control nationally was part of the system of price controls enacted during World War II. When wartime controls ended, Congress allowed municipalities to retain rent control as a local option. New York retained it longest and still has about 20,000 units subject to rent control and almost a million subject to the looser regime of rent stabilization, where rent increases are limited according to a formula. In New York's complex system, another 258,000 units are subject to some other form of rent regulation. Elsewhere, rent control has been mostly phased out, though it has been reinstituted on a statewide basis in the past decade in Oregon and California as a brake on rapidly rising rents. In addition, some municipalities in New Jersey, Maine, Maryland, and Minnesota have imposed rent control.

The economic arguments against rent control are less persuasive in an era of windfall landlord profits. Even with rent control, owners in hot housing markets have ample returns on their investments. That said, rent control is a stopgap at best.

The Case for True Social Housing

Because of the underinvestment in public housing in the United States, and its association with the poorest of the poor, American public housing carries a stigma. "The projects" are considered dangerous places, spots to be avoided if other options are available. But municipal housing has a very different meaning in some other countries. Austria and the Netherlands provide powerful counterexamples.

Municipal Housing in Vienna.[11] In the 1920s, Vienna was governed by a socialist municipal administration, and one of its priorities was to build attractive worker housing. Over time, the municipal housing in Vienna has become a worldwide model. It has won architectural awards and is considered an appealing place to live, for the middle class as well as for the poor.

Today, about 24 percent of all housing and 46 percent of all rental housing in Vienna is municipally owned. For a single person, the annual income limit is about $42,000; for a family, it can be as much as $92,000, or well above the Austrian median income. Residents are not evicted if their income rises but pay rent on a sliding scale, generally around 25 percent of income.

About 500,000 people, more than a quarter of the city's population, live in some 1,800 complexes of different sizes and designs. Because this housing is valued and well-maintained capital stock, most of which has long since been amortized and is largely free of debt, rents cover most of the operating cost; the ongoing cost of public subsidy is modest at around $300 million annually. This is a benefit of creating and then maintaining a substantial social housing sector.

There are economic benefits as well. According to the city government, Vienna's social housing program creates 23,300 jobs in the city in the short term and safeguards 30,100 in the long term, or about 3.5 percent of jobs in Vienna. Municipal housing is also a leader in green design. And because the municipality is the city's largest landlord and keeps rents low, private sector rents face competition and are also moderate.

Nonprofit Social Housing in the Netherlands. The Dutch system uses nonprofit housing associations as owners of social housing.[12] This sector is subsidized by the state, increases the stock of affordable rental housing over time, and today accounts for

11
"Municipal Housing in Vienna," City of Vienna, accessed Jan. 17, 2023, https://social housing.wien /tools/municipal -housing-in-vienna.

12
Hanneke van Deursen, "The People's Housing: *Woningcorporaties* and the Dutch Social Housing System," Part 1: The History, working paper, Joint Center for Housing Studies, Harvard University, June 2023, https://www .jchs.harvard.edu /sites/default/files /research/files /harvard_jchs_the _peoples_housing _history_van _deursen_2023.pdf.

13
"Allocation by Housing Associations," Dutch Housing Policy, accessed Jan. 17, 2023, https://www .dutchhousing policy.nl/topics /allocation-by -housing -associations /allocation-rules.

14
"Dutch Social Housing in a Nutshell," AEDES, Dutch Association of Social Housing Organisations, accessed Jan. 17, 2023, https:// dkvwg750av2j6 .cloudfront.net /m/6c2c81c93f 5a9522/original /Brochure-Aedes -Dutch-social -housing-in-a -nutshell-examples -of-social -innovation-for -people-and -communities-2016 .pdf.

15
Frans Schilder and René Scherpenisse, *Policy and Practice: Affordable Housing in the Netherlands* (The Hague: PBL Netherlands Environmental Assessment Agency, 2018), https://www.pbl .nl/sites/default /files/downloads /PBL2018_Policy -and-practice -affordable -housing-in-the -Netherlands _3336_0.pdf.

16
Homes for All Act of 2019, H.R. 5244, 116th Cong. (2019–20), https:// www.congress .gov/bill/116th -congress/house -bill/5244?s =1&r=33.

about 75 percent of the roughly 3 million rental units in the Netherlands. As in the case of municipally owned housing in Austria, these units can never leave the social housing sector. In recent years, social housing has accounted for about half of all new housing construction in Holland.

Rents are capped at about €750 a month, and 80 percent of the units must be rented to people with an income limit of about €43,000, very close to the Dutch median income. These financial guidelines mean that social housing in the Netherlands does well at integrating the middle class with the poor.[13]

Because this housing is operated by some 300 different nonprofit housing associations, strategies and secondary goals are widely varied. As a whole, the Dutch system of social housing targets clean energy and tenants with special needs. The housing associations learn from each other and exchange information through AEDES, their national association. AEDES explains, "The social housing sector is a closed system in which all revenues must be reinvested. Essentially, it acts as a revolving fund."[14] According to one study, in 2016, the value of all residences owned by housing associations was €250 billion, financed with €87.5 billion of long-term debt and representing €173 billion in equity.[15] The government spends a billion euros per year to underwrite new housing construction in the social sector.

The key point in both the Austrian and the Dutch systems of social housing is that these units remain permanently in the social sector. The benefit of the subsidy to housing supply cumulates over time. Unlike so much subsidized housing in the United States, there is no ongoing leakage to the market sector. A second benefit is that this approach creates and maintains a highly competent cadre of public and nonprofit housing professionals.

The United States: If You Build it, Will They Come? The experiences from other countries suggest that municipally owned housing or large-scale nonprofit housing can address several problems. It can increase the supply of high-quality affordable housing, which will attract the middle class as well as the poor over time; ameliorate the social isolation of the poor; create valuable capital stock insulated from market pricing pressures; and reduce the need for annual subsidy.

Fiscally, it would be necessary to jump-start the process with a large capital outlay. Given the extreme shortage of affordable housing and the net loss of affordable housing under consolidation strategies such as HOPE VI, any new socially owned system of housing construction would have to be at a scale large enough to produce plenty of units for lower-income people as well as some for the middle class.

Some proposals to take public housing to a much larger scale have been introduced in Congress, but they are political long shots sponsored by left-wing legislators. Representative Ilhan Omar has introduced the Homes for All Act, which would underwrite 8.5 million new public housing units.[16] Senator Bernie Sanders and Representative Alexandria Ocasio-Cortez introduced the Green New Deal for public housing legislation—co-sponsored by Senator Elizabeth Warren along with 23 other congressional Democrats—which would invest $172 billion to modernize existing public housing units and retrofit them to be carbon neutral and energy efficient.[17]

Urban Land Trusts. The other major model of proven social housing is the urban land trust. This approach has produced some recent successes in the United States, but at a small scale. With a land trust, the land is socially owned and permanently protected from market pricing pressures. It can never be sold to the highest bidder—or to any bid-

17
Jeff Andrews, "Sanders, AOC Introduce Green New Deal for Public Housing," Curbed, Nov. 14, 2019, https://archive.curbed.com/2019/11/14/20964763/green-new-deal-public-housing-bernie-sanders-alexandria-ocasio-cortez.

18
Brenda Torpy, "Champlain Housing Trust," Center for Community Land Trust Innovation, 2015, accessed Jan. 17, 2023, https://cltweb.org/case-studies/champlain-housing-trust/.

der. Various forms of social housing can be built on the land: limited equity co-ops, non-profit rental housing, or moderately priced owner-occupied housing, where the owner gives up all or most capital appreciation in exchange for an affordable home.

Different community land trusts have different models, and some combine different housing forms. For example, Vermont's Champlain Housing Trust, founded in 1984, oversees 565 owner-occupied homes and 2,200 rental apartments.[18] Producing adequate volume with this model would require federal funding to provide the capital for land acquisition; the trust, however, would be organized and operated locally.

This approach not only protects the current supply of social housing but increases it over time. Land trusts encourage local forms of experimentation and do not depend on a government housing bureaucracy. It seems far better to expand land trusts than to continue subsidizing a market sector that grows ever less affordable and supplies insufficient affordable housing. If capital grants can pay to acquire the land, then the housing will be far more affordable and will not require deep ongoing subsidy over time.

Limited Equity Co-Ops and the Challenge of Wealth Accumulation. One more variant of social housing, sometimes used in tandem with urban land trusts, is the limited equity co-op. In exchange for living in an affordable unit, a member of a limited equity co-op gives up the chance to profit from the market appreciation of the unit if or when he or she chooses to move elsewhere. This agreement keeps the unit affordable for the next resident. Some variants allow residents to take out some limited equity. These co-ops are a promising approach, but so far on too small a scale.

In the United States, the roughly two-thirds of Americans who own homes use homeownership as a strategy to amass wealth over a lifetime. This secondary benefit of homeownership is not available to renters generally, even with a social housing sector that provides an adequate supply of affordable housing. The problem cannot be solved through rental housing policy, except to a very limited extent via limited equity co-ops. The challenge of wealth accumulation for renters requires complementary policies, such as better pensions or so-called baby bonds, to facilitate wealth accumulation for the underprivileged—and that is a subject for another day.

Affordable Housing: Forgotten Factors

Michael Gecan

is the former co-director and current senior advisor to the Industrial Areas Foundation. He is the author of the books *Going Public: An Organizer's Guide to Citizen Action* and *After America's Midlife Crisis*, as well as essays for the *Boston Review*, *Village Voice*, *Nation*, and other publications.

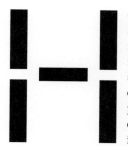

ousing production—or the lack of it—is directly related to the amount of power communities have over their own space, time frame, and trajectory. There aren't many discussions of this factor in the large and ever-expanding literature on housing trends and struggles in the United States. Many books and articles focus on financing options, zoning and density matters, exclusionary practices and covenants, neglect and abuses, materials and design elements used in housing construction or renovation, and political issues or policy disputes. These issues merit discussion. But so does the role once played by powerful unions and currently played by several powerful citizens' organizations like East Brooklyn Congregations in New York and United Power for Action and Justice in Chicago, both affiliates of my group, the Industrial Areas Foundation. In most cities, however, the vacuum left by declining unions has been filled by market developers, if at all.

A report prepared in 2021 by Sam Khater, a chief economist for Freddie Mac, described the decline in the production of starter homes: "In the span of five decades, entry level construction [i.e., houses of 1,400 square feet or less] fell from 418,000 units per year in the late 1970s to 65,000 in 2020." He also noted, "We estimate that the housing shortage increased to 3.8 million units by the end of 2020." Other knowledgeable sources believe the shortage might be even higher—more than 5 million.

This shortage has major implications for many constituencies. Consider the 72 million millennials entering the housing market. Fewer starter houses means more years at home with parents, more doubling or tripling up, more years of renting. In the past, when those 418,000 units were being built annually, these years would have enabled buyers to begin to build equity. But today, those making modest or even moderate wages, particularly blue-collar workers in African American and Hispanic neighborhoods in our cities and in White and more rural and exurban counties, have no starter home to buy and no way to start to generate wealth. The obstacles to economic equity created by this housing shortage are clear, especially with 60 percent of the resources of all but the wealthiest Americans residing in the value of a home. And beyond the damage done to individuals, families, and communities, many of our largest cities, metropolitan regions, and rural counties pay an ongoing price for this shortage.

No amount of financial engineering or policy tweaking will break this cycle. What is needed instead is a robust and expansive effort to construct starter houses. But where is the power base, where are the concentrations of organized people and organized money, that can demand this effort and monitor its implementation?

Fortunately, it's not hard to point to examples where people *did* build that base, *did* create that organization, *did* use that power to demand just the kind of starter homes discussed by Sam Khater. Historically, in New York City, major labor unions once produced a total of more than 50,000 units of affordable housing for their members, not exactly starter houses but starter co-ops. As David Chen wrote in the *New York Times* in 2004, "The meat cutters had Concourse Village in the Bronx. The garment workers had Seward Park Houses in Manhattan. The printers had Big Six Towers in Queens." Rochdale Village in southeast Queens and Penn Station South in Manhattan were other examples. The title of Chen's article—"Electchester Getting Less Electrical; Queens Co-op for Trade Workers Slowly Departs from Its Roots"—describes how the drive to provide this housing slowed and the connection between the vision and values of the unions and the union members who once lived there faded over time. By the 1970s, that drive had come to a halt. Today there is little understanding or appreciation of the contributions that unions made to the city's housing stock and to the well-being of their working-class members.

But as the unions were fading, a new group of citizen organizers was quietly and unexpectedly beginning to assert itself. Beginning in 1983, East Brooklyn Congregations began a home-building and equity-generating effort called the Nehemiah Plan. In the abandoned and burned-out blocks of two neighborhoods, Brownsville and East New York, the largely African American and Hispanic leaders of EBC proposed building 5,000 new, affordable, single-family town houses of 1,170 square feet each. EBC was one of a new generation of organizations rooted primarily in religious institutions and staffed by organizers trained and supported by the nation's oldest and largest network of locally based citizens' power organizations, the Industrial Areas Foundation.

EBC needed three things from New York City: $10,000 no-interest second mortgages with lien, which would reduce the cost of the residences from $50,000 to $40,000; free land; and expedited review by city agencies. EBC also needed, and received, below-market money for first mortgages from the State of New York Mortgage Agency, at the time headed by Herman Badillo, who worked for then governor Mario Cuomo. This funding reduced by at least 2 percent the sky-high interest rates of the early and mid-1980s. The organization wanted to build houses that those who already lived in or near those communities could afford to buy with mortgages they could maintain and to provide residents in an overwhelmingly rental environment with an opportunity for ownership and equity equal to that of all other ethnic and racial groups in New York. The initial reactions to this proposal, which stunned then mayor Ed Koch and his administration, begin to explain how the nation decided to stop building starter homes.

Reaction one: Don't build anything. When EBC made its proposal known in 1982, the city was emerging from near bankruptcy and was plagued by high crime and population loss. Many observers predicted that New York would never recover and that the best option was to consolidate viable neighborhoods and let the distressed ones continue to shrink. The policy types even had phrases for this: "planned shrinkage," "benign neglect." EBC leaders and IAF organizers argued that this defeatist attitude would lead to more decline. Besides, no one asked the residents of East Brooklyn and the South Bronx, of upper and lower Manhattan, of central and southeast Queens whether they thought the neglect was in any way benign. It's important to mention that even most of those who considered themselves progressives bought into this mindset.

Reaction two: Build more high-density rental. This course of action would have added to the already overwhelming stock of high-density rental housing rather than creating single-family ownership housing. A racial component characterized this reaction. Administrators and advocates claimed that people needed to be "managed," that they could not be counted on to buy, maintain, and improve their own homes. There was also a new trend in the wind: the Reagan administration began to make deep cuts in federal support for housing. Then, in 1986, Congress passed Low-Income Housing Tax Credit legislation, which, as I wrote in the *Boston Review* in 2021, "became the dominant [development] tool of a vast network of nonprofits, developers, academic and technical consultants, financial intermediaries, and others." In short, subsidized rental housing emerged as the consensus solution in most cities and counties. This accord was not reached for sinister reasons, or because public officials were opposed to ownership options. In fact, many housing officials, agency heads, community development corporation executives, and affordable housing lenders thought of themselves as progressive or liberal and acted out of estimable motives. But self-interest tugged the entire industry away from large-scale construction of starter homes and into a decades-long pattern of production of affordable rental housing.

Reaction three: Start small. Among the few who thought that the EBC proposal had merit, the recommendation was to build a small number—10 or 20—to prove that people would buy homes in devastated areas. The view held by IAF and EBC was just the opposite. The communities were so distressed, and the chain reaction of negative experiences so powerful, that a critical mass of new ownership housing was needed. Not 10 or 20, but first 1,000 and eventually 5,000. Our instincts told us that only a fundamental rebuilding effort would send a signal to those who might buy, thus prompting a positive chain reaction—new homes, rebuilt blocks, more eyes on the street, new stores, schools that would no longer be threatened with closure because of declining student populations.

Reaction four: Assume that communities cannot initiate or implement long-term improvement strategies. So many professionals—planners, finance experts, administrators, lawyers, elected officials, foundation staff, nonprofit executive directors, academics, researchers, and others—dominate the world of housing production and housing discussions that there is little regard for the agency that organized communities can generate and demonstrate. Housing professionals have their own language, patterns, and relationships. While they sometimes design "listening procedures," as I described in the *Boston Review*, these mechanisms are usually carefully controlled and fail to engage credible and respected local leaders who might have different points of view from the professionals. As a result, much housing development is executed without the social knowledge that only local leaders and residents can provide and is based on assumptions about the limitations of local engagement that become self-fulfilling prophecies. Even when local communities succeed in building housing on their own, as the unions did for many decades, their achievements are often overlooked because they do not fit into the entrenched patterns of thought and activity where housing professionals—oriented more to the market and to affordability—find themselves stuck.

The conventional wisdom regarding affordable housing helps explain why those reacting to the proposals put forward by East Brooklyn Congregations did not understand exactly what was happening in New York at that time. As investigating journalist (and East Brooklyn resident) Wayne Barrett famously wrote, as EBC emerged, the establishment kept asking, "'Who are these guys?'" An affiliate of IAF, EBC comprised more than 40 local congregations. Leading the effort was a strategy team of clergy and lay leaders with deep knowledge of these communities and great credibility among their members. A small professional staff—two organizers and one administrator—supported the strategy team. The organization could bring 1,000 or more residents—not a random selection but people whom the leaders knew and respected—to planned community action assemblies on a regular basis. For larger events, often held outdoors, 5,000 to 8,000 local EBC members could gather when needed. EBC was financially independent, funded by dues from the member institutions. It thus had the two critical components of power: organized people and organized money. But the leaders and organizers were also ambitious and entrepreneurial, building relationships with journalists like Tom Robbins and Michael Powell; housing innovators like Michael Lappin of the Community Preservation Corporation; and no-nonsense housing agency heads like Felice Michetti, who would become commissioner of the city's Department of Housing Preservation and Development.

Bearing in mind an old business maxim—never go to power *for* a decision, go *with* a decision—EBC built a team and designed a plan that emerged from the needs and interests of its own members and its own struggling and written-off communities. They found partners with housing expertise who both respected the primary role of the EBC leaders and could help them deliver the thousands of houses they proposed to build: general manager I. D. Robbins in the 1980s (Robbins, with his cousin Lester Robbins, had built Big Six Towers in Queens for the Typographical Union); general manager Ron Waters and architect Alexander Gorlin in the 1990s and 2000s; Nick Lembo, Peter Hansen, and Kirk Goodrich of Monadnock Construction and Monadnock Development in more recent years.

When EBC and its team approached the City of New York in 1983, it was *with* a decision to build 5,000 affordable owner-occupied homes, along with $8 million in no-interest revolving construction financing, something no one else had done. The organization was able to assert the need for critical masses of these entry-level homes, in part to complement the growing scale of rental construction. Insisting on starting big, not small, EBC mounted a campaign that convinced the mayor and his administration, grudgingly at first, enthusiastically as the year went on, to provide the subsidy, the land, and the expedited processes needed to build the first 1,000 houses. From 1983 to 1987, EBC built 1,100 Nehemiah homes in Brownsville. From 1987 to 1991, the organization constructed another 1,100 houses in East New York. Beginning in 1996, 700 homes filled a mostly deserted section between the two areas. And starting in 1996, EBC began construction on the world-class Spring Creek development—a new community of more than 3,000 fully affordable houses and apartments, schools, parks, and more than 1 million square feet of retail built and managed by the Related Companies.

The original buyers of one of the now more than 5,000 Nehemiah homes realized an increase in equity of about $250,000. Almost all of these first-time buyers were either African American or Hispanic. And almost all had previously lived in or near the East Brooklyn communities where EBC began its effort.

Other powerful organizations noticed EBC's project and applied some of the universals used and lessons learned to their own areas. For instance, South Bronx Churches, another IAF affiliate, built 1,000 Nehemiah homes in that area. Jersey City Together, the New Jersey IAF partner, has led an effort to guarantee that a site called Bayfront (cleaned of chromium thanks to the IAF's efforts over several decades) will designate 30 percent of its thousands of new units as affordable apartments or condos. Chicago's United Power for Action and Justice, also an IAF affiliate, is beginning a similar effort there.

In a very real sense, the entire country finds itself in a position similar to the one that the people of East Brooklyn occupied nearly 40 years ago. In hundreds of inner-city neighborhoods in scores of cities big and small, the streets and blocks resemble the once abandoned, deserted, and debris-strewn acres along Stone Avenue (now Mother Gaston Boulevard) or Livonia Avenue in Brownsville or too many streets and avenues to count in much of eastern and central Brooklyn, southern and mid-Bronx, Harlem and East Harlem, and the Lower East Side. The dispiriting visual signs of decline are not immediately evident in rural counties or aging suburbs, but a closer look encompasses abandoned storefronts, deteriorating mobile home parks, sagging rental buildings. East Brooklyn has benefited from nearly 40 years of consistent reconstruction. Most other communities have suffered from nearly 40 years of steady decline. And as the sage Yogi Berra used to say, "It's getting late early."

This state of affairs means that organizations like EBC need to be created in those areas and among those constituencies, including the famously institution-averse millennial camp. Without those deep and credible power formations, without the innovation and pressure that those groups can bring to bear, without the ability to filter out false friends and identify those who have both expertise and a sense of their critical but limited roles in the construction of new affordable ownership housing, it is hard to see how the scarcity that the nation faces, deepening each year, will ever be addressed. Any solution requires relentless and imaginative organizing along with a new generation of relentless and imaginative organizers.

Addressing the nationwide shortfall in affordable housing also depends on a new kind of maturity among political leaders and others in the professional classes. In the early 1990s, as IAF/EBC efforts in Brooklyn reached scale and attracted attention, I received a call from the mayor of a major midwestern city. He had been talking to people in New York and elsewhere, he said, and he was very interested in replicating the Nehemiah Plan in his city. I flew there a week later and was ushered into his office. He said, very directly, "I love what you are doing in Brooklyn. I want one of those Nehemiah Plans here." I had never really heard a mayor be so positive and forthright, contacting an IAF organizer and organization and inviting us in. That was great to hear, I said.

But I then laid out the fact that we really didn't work for mayors or governors directly, as tempting as that might be at times. We worked for organized communities like the pastors, lay leaders, and local civic leaders who spearheaded EBC. I said that critical to Nehemiah's success was an *organized base* of people who desired it, who designed it to suit their own priorities and goals, and who, politically speaking, *owned* the enterprise. The mayor nodded, then said, "Look, I got a pastor I'll give you for that." That wouldn't suffice, I told him. If he had the patience to let us build a deep and broadly based citizens' organization, one that would be powerful enough to engage with the city, state, and private sector power people effectively, that would at times hold him and others accountable, then we would be interested. He asked for some time to consider my observations. I never heard another word.

Years, even decades, have been squandered in city after city because the political and professional classes have not reconciled themselves to a different kind of relationship—reciprocal, accountable, complex—with an organized group like EBC. In Chicago, 15 years ago, United Power for Action and Justice raised a construction fund, identified sites, and put forward an ambitious reconstruction plan for the fast-fading neighborhoods of the West and South Sides. But the then mayor deferred to the local alderman, as he and most others had always done, in return for his support of the mayor's wishes on real estate, finance, airports, insurance, and other priorities. Chicago's aldermen and -women have de facto veto power over developments in their wards, which they often use to shake down builders and nonprofits on a scale that would make the most brazen burglar blush. Unwilling to play into this corrupt dynamic, unable to convince the mayor and his minions that this was not just a local strategy but an attempt to reverse what was, by then, four decades of population loss, we stopped construction after building 100 homes. Had the political culture been healthy, we could have completed the reconstruction of the West Side and parts of the equally distressed South Side. It is essential that existing political figures reflect and change or, alternatively, that a new generation of more confident leaders, with a better, broader vision, replaces them.

Reversing the decline of American cities will require that the professionals who want to help rebuild communities—urban, older suburb, exurban, rural—reexamine their tendencies and revisit their roles. Finding and deciding to partner with a credible, local, sustainable citizens' power entity, which might look very different in different places, seems to me to be the most important decision the professionals can make. In some places, IAF affiliates represent such an entity. In other places, proven citizens' organizations have been founded and supported by other networks. In more rural or exurban areas, a combination of groups—teachers' associations, health care workers, other public sector unions, big box employees, small business owners—might need to collaborate to create a pragmatic modern housing production strategy.

And again, those millennials. Many young women and men emerging from colleges or grad schools face a bleak future when it comes to home buying and wealth building. Even if recent graduates are equipped with the skills that enable them to demand a good salary, they will likely find a major portion of that salary will be devoured by ever-rising housing costs in the hot employment centers. The reality of the 2010s and earlier should be enough to convince this cohort that they are going to need a bigger boat, that whatever alumni association or fraternity or sorority group they carry with them into the public arena might consider fashioning a new kind of housing campaign, one that breaks the scarcity stranglehold and generates hundreds of thousands of starter homes every year, not just the 65,000 built in 2020.

These efforts will not be easy or quick. But in the early 1980s, no one thought communities like East Brooklyn could ever be rebuilt. On the contrary, nearly everyone was betting that they were down for the count. So if the working class and poor leaders and members of EBC, who had never collectively raised more than $100,000, who had never spearheaded a housing effort of any scale, and who had had to overcome obstacle after obstacle in the start-up and implementation phases of their work—if those leaders could do it, then others can too.

They made it there, goes the old saying. Now others need to make it everywhere.

The Housing System and Homelessness

Rosanne Haggerty is president and chief executive officer of Community Solutions, a nonprofit organization that develops strategies to end homelessness. Haggerty also founded and led Common Ground, which creates permanent and transitional supportive housing in New York City in addition to providing services for those experiencing homelessness.

One day in 2003, I sat in front of a whiteboard with thirty or so colleagues. In the group were people experiencing homelessness and staff members from the community agencies and organizations responsible for helping them in various ways. Our assignment was to map, step by step, the process of connecting a person with a home, noting which agency was in control of which step and how long each step would take.

More than three hours later we looked at each other in alarm. The whiteboard looked like a game of Chutes and Ladders. The 46 steps we had charted would take more than 340 days to complete—at best. *If* all the documents for each organization were in order, *if* the hand-offs between organizations were fumble-free, *if* individuals staying in shelters or on the street could be notified of mandatory appointments—if all of this and a host of other tasks could be completed before various authorizations expired, a period of 340 days was achievable.

The exercise revealed barriers to ending homelessness that could only be seen by focusing on the surrounding system, not on those experiencing homelessness themselves. It exposed the absence of any guarantee that available housing units, rental subsidies, and case management services would reach those who needed them desperately. Most strikingly, it showed that there was no single person or group in charge of making sure that the myriad activities of all the organizations responding to homelessness in any community actually added up to fewer people experiencing homelessness. While we noted an abundance of programs, it was also clear that no unified, coherent, accountable system existed for preventing and ending homelessness.

When the modern era of homelessness emerged in the late 1970s, policymakers and the public were slow to understand what was happening. Observers drew conclusions about the people who were appearing on the streets in growing numbers, about their personal traits and misfortunes. The belief that homelessness reflected individual problems informed key programs and policies and shaped stories and debates that continue to this day: about whether it is a choice, about mental illness and addiction among those experiencing homelessness, about how to manage the behavior of those living in public spaces.

Four decades later, we are learning that we have been trying to solve the wrong problem. We failed to recognize that the assorted zoning and land-use policies, housing design standards, housing finance tools, property tax policies, rental subsidies, building department review practices, occupancy rules, brokers' fees, shelter policies, eligibility criteria, subsidy priorities, code enforcement laws, construction technologies, and other activities that determine what housing is built, how it is operated, what it costs to occupy, who has access to it, and the quality of services that are available to support those with mental health, addiction, or other disabilities in securing and maintaining housing constitute a dynamic housing *system* that requires rigorous collective action. By attributing homelessness to those experiencing it, we missed the evidence that the housing system itself was failing.

Donella Meadows, a pioneer in the study of systems theory, defined a system as "an interconnected set of elements that is coherently organized in a way that achieves something."[1] Complex systems are those with many interdependent parts: healthcare, for example, or the economy. The operations of complex systems cannot be easily predicted or controlled because they move and transform as their elements interact and respond to change. Effectively guiding a complex system is a coordination challenge involving the regular and continual adjustment of many moving parts to achieve a common goal. This requires reliable and timely information, ways of working matched to the constantly evolving ways in which the system operates, and above all leaders who understand that the task is a continuous one: to respond nimbly to changes in the system in order to stay on course.

Failed systems—those that do not operate with intention or accountability toward a collective goal—are still systems. But lacking a unifying, measurable goal to guide necessary collaboration, fragmentation wins. Policies and initiatives fail to deliver promised results, opportunities are squandered, and the most vulnerable, who rely on effective public systems, suffer avoidable harm while typically being blamed for being the problem.

With respect to housing and homelessness, failing to address the broken system problem thwarts single initiatives. The same scenario plays out time after time: officials make bold pledges or voters support funding for new affordable housing only to see plans undermined—perhaps by local zoning and land-use policies, or by weaponized public review processes, or by bureaucratic cultures that reward compliance over problem solving. Innovation is stymied, especially the innovation needed to create types of housing aligned with current demographics. Outdated building regulations, design requirements, and occupancy regulations reinforce the status quo.

Inattention to the whole housing system also means we lose ground. Unenforced housing maintenance codes and corporate acquisitions of rental properties result in

1
Donella H. Meadows, *Thinking in Systems: A Primer* (White River Junction, VT: Chelsea Green Publishing, 2008), 11.

affordable housing disappearing more quickly than new units can be built. Policies such as waiting lists and lottery requirements to award government-assisted housing by chance, not by urgency of need, are mismatched to the current crisis. And alarmingly, developers of affordable housing often aren't aware of, much less collaborative with, organizations serving the homeless. Absent a coherent, accountable, and coordinated housing system, the United States, with all its wealth and creativity, finds itself with more than 580,000 people experiencing homelessness—disproportionately Black and Native Americans, those with disabilities, the elderly, and children—at the time of the last national estimated count.[2] More than twice that number seek emergency shelter over the course of a typical year.[3]

In a failed system, communities spend more to achieve poorer results. Prior to the pandemic, federal, state, and local governments together spent more than $12 billion each year on responses to homelessness. Yet in many places the number of people experiencing homelessness grew, often most sharply in communities spending the most on emergency responses. This demonstrates another system principle: putting more money into a broken system without fixing it usually makes the problem worse.

And there is so much at stake. Homelessness for many is a death sentence. Nationally, the average life span of those experiencing homelessness is almost 30 years shorter than the average American's.[4]

We have come to a moment when the failures of our national, state, and local housing system are more costly to ignore than to solve. How might things be different? What can we learn from other sectors that have placed the safety of people at the center, taken responsibility for mastering complex problems, and transformed the way they work?

———

The eradication of smallpox offers many lessons. Although a smallpox vaccine was developed in 1796, the disease persisted in countries that lacked an effective system for delivering the vaccine, killing more than 300 million people in the 20th century alone. Ultimate success was achieved when the Intensified Eradication Program, with the objective of ridding South America, Asia, and Africa of the disease, was launched in 1967. The international commitment to an urgent, collective goal supported by determined leaders unleashed technical innovations in vaccine storage and needles; workforce innovations to broaden the role of community health workers; governance innovations in how agencies worked together and disseminated knowledge; and innovations to interrupt the process of disease transmission and eliminate its spread through targeted vaccination efforts.

Plans to eliminate or eradicate polio, malaria, and other diseases have successfully applied the lessons of the smallpox campaign: they set a clear aim, build a coalition, collect accurate and timely data, and prepare to learn through continuous monitoring and data-driven, targeted improvement efforts how and when to adjust strategy as conditions change. These lessons have implications for improving systems beyond the containment of infectious disease. The Vision Zero initiative is just one example.

By the early 1990s, traffic engineer Claes Tingvall of the Swedish Transport Administration had seen too many avoidable deaths on his country's roads. Inspired by the success of smallpox eradication, he proposed to his colleagues that they aim for the elimination of road traffic deaths and serious injuries. "Success in both safety and health

2
The 2022 Annual Homelessness Assessment Report (AHAR) to Congress, report (US Department of Housing and Urban Development, Dec. 2022), https:// www.huduser .gov/portal/sites /default/files /pdf/2022-AHAR -Part-1.pdf.

3
All In: The Federal Strategic Plan to Prevent and End Homelessness (United States Interagency Council on Homelessness, Dec. 2022), https://www.usich .gov/All_In _The_Federal _Strategic_Plan_to _Prevent_and_End _Homelessness.pdf.

4
All In.

can be represented by the idea of zero," wrote Tingvall and his coauthors, "whether that zero stands for zero deaths from disease or crashes, or zero illnesses or injuries or collisions."[5] Tingvall started by reframing conventional assumptions about traffic deaths. First, they were a public health issue, not simply a product of individual misfortune or error. Second, they were not a fact of life since road systems could be designed to protect users from human error.

Implementing the traffic reform plan that became Vision Zero required private, public, and governmental sectors to work together in new ways toward a bold, shared aim. It meant aligning policies and resources behind the goal and testing new practices rigorously and openly before implementation. At the heart of Sweden's new road safety system was information. Teams were trained to collect and analyze data on crashes and near misses to continuously improve safety as new issues came to light. This transformation necessitated strong management, the creation of standards for high-performing road safety systems, and sustained political will to continue learning and improving. Since 2000, deaths from traffic accidents in Sweden have been cut in half. And as of 2023, another 25 countries and 45 US cities have adopted Vision Zero.

It was far from evident at the outset that something like a road safety system could be realized by creating a culture of shared responsibility for the prevention of harm. In fact, cultural shifts to protect the safety of vulnerable individuals tend to begin with this sort of imaginative leap. A vision of a new system aimed at solving a problem all the way through permits beliefs and roles to be inverted, new relationships, rules, information, designs, behaviors, resources, and decisions to be considered. Progress toward zero traffic fatalities and serious injuries has involved organizations working across sectors and pulling multiple levers, from national and local policies on road design and use—such as creating roundabouts instead of intersections, installing crash barriers, limiting truck access to certain roads, and reducing speed limits—to collaboration with car manufacturers to improve vehicle safety features.

The same system-level thinking is applicable to housing. It's possible to imagine local housing systems designed to achieve similarly fundamental, measurable goals: eliminate homelessness, severe housing cost-burden, unsafe living conditions, and discrimination. Many communities are already on their way.

In the late 1990s, colleagues and I interviewed 127 individuals living on Manhattan streets to learn what they needed to escape homelessness. The responses were strikingly similar: someplace private, clean, safe, and free of excessive rules. The amount of space didn't matter. Individuals described being able to pay for the housing they desired—on average, they had $10 to spend each night for accommodation that met these basic standards—but also needing flexible terms, such as paying by the night or by the week to match their source of income.

What if the challenge is this basic and straightforward: to align all housing-related activities, rules, and investments into a system that can provide a safe, clean, private living space to anyone who needs it?

Homelessness illustrates the need for system-level approaches to housing. The relationship between housing costs, vacancy rates, and levels of homelessness[6] illustrates the dynamic nature of the challenge and the need for close coordination of policies

5
Karin Edvardsson Björnberg, Sven Ove Hansson, Matts-Åke Belin, and Claes Tingvall, eds., *The Vision Zero Handbook: Theory, Technology and Management for a Zero Casualty Policy* (Cham, Switz.: Springer, 2022), https://doi.org/10.1007/978-3-030-23176-7.

6
Gregg Colburn and Clayton Page Aldern, *Homelessness Is a Housing Problem: How Structural Factors Explain U.S. Patterns* (Oakland: University of California Press, 2022), 29.

and interventions. The way a community understands the dynamics of homelessness affects what happens on the street, as does the loss of certain types of housing and many other factors. Houston, for example, with no restrictive zoning and a well-coordinated response team, has reduced homelessness by 63 percent since 2011; other Texas communities, by contrast, saw steady increases.[7]

Before the 1970s, economic and demographic shifts were catalysts for innovations in housing. As the country industrialized, lodging houses and cubicle hotels appeared to accommodate the laborers who were building city infrastructure. The YMCA created a national network of urban dormitories, supplying 100,000 rooms for young men leaving farms for the city. A single-room-occupancy-hotel building boom followed World War I, offering modestly priced, basic housing to waves of returning soldiers. As late as 1960, New York City alone had more than 129,000 SRO units that provided inexpensive private accommodation for single adults.[8]

In fact, most older cities are living case studies of need-driven housing innovation. It is this innovation that we are missing today, and what an accountable housing system would deliver. In the small New England city where I live, the blocks near downtown are dense with housing arrangements fashioned during the city's initial period of growth in the late 19th century. There are apartment buildings originally built as worker housing for nearby factories and former rooming houses where law students can still rent a room by the month. Alleyways lead to houses sitting in the center of blocks, wedged behind other houses in defiance of current zoning codes. Land and structures were developed to meet the community's basic housing needs because that's what the community, at that time, expected.

It is this same expectation—that basic housing needs will be met, for everyone—that should drive a well-functioning housing system now. A commitment to this end state would create an imperative for flexibility and innovation in testing new forms of housing and living arrangements and for unlocking all the tools at hand to deliver expected results.

We are not beginning at square one in imagining what the basic housing options might look like. Solutions to earlier generations' needs remain relevant. After more than 100,000 SRO units were lost in New York City between 1955 and 1985—tax incentives hastened their demolition or conversion to apartments[9]—this housing type was belatedly recognized for the essential role it played in housing lower-income single adults. Remaining SROs have found new life in New York and elsewhere as permanent supportive housing for disabled individuals experiencing homelessness. In most of these preserved and renovated buildings, individuals have a lease to their own small apartment. Services come to them, providing health, mental health, and employment supports as needed.

The cubicle hotel concept has also been rediscovered. What were essentially bare-bones private sleeping spaces with shared bathroom and kitchen facilities in cities' skid row districts, offering inexpensive nightly or weekly rates, have reemerged in new form as "co-living," a shared housing concept embraced by students and young professionals.[10] Shared arrangements like the rooming houses of old have also been revived, including for the purpose of providing a path out of homelessness.

Many of the new forms of housing required to meet our country's current needs—more of us poorer, aging, living alone, working remotely, burdened by debt and with higher rates of mental health and addiction issues—have already been created. Various

7
Michael Kimmelman, "How Houston Moved 25,000 People from the Streets into Homes of Their Own," *New York Times*, June 14, 2022, Feb. 13, 2023, https://www.nytimes.com/2022/06/14/headway/houston-homeless-people.html.

8
"History of Homelessness In NYC," Homelessness & Affordable Housing NYC, https://eportfolios.macaulay.cuny.edu/affordablehousingnyc/.

9
Brian J. Sullivan and Jonathan Burke, "Single-Room Occupancy Housing in New York City: The Origins and Dimensions of a Crisis," *City University of New York Law Review* 17, no. 1 (winter 2013), https://doi.org/10.31641/clr170104.

10
Podshare, https://www.podshare.com/; Coliving, https://coliving.com/.

11
New York Citizens Housing and Planning Council, *Making Room*, https://chpcny.org /making-room/; *Making Room: Housing for a Changing America*, National Building Museum, Nov. 18, 2017–Jan. 6, 2019, https://www.nbm .org/exhibition /housing/.

12
US Department of Housing and Urban Development/US Census Bureau, American Housing Survey, https:// www.census.gov /programs -surveys/ahs.html; Kyle G. Horst, "A Look under the Hood of Housing Adequacy," MReport blog, Aug. 5, 2022, https:// themreport .com/news/data /08-05-2022 /housing-adequacy.

13
Research Memo: New AFR Research Estimating Minimum Number of Private Equity-Owned Housing Units, report, Americans for Financial Reform, June 2022, https:// our financial security.org/2022 /06/letters-to -congress-new -afr-research -estimating -minimum-number -of-private-equity -owned-housing -units/.

solutions to the mismatch between the nation's demographics and its housing options were gathered by the *Making Room* project of the New York Citizens Housing and Planning Council and the Architectural League of New York and by the *Making Room: Housing for a Changing America* exhibition at the National Building Museum; these provide practical starting points for any community.[11]

Meeting basic housing needs also requires preserving and maintaining the quality and affordability of existing housing and increasing access to it. Familiar and newer threats include neglect, predatory investors who disrupt local housing markets with rapid rent increases, and climate change. The latest American Housing Survey found that 5 percent of the nation's occupied housing was substandard, undermining the health of the estimated 15.5 million residents of those homes.[12] Private equity firms are estimated to have acquired and raised the rents on more than 1.6 million properties.[13] And climate events routinely destroy homes in vulnerable environments. A properly functioning housing system would attend as closely to the quality and preservation of existing affordable units as to the enablement of new supply.

What keeps communities from having the housing they need and preserving the housing they have? Increasingly, evidence points to the absence of a system-level view, beginning with the housing development process itself.[14] Almost universally, its complexities, uncertainties, lack of urgency, cost, misused public approval processes and environmental reviews, and restrictive zoning mean that communities are unable to create the housing they need.

The challenges of producing and maintaining sufficient housing options for a community and of connecting everyone to the safety of a home are distinct but interrelated elements of the same system. Removing barriers to achieving that aim in the United States will require following in the footsteps of Claes Tingvall, that is, starting with a vision and a commitment to solve a complex, urgent, life-or-death problem at the population level and to build an effective national housing system that delivers acceptable results in every community.

As in global health, traffic safety, and many other fields, creating an effective solution for housing will mean establishing a shared aim, relentless collaboration, and timely and accurate information on what is happening; policies and practices that adapt in response; and communities—including all levels of government—that are prepared to hold themselves accountable to new standards and to the expectation that everyone has the safety of a home.

———

Until recently, the idea that the fragmented activities and policies that make up the housing sector could operate as a coordinated system seemed far-fetched, despite widespread awareness that this coordination is desperately needed. To operate with the same accountability, public purpose, and urgency to protect people from harm that define emergency management and public health, communities in the Built for Zero movement start with the idea of zero homelessness and work backward to create a housing system with that goal. More than 100 cities, counties, and regions of all sizes and types have adopted this approach.

Participating communities begin with key actors—not-for-profits; city, county, and housing authority leaders—committing to work together to reach "functional zero"

14
Jenny Schuetz,
*Fixer-Upper:
How to Repair
America's Broken
Housing Systems*
(Washington,
DC: Brookings
Institution Press,
2022).

homelessness. Functional zero is a measure of a housing system in equilibrium, one where homelessness is rare overall and quickly detected and resolved when it does occur. Cooperation among the players involves the same transformation in thinking and behavior found in all movements aimed at eliminating avoidable harm: it is the responsibility of professionals to anticipate human error and vulnerability and to design systems that protect people.

Measurable progress toward functional zero homelessness has been made in more than half the Built for Zero communities. Among these, 14 communities have reached functional zero for one or more groups (veterans, the chronically homeless) on their path to ending homelessness altogether. Their progress is driven by four fundamental practices that any community can adopt.

First, the primary organizations work as an integrated, nimble team toward the community's overall aim rather than toward organization or program goals alone. The structure is similar to that of an emergency command center during a crisis.

Second, the team can see the entire picture of homelessness in one place, at the level of both the individual and the population. This requires gathering and maintaining real-time, person-specific data on everyone experiencing homelessness. Communities implement privacy-protected data sharing arrangements to build a comprehensive view of the dynamics of homelessness. This allows individual service providers to have complete and timely information on the needs of each person and the community team to monitor overall progress. Interventions and improvements can be pinpointed to places where the data indicates the highest-impact opportunities at the population level. Among these interventions are preventing new "inflow" into homelessness and improving the speed and quality of connections to housing.

Third, the group develops flexible resources to address the limitations of government programs, especially housing programs with the narrow eligibility criteria that characterize most government assistance. Committing adequate resources also means the creative use of a community's existing assets, such as buildings, landlords, service providers, local businesses and hospitals, public sector staff, philanthropy, faith-based organizations, and community volunteers to fill the inevitable gaps.

Finally, no local housing team reinvents the wheel. They draw on other communities in the network for insights on challenges and lessons from their efforts. Teams focus on improving their system; on growing their skills in data analytics, outreach, case conferencing, and housing search; and on using quality-improvement principles to test and refine new strategies and adapt relevant practices from other network members for rapidly and sustainably reducing homelessness.

These efforts demonstrate the power of a housing sector that operates as an intentional, aligned system. The changes in practice, behavior, and outcomes in Built for Zero communities have not come about because of new funding or policies but because of a shared aim driving a new culture of shared accountability, learning, and continuous improvement enabled by reliable data.

———

After our hours-long effort to map what it took to connect those experiencing homelessness to a home, our group considered a second question: what the system should look like if the goal was to end homelessness. This exercise took no time at all.

The group discarded requirements that served little or no purpose, such as mailed paper forms and redundant identity requirements. They reassigned work, and even contracts, to build on the strengths of each organization. They expedited document verification, apartment inspections, and lease signings with improved communications between groups. They engaged private landlords—who control the most housing in any community and hold the key to reducing homelessness in most communities—as a shared project and improved support to individuals once they moved into a home to prevent a return to homelessness. A single agency was designated to manage the work of the group, implement a streamlined housing process, and establish targets for reducing the routine time from homelessness to housing placement.

"What keeps us from working this way?" asked one participant. "Permission," said a second, as others nodded agreement.

There was excitement and longing in the room. The group had glimpsed an alternative to the ineffectiveness, unintended cruelty, and overall absurdity of current US housing practices. They imagined themselves, along with others drawn to housing, designing it, building it, enabling it through policy and finance, and managing it as part of a housing system capable of achieving so much more.

Racial Injustice and Housing

Race, Housing, and Democracy

J. Phillip Thompson is associate professor of urban planning and politics at the Massachusetts Institute of Technology. His research focuses on Black politics, community development, and political economy. Thompson's extensive experience in city government includes his 2018–21 position as deputy mayor of New York City for strategic policy and initiatives.

The housing affordability crisis, a key component of the gaping inequality that currently sears the nation, is putting to the test our democracy's binding beliefs in justice and equality. Large numbers of people are concluding that the basic requirements of living—such as decent housing—are increasingly out of reach. Yet by planning the right kind of affordable housing, infrastructure, and employment, government can enable a more inclusive and prosperous democracy in our emerging multiracial era.

Unaffordable housing has been a central characteristic of the Black condition in the United States since African Americans first moved into cities in the early 20th century—and has been neglected by the government for just as long. The current "crisis" has arisen because the problem is growing more widespread: large segments of the White population now also find housing costs unsupportable. It is no longer politically feasible to blame the victims, as past practice has been with African Americans. While housing unaffordability is heightened by increased economic inequality between rich and poor across race, it is more fundamentally about the integrity of American democracy.

The integrity of American democracy is what connects the housing affordability crisis to America's enduring race crisis. Many communities believe that they are being left behind—and that their government doesn't care. This widespread feeling is compounded by the major social and economic forces tied to climate change, job displacement through automation, and racial/demographic shifts. These commanding change agents are on course to transform our way of life.

We are in a perilous historic moment: there is an urgent need to instill in the public the confidence that freedom and opportunity have meaning for all Americans. Such an overarching effort can only be accomplished by government. It must include transforming the nation's crumbling infrastructure while addressing climate change; training workers for a digital-tech economy; broadening worker ownership of firms, land trusts, community-owned energy, and broadband infrastructure; and encouraging robust labor and community organizing and engagement in democracy.

What this plan would amount to is an updated, inclusive version of Thomas Jefferson's vision of widespread citizen ownership of and participation in the productive economy—economic democracy as the corollary to political democracy. (Though Jefferson is rightly criticized for his dealings with enslaved people and Native Americans, this Founding Father was on the right track when he noted the contradiction between building a nation asserting democratic principles and maintaining the deeply anti-democratic economic structure of slavery.)

Our Past

In early America, given the omnipresence of slavery, freedom was understood as the *absence* of enslavement—being White and being free were indistinguishable concepts. America's founders couldn't reconcile their Christian beliefs and advocacy for democracy with African enslavement, so they created the lie that Blacks were subhuman.[1] It took the extreme violence of the Civil War to end slavery. The lie was forcefully challenged, and abolitionists hoped the Constitution's 13th, 14th, and 15th Amendments would make US democracy secure.

But struggle over the course of the nation continued during Reconstruction. What Martin Luther King Jr. would one day call a "poisonous fog of lies" was once again spun, this time to justify a new system of Black subordination: racial segregation through Jim Crow laws. Segregation lasted almost 100 years and has thoroughly defined the modern era. The Civil Rights Movement, and the 1960s legislation it spurred, made some progress in dismantling formal segregation and protecting Black people's right to vote. Yet key Black demands for economic change—including quality employment for all, fair housing, and school integration—were never met. Believing the old lie, many Whites saw (and still see) racial integration as a threat to physical and material security.

Despite recent advances in Black political representation, the nation has not moved far beyond where it was during King's time. America is still a bitterly torn society, a circumstance reinforced physically by our racialized infrastructure. Integrating housing, neighborhoods, and schools would be the surest sign that the United States is moving toward an inclusive, multiracial democracy.

Climate change, technology, and demographic shifts toward a non-White majority are now forcing the nation to rethink its infrastructure. We have fateful choices to make: whether to create new infrastructure that draws people together or to re-create an older one that keeps people apart. For like a slow-moving ocean barge, large US cities are growing predominantly non-White. Within a few decades, the entire nation will follow suit. For some, the nation's changing racial (and political) demography is even more frightening than climate change and tech disruptions. We have only to look at rising far-right White nationalism and its conspiracy theories about the "replacement" of White hegemony.

Government's role here is key. Though the government created racial segregation and inequality over centuries, it has never used its full power to remedy these wrongs. In

1
Eddie S. Glaude Jr., *Begin Again: James Baldwin's America and Its Urgent Lessons for Our Own* (New York: Crown, 2020).

housing, privatization has for decades served as an escape hatch for shunting to the side the democratic demand for affordable housing—in other words, for allowing the free play of prejudiced real estate brokers and bankers. The "toxic mortgages" at the root of the 2008 financial meltdown were often concentrated in Black communities because government neglected its obligation to guard against racial discrimination.

Intentions and trust, not resources, have been the main obstacle to creating more affordable housing. Aside from government investments, for example, labor unions have significant pension fund resources. What would make investing their members' retirement savings in affordable housing doable is the belief that government is committed to supporting people in need of affordable housing. Again, King put it well: "It is a constitutional right for a man to be able to vote, but the human right to a decent house is as categorically imperative and morally absolute."

Change won't be easy. The myriad challenges created by the nation's original sin of slavery have led to a society where racial inequality seems normal. Recent movements for racial equity—such as the 2020 Black Lives Matter protests—were an attempt to unsettle this normalization of injustice and remind the US public that slavery and segregation facilitated extreme economic exploitation of African Americans and other people of color, and thereby created much of the wealth the nation now enjoys.

By the early 20th century, millions of African Americans had fled Southern Jim Crow repression in search of good jobs and democracy in the industrialized North. Yet their hopes were crushed as they pushed against the limits of Northern White liberalism.

Shortly thereafter, in the 1930s, both the soaring aspirations and the unbearable restrictions of White liberalism were on display in the New Deal. During the Great Depression, as tens of millions of people lost jobs, President Franklin D. Roosevelt and his New Deal allies put tremendous effort into aligning the US economy with democratic principles by using the power of government to raise living and work standards. But confronted by strong Republican opposition, Northern liberals abandoned their fight for Black democratic rights in order to secure Southern Democrats' support for progressive government programs.

Efforts to reconstruct America's society and economy were regularly cut short at the color line. The 1935 Social Security Act, which provided vital relief for millions during the Great Depression, excluded farm workers and domestics—sectors largely consisting of African Americans. The 1934 National Labor Relations Act, which protected workers' rights to organize unions, had the same exclusions. Another condition for Southern legislative support was that states administer New Deal programs, which enabled Southern officials to deny help to needy African Americans.

The 1944 GI Bill similarly transformed America—and also deepened racial segregation. The $95 billion bill helped more than 200,000 veterans start businesses or buy farms. Over 2 million veterans attended colleges and universities since the bill covered tuition and living expenses. Another 5.6 million veterans went to vocational schools, learning vital skills in the building trades or car and airplane repair. Black veterans, however, were excluded from most of the bill's benefits due to a "combination of entrenched racism and willful exclusion."[2] The program of home loans provided by the Department of Veterans Affairs offers a good example. On the surface, it was not discriminatory. But the VA did not make direct loans—it merely guaranteed them. When local banks proved unwilling to issue loans to Blacks, the Federal Housing Administration, which purchased

2
Ira Katznelson, *When Affirmative Action Was White: An Untold History of Racial Inequality in Twentieth-Century America* (New York: W. W. Norton, 2005), 117.

3

Keeanga-
Yamahtta Taylor,
*Race for Profit:
How Banks
and the Real
Estate Industry
Undermined Black
Homeownership*
(Chapel Hill:
University of North
Carolina Press,
2019), 10, 35.

4

Mindy Thompson
Fullilove, "Root
Shock: The
Consequences of
African American
Dispossession,"
*Journal of Urban
Health* 78, no. 1
(2001).

5

Joe William Trotter,
*Workers on Arrival:
Black Labor in
the Making of
America* (Oakland:
University of
California Press,
2019), 100.

6

Alex Marshall,
*The Surprising
Design of Market
Economies*
(Austin: University
of Texas Press,
2012), 124.

7

Debra Kamin,
"Widespread Racial
Bias Found in
Home Appraisals,"
New York Times,
Nov. 2, 2022,
https://www
.nytimes.com/2022
/11/02/realestate
/racial-bias-home
-appraisals.html.

mortgage loans from banks, refused to impose antidiscrimination requirements on the financial institutions.

The federal government, through the GI Bill and other mechanisms, essentially perpetuated racial segregation in housing. Beginning in the 1920s, the FHA put racist criteria into the underwriting manuals it prepared for the real estate industry. In line with this guidance, the National Association of Real Estate Boards in 1924 threatened to revoke the membership of any broker who disrupted patterns of racial homogeneity in a neighborhood. The 1949 National Housing Act set a national goal of "decent" housing for all citizens, yet ten years later, "less than 2 percent of FHA-insured property went to non-whites."[3]

The same year the Housing Act was passed, the federal government initiated urban renewal to clear slums in inner cities. The programs, according to some estimates, forcibly uprooted close to half of Black families in cities. Although African Americans were 10 percent of the population, they made up 66 percent of those slated for removal.[4] Many were moved to public housing, but far fewer replacement units were developed than urban renewal destroyed. The effect was to intensify housing shortages for Black families, already redlined out of White neighborhoods by the real estate industry and banks. Unscrupulous real estate brokers then inflated the costs of housing in de facto segregated Black neighborhoods, even for substandard residences. The Black home buyers who did manage to purchase in White neighborhoods frequently faced violent attacks.[5]

Strengthening democracy and building quality public infrastructure have always been tightly interrelated. Infrastructure, as one author has written, "is a physical manifestation of our willingness to do something together, to be our brother's keeper. Because of this, it's appropriate that infrastructure be built with élan, with style, expressing physically some of the ideals it embodies."[6] The infrastructure built to serve the millions of African Americans fleeing Southern segregation was invariably limited to public housing. The poor design and isolated locations of these structures visibly manifested America's commitment to racial exclusion. The resulting combination of relentless poverty, dilapidated housing, police repression, and acute Black disappointment ultimately led to the urban explosions of the late 1960s.

Despite passage of anti-discriminatory Fair Housing legislation in the 1960s, the redlining policies sponsored by the financial system continued into the 21st century, if often covertly. Such practices were one reason why African Americans, including middle-class African Americans, were regularly targeted with predatory home-loan policies. As recently as 2022, studies revealed that racist practices sluice through the housing market,[7] affecting everything from home appraisals to sales to loan financing. Market solutions, without government oversight and commitment to racial inclusion, not only failed to fix this problem, they made it worse.

A New Direction?

Many observers have argued that a tech-based economy will help fix our society's many problems. But the Tech Revolution has been too slow and too myopically profit-driven to be a wave that lifts all boats: Apple iPhones, for example, are manufactured in low-wage foreign factories. Meanwhile, big-box facilities, like Amazon's warehouses, are already deploying robots to replace workers. Some scholars estimate that 50 percent of current jobs in the United States are at risk of being replaced by machine automation.[8]

8
Carl Benedikt
Frey and Michael
A. Osborne,
*The Future of
Employment*,
working paper
(Oxford: Oxford
Martin Programme
on Technology
and Employment,
2013), 38; https://
www.oxfordmartin
.ox.ac.uk
/downloads
/academic
/future-of
-employment.pdf.

9
Joseph R. Blasi,
Richard B.
Freeman, and
Douglas L. Kruse,
*The Citizen's
Share: Reducing
Inequality in the
21st Century*
(New Haven: Yale
University Press,
2013).

The disruptive nature of postindustrial technology (and climate economics) is poorly understood. In traditional mainstream economic thinking, government is agnostic as to what business produces and where it is produced. Neither position is tenable in a sustainable democracy. Unguided markets do not provide a steering mechanism sufficient to effectively respond to the level of risk the nation and the planet are facing because of the climate crisis and postindustrial technology. An alternative, as was clear to Jefferson even in the 18th century, is widespread worker and community ownership.[9] If employees owned Amazon, for example, it is unlikely they would use robots to lay themselves off or ship their jobs to low-wage countries.

Participation in daily economic affairs, which is normally part of ownership, also addresses one of the nation's most critical needs: improved civic discourse. Participatory co-ops and other social ventures train citizens in the arts of democracy: listening to others, negotiating differences, taking responsibility, acknowledging mistakes. Increasing public capacity for civic dialogue is vital to meet impending demographic changes like the transition to a majority non-White US population and the growing numbers of young progressive Whites in cities. Government will likely face intense pressure to build a unified, multiracial democracy and an equitable economy that respect and include historically marginalized communities. This shift could be one of the best things that has ever happened in America. It would mean finally unleashing into the economy the suppressed talents of nearly half the population while redirecting resources from managing damage created by the current system (prisons, militarized policing, drug addiction) to social-emotional healing, education, and beautification of cities.

Recent actions in New York City could show the way. In November 2022, voters overwhelmingly approved the ballot initiatives proposed by the Charter Revision Commission, which focused on racial justice. One change was a new preamble to the City Charter, which pledged justice and inclusion to all and cited past injustices against racial minorities, people with disabilities, LGBTQ residents, and women. Equally important, the commission made clear that addressing racial injustice does not mean replacing "White supremacy" with "Black supremacy" or "people of color supremacy." Rather, it is a call for an end to all supremacies.

While New York is on the way to improved efforts toward equality, the federal government is too divided to devise a national plan for racial reconciliation. But we needn't wait for federal action. Local government is already well-positioned to play a leading role in addressing America's challenges. It can ignite federal action with powerful local social justice programs—such as building affordable housing.

Affordable Housing and Jobs

Addressing the affordable housing crisis is also an opportunity to chart a new course for the redevelopment of cities as green, high-tech, and equitable. Public housing can be re-created as mixed-income, racially diverse, and well-designed places to raise a family. Originally, New York City Housing Authority buildings were meant for one-third low-income residents and two-thirds moderate- and middle-income families but instead were used as "housing of last resort" to warehouse those too poor to afford housing, including those experiencing homelessness. The original formula worked and should be restored.

New York could take a giant step toward dramatically reducing poverty and crime by reimagining affordable housing. For starters, public housing residents and other low-income city residents can be trained and hired to do the work of rebuilding housing in the city. The federal government, through new legislation, has allocated billions of dollars in infrastructure funds, which New York could leverage for blocks of new residential buildings.

Other shortcomings can be resolved at the same time: Locating new public housing near grocery stores, parks, schools, libraries, restaurants, and public transportation would avoid isolation and exclusion from civic life. Communal facilities like kitchens, laundry, safe play areas, and gardens would foster pride of place. Landscaping with trees, shrubs, and flowers would improve quality of life for both residents and the environment. State-of-the-art training centers—like the modern teaching facilities for plumbers, electricians, and carpenters in the Martin Luther King Jr. Houses in Harlem in the 1950s—could make available instruction for jobs in the tech sector.

Resident participation in design, management, and ownership adds value to the community and builds civic engagement. After the devastation of Hurricane Katrina, low-income residents in the Tremé section of New Orleans specified important design criteria to be used for rebuilding. They wanted front porches, for example, to maintain their tradition of neighborly socializing while collectively watching over their streets.[10]

In New York, NYCHA has built affordable housing on some of the nation's most valuable real estate. Many of the properties are not built to maximum allowable density. This unutilized square footage presents an opportunity to secure private financing for the addition of market-rate units. A key challenge in attracting higher-paying tenants will likely be concern about poverty and crime—and central to both these ills is the lack of good jobs.

Besides creating a great many new jobs, new infrastructure funding could also be instrumental in addressing climate change. Existential changes in weather patterns have enormous implications for cities. Potential disruption of public transit due to rising seas, for example, could severely threaten metropolitan regions. So tackling climate change in conjunction with affordable housing offers a historic opportunity to address long-standing social problems.

Reducing carbon emissions is essential to protecting the environment. Most carbon emissions in urban settings come from buildings. New York City alone has almost a million buildings that must be retrofitted to decrease carbon usage. Reconfiguring these buildings by installing building components that reduce or lead to reduced carbon emissions—energy-efficient windows, improved insulation, solar panels, or green rooftops—makes them more cost-efficient generally. Meanwhile, skilled workers would be needed to implement these changes to building envelopes or systems, providing well-paying jobs for current and future generations.

Larger-scale green energy systems such as solar- and tide-powered microgrids also require specially trained workers. Rising sea levels have already led to restructuring some of the tunnels essential to New York's transportation system; in the future, it may also be necessary to evacuate some low-lying areas and build new housing for the relocated residents. In this way, a major climate retrofit could be an effective jobs-creation program that cuts poverty.

The outline for such an approach already exists. In 2019, New York reached a Project Labor Agreement with the building construction trades: 30 percent of workers on city-funded construction projects must reside in public housing or in zip codes that have a 15 percent or higher poverty level. This PLA could be a first step in creating a pipeline from poverty to prosperity: construction, retrofitting, broadband installation and

10

J. Phillip Thompson, "Race in New Orleans since Katrina," in *Searching for the Just City: Debates in Urban Theory and Practice*, ed. Peter Marcuse et al. (New York: Routledge, 2009).

maintenance, and other infrastructure projects require specialized, highly paid trades, including plumbers, electricians, and HVAC specialists.

Preparing workers for such careers will require robust training and apprenticeship programs. These programs, in turn, generally require 12th-grade reading (in English) and math levels. A large proportion of young, inner-city high school graduates (as well as those who dropped out) would likely need remedial education. Moreover, an estimated million immigrant workers are not proficient in English. Strong pre-apprenticeship and English-as-a-second-language programs might be needed to prepare them for jobs in the green and tech economies.

By taking a lead in tackling climate change, and given New York's remarkable diversity—both human and in the built environment—the city could be well-positioned to create businesses capable of exporting programs and tactics for addressing these issues around the world. Estimates project that climate mitigation will, by 2030, generate $26 trillion in global business and create 65 million new jobs. The opportunities will be in areas such as climate diagnostics, including data analysis and forecasting using artificial intelligence; resilience businesses, such as early warning systems and ocean acidification reduction; and climate response, including geothermal heating and cooling.

More broadly, America's pattern of suburban sprawl is carbon intensive and unsustainable. The alternative is to create more affordable housing in cities even though urban accommodation is constrained by land and zoning limitations. The rise in sea levels could make land even more scarce—heightening the already acute need for affordable housing. Without government intervention to protect tenants, environmental pressures will worsen housing affordability as existing property owners will likely continue demanding higher rents for scarce land, thus sucking the life out of other parts of the economy and ruining young renters' futures. Two solutions seem inevitable: government must protect affordable housing from the pernicious effects of real estate speculation; and cities must allow taller buildings.

Unions are an important part of the solution. Union pension funds are estimated to be between $3 and $6 trillion,[11] which for the most part is invested in corporations, hedge funds, and private equity funds. Only a relatively small amount goes toward affordable housing. The fundamental tension in pension fund management has been between using the money to advance workers' interests as workers or to advance workers' interests as long-term shareholders. Although these two aspects of workers' interests may at times conflict, they needn't. Some public employee pensions governed by state law—such as those of New York City employees—do not invest in businesses that take jobs away from government employment.

The logic is simple. It is hard to see how, for a public employee, earning a slightly higher return on retirement investment through privatizing city functions is worth putting one's own job at risk. Affordable housing is of similar vital interest to workers. Using retirement savings to create more affordable housing is in workers' best overall interests. During the mid-1960s, applying similar reasoning, unions invested heavily in New York City cooperative housing, creating affordable housing for 60,000 people at Co-op City in the Bronx alone. Crucially, New York State guaranteed the union housing investments through the Mitchell-Lama program. Since then, although pension funds have grown—and the need for housing among their members hasn't abated—unions have played a lesser role in affordable housing.

11
David Webber, *The Rise of the Working-Class Shareholder: Labor's Last Best Weapon* (Cambridge, MA: Harvard University Press, 2018), xii.

Part of their reluctance is linked to diminished federal support for building affordable housing. But here again, local and state government do not have to wait for Washington. In New York, greater cooperation and planning between the city and the state could go a long way. Suburbs around New York City, for example, such as Mount Vernon and Peekskill, have far cheaper land, and they offer public rail transit into the city. New York State could guarantee pension investments for affordable housing in the suburbs, while the city could relax restrictions preventing its workers from living outside the five boroughs.

Labor unions should also contribute to the concept of reinventing public housing. The idea of building taller, mixed-income buildings on NYCHA sites is not new. Current residents in NYCHA housing, however, have vigorously opposed such redevelopment in the past, for fear of displacement by the wealthier tenants that private developers prefer. Their fear is not without reason: when public housing residents were forced to vacate their apartments in other cities, such as Chicago, replacement housing for many never materialized.[12]

Ensuring a "right of return" is another place where labor unions could play a key role. Because many union members live in NYCHA buildings, and many more could live in future renovated buildings, unions are far more trusted as development partners by current residents than are real estate developers and banks. Union investments can also calm residents' fear of predatory financing. Unions have an interest in keeping housing affordable to their members and their families, not only in making a profit. To provide residents even more assurance, NYCHA land could be converted from public ownership to community land trusts, with current residents assigned seats on the board.

Such a model of collaboration between NYCHA residents, labor unions, pension funds, and developers, along with nonprofits and educational institutions, is the kind of approach needed to shift New York and other cities to a prosperous, green, tech-savvy, and equitable future. Public housing, precisely because it is where the ills of the past are concentrated, is the right place to begin.

12
Lawrence J. Vale, *Purging the Poorest: Public Housing and the Design Politics of Twice-Cleared Communities* (Chicago: University of Chicago Press, 2013).

How Land-Use Policies Discriminate Against People and Neighborhoods

Problems that remain persistently insoluble should always be suspected as questions asked in the wrong way.
—Alan Watts, *The Book: On the Taboo Against Knowing Who You Are,* 1966

Margery Perlmutter is a land-use lawyer and architect. Her consulting firm, Urban Factors, has studied affordable housing systems in the United States and Europe. As chair and commissioner of the New York City Board of Standards and Appeals from 2014 to 2022, Perlmutter created a new form of zoning variance to encourage development of more low-income housing along with other initiatives.

Prior to the enactment of New York City's first zoning resolution in 1916, the city had organized itself organically. "Unfettered urban industrialization" and laissez-faire economic policies[1] had encouraged developer speculation that divided the city into neighborhoods for the poor, the middle class, and the wealthy, concentrating the poor around polluting factories, slaughterhouses, and working waterfronts. The introduction of public transportation in the early 19th century and the construction of the major bridges in the late 19th and early 20th centuries enticed the wealthy and middle classes to move their homes away from the city's lower and mid-Manhattan business centers to burgeoning, sprawling suburban developments in Brooklyn, Queens, the Bronx, and the northern portions of Manhattan. Consequently, many of the vacated two-to-four-story row houses that had been built for the middle classes were converted into densely occupied tenements; others were demolished and replaced by five-story tenement buildings that housed many dozens of poor factory and piece workers and their families but lacked proper sanitary facilities or ventilation. These crowded, underserved neighborhoods rapidly became slums from which those with the means to do so fled. It is an old story, one that has been replicated in every city in the world: refuse or neglect to provide basic services to a population that has no resources to provide such services for itself, frighten away the population that might have facilitated neighborhood improvement, and watch the inevitable downslide to slum.

In 1893, social critic, reformer, and author Benjamin Flower wrote of legislation that undermined efforts to provide for the poor:

1
John F. Bauman, Roger Biles, and Kristin M. Szylvian, eds., *From Tenements to the Taylor Homes: In Search of an Urban Housing Policy in Twentieth-Century America* (University Park: Pennsylvania State University Press, 2000), 9.

2
B. O. Flower, *Civilization's Inferno; or, Studies in the Social Cellar* (Boston: Arena, 1893). In 1921, Bruce Blivens urged direct government funding and control of housing development, as was the model in Europe. He observed, "This sort of state interference in private business goes against a stubborn grain in the American character … Whatever the great god of Business doesn't take on itself ought not be done at all." Blevins, "Do Working Men Deserve Homes?" *New Republic*, Mar. 5, 1924, 39–41.

3
See NYC Housing Maintenance Code, Admin. Code Title 27, ch. 2 (1968), and NYS Multiple Dwelling Law (1929).

4
"Our present laws regulating taxes favor the mainte-

If our people had boasted less and observed more during the past three decades, they would have seen behind the vicious class legislation which has fostered plutocracy and virtually placed the reins of the government in the hands of organized capital [in order] to maintain the unjust and inequitable conditions through which the few reap the harvests of the many.[2]

Many tenement house occupants in the late 19th and early 20th centuries were poor immigrants, mostly from Eastern Europe, who lacked the social, cultural, technical, and language skills needed to integrate into American society. Housing reformers wondered whether the miserable housing and neighborhood conditions in which these poor immigrants lived led to these groups' decline or whether, instead, the lack of "American" skills brought down the neighborhoods and degenerated the housing stock. This attitude toward the immigrant poor—inherently racist at a time the eugenics movement was enjoying increased popularity—ensured that housing designed to improve conditions would remain removed from middle- and upper-class neighborhoods. Such thinking, attached subsequently and now to groups deemed to be "outsiders," has endured through the generations and continues to inform housing reform and land-use policy.

Reformers of the early 20th century targeted poor maintenance, overcrowding, and inadequate sanitary services and set minimum standards for natural light, ventilation, plumbing, room sizes, occupancy, and fire protection. These measures led to the enactment of laws that still apply to all existing and new multiple-family housing in New York City.[3] Such standards were necessary because slumlords would not invest in building-wide improvements without laws that would force them to do so, especially since there were otherwise no financial incentives associated with the related expenditures, such as mandated rent increases or public subsidies.[4] Similarly, tenement house developers would continue to build substandard buildings unless compelled by law to do otherwise. Even with laws that prohibit neglect, and even where significant opportunities to fund essential improvements through government-subsidized low-income housing finance programs are available, avoided building maintenance, compounded by poor construction materials and methods, persisted over the 20th century and remains a cause of urban deterioration. Legislated disincentives continue, as they did in Flower's day, to discourage maintenance of the older properties that would be affordable to low-income tenants. Widespread homelessness has resulted in the same sort of overcrowding decried in pre-1880s tenement house times.[5]

Housing reformers and architects have long argued that well-planned and -designed housing with equally well-planned and -designed public spaces and amenities, constructed with good-quality, durable materials, will foster "pride of place" in the occupants, who will care for their surroundings and prevent neighborhoods from degrading into slums. But this system can work only when residents are in control of their buildings and grounds and have the means to make essential improvements. Predatory landlords, underregulated lending practices, and even construction trades prey on poor neighborhoods and inexperienced property owners or managers, leading to building and neighborhood decline. On top of that, a lack of correspondence between rent protections for tenants and increased operational costs may discourage even the most modest investment in existing buildings, resulting in ever worsening conditions and warehousing or shuttering of unoccupied units.[6] Additionally, lending and affordable housing grant programs are structured to discourage better site design and planning or urge against the

nance of miserable old buildings, for we fine industry and discourage improvements by taxing them." Flower, *Civilization's Inferno*, 83.

5
Homeless or underhoused families double or triple up in housing intended for a single family. See, e.g., Molly K. Richard et al., "Quantifying Doubled-Up Homelessness: Presenting a New Measure Using U.S. Census Microdata," *Housing Policy Debate* (2022), https://doi .org/10.1080 /10511482 .2021.1981976.

6
Real Estate Board of New York, "Summary of Housing Stability and Tenant Protection Act of 2019," reporting on A.8281/S.6458 (C.36 of the Laws of 2019, NYS Legislature). This legislation disallows certain kinds of deregulation and also severely limits expenditures on apartment renovations, encouraging the warehousing of over 25,000 rent-regulated or low-rent apartments. See Suzannah Cavanaugh, "Landlords Offer to Re-Open 20K Warehoused Apartments* *If Albany Allows a

mixed-use developments that would have evolved naturally to include the commercial and community spaces that are essential to safe, vibrant, and healthy neighborhoods.

Planning the Plan and Then Ignoring the Plan

In 1916, New York City planners, following many years of study of neighborhoods in the city and with an eye to encouraging future development of business, manufacturing, and residential activities in all the right places, specified on zoning maps which uses and what building massing would be permitted in newly designated zoning districts. The elaborately researched and data-supported plan considered the locations of the recently completed subway and elevated train stations, retained manufacturing near the waterfront for convenient and easy access to waterways and rail lines, and situated new, limited-density housing near parks to support healthful living.[7]

Meanwhile, housing reformers and related legislative initiatives struggled with how to better house low-income workers. But their interests collided and continue to collide with developers' entrepreneurial designs on more desirable sites in nicer neighborhoods, and their plans encountered successful pushback from their better-off neighbors. As reform efforts began to take effect in the early 20th century, privately or publicly financed middle- and high-rise developments for the poor emerged on cheap, less desirable land located adjacent to or even within areas that, under the 1916 Building Zone Resolution, had been designated as "unrestricted" (i.e., manufacturing) districts. Among the New York City Housing Authority's then-developing portfolio was Queensbridge Houses. Completed in 1939, it was and still is the largest public housing project in the country, consisting of 26 six-story apartment buildings on 49.5 acres of industrial land organized into six superblocks.

The zoning maps of 1916 reserved for manufacturing the Queens waterfront along the East River to the north and south of the Queensborough Bridge. Nonetheless, site selection for the Queensbridge Houses ignored this classification, ostensibly constrained by the 1937 US Housing Act and the US Housing Authority mandate to build public housing on cheap land with reduced construction costs. Although siting large-scale housing developments along the edges of the city and adjacent to industrial or transit-oriented areas was common at the time—because large swaths of less expensive land were available there—the zoning regulations were usually adjusted to accommodate these changes by allowing new residential or mixed-use construction projects to filter into the established housing developments and expand around them.[8] Not so for Queensbridge. Built shortly after the wave of better-quality housing developments aimed at the middle classes, Queensbridge suffered immediately from its "no frills"—that is, reduced—construction budget, which resulted in poorer materials and methods that economized on details and quality, eliminated community-enhancing amenities, and made building maintenance more challenging.[9] Encouraged by discriminatory finance practices that favored and attracted White working families to seek better housing opportunities elsewhere, by the late 1950s, the working-class, low-income, mostly White population that had moved into Queensbridge initially was replaced by poor, underemployed minorities. As in the 1950s, today's occupants are mostly Black or Latino, with median annual household incomes of $15,843.[10]

Complexes such as Queensbridge became known as the "projects" of the mid-20th century and as "housing for the poor,"[11] committing neighborhoods evermore to unaesthetic conditions and worsening neglect—that is to say, undermaintained, underserved,

Vacancy Reset on Rents," *Real Deal*, Apr. 6, 2022.

7
City of New York Board of Estimate and Apportionment Committee on the City Plan, "Commission on Building Districts and Restrictions, Final Report," June 2, 1916.

8
For instance, Sunnyside Gardens, Queens (1928), and Tudor City, Manhattan (1929–32).

9
Bauman, Biles, and Szylvian, *From Tenements*, 112. Lewis Mumford described the project as "unnecessarily barracklike and monotonous" with interior planning that was unadaptable, "frozen tight, committed to their mistake till the buildings are demolished." Lewis Mumford, "Versailles for the Millions," The Sky Line, *New Yorker*, Feb. 17, 1940, 44, 45.

10
Corey Kilgannon, "Amazon's New Neighbor: The Nation's Largest Housing Project," *New York Times*, Nov. 12, 2018.

11
Bauman, Biles, and Szylvian, *From Tenements*, 115.

substandard, and eventually unsafe lifestyles and crime-ridden environments. These circumstances passively (aggressively) discouraged entrepreneurial investments into new residential buildings, new businesses, and neighborhood amenities, which might have attracted middle- and upper-income residents to the area. In addition, federal and state funding programs, such as the Low-Income Housing Tax Credit program, encouraged, through regulatory preference, development of new low-income housing in poor neighborhoods rather than in middle- or upper-income ones—in short, adding ghettos to ghettos. These programs thus further reduced, if not eliminated, any opportunity for improved outcomes on every front: urban design, architecture, environment, aesthetics, amenities, commerce, employment, education, upward mobility, crime-free safety, and health.[12]

At Queensbridge Houses, the conditions that typically attach to the projects were exacerbated by zoning regulations that continued to designate the surrounding area as unrestricted. In 1961, 20 years after the project was completed, new zoning maps provided with the enactment of the 1961 Zoning Resolution persisted in designating the same surrounding area a high-density manufacturing (M1-3) district rather than rezoning it to allow new residential and mixed-use development to filter into and incorporate Queensbridge into its urban fabric.[13] In 1990, one large area several blocks to the east of the Queensbridge Houses was designated a high-density manufacturing district that permitted residential use (M1-3D) only through a costly New York City Planning Commission authorization process intended to protect existing commercial and manufacturing uses from residential conversion or development. Notably, the manufacturing zoning districts around the Queensbridge development were also designated an Industrial Business Zone, with promises by city government to leave business uses in the area untouched by residential development. Today the waterfront area adjacent to Queensbridge Park, and onto which portions of the superblocks open, is still zoned for heavy industrial use (M3), while the M1-3D district was rezoned in 2008 to expand the thriving mixed residential and commercial Long Island City Special Purpose District. As of 2018, 40 new high-rise apartment and office buildings have been constructed in the Long Island City mixed-use district, and the average price of apartments is over $1 million.[14] But Queensbridge Houses remains use-locked, bordered by the Queensborough Bridge to the south, Queensbridge Park and the East River to the west, and manufacturing districts that include a major electric power plant (Con Edison's Ravenswood Generating Station) and industrial buildings to the west and north.

Although some enhanced retail and hotel development has recently appeared in the manufacturing districts close to the Queensbridge Houses, likely responding to the draw of a burgeoning Long Island City and adding new light-impact uses to the area that may animate the otherwise deserted and dangerous streets at night, hotel development in districts designated for manufacturing uses has been almost entirely prohibited since 2018 to appease hotel union workers' lobbying demands. Hence the range of possible residential-friendly uses remains limited, impeding the intermingling of compatible functions within and around the Queensbridge Houses.

Furthermore, had a 2018 proposal for rezoning a high-density manufacturing zone (M1-4) to allow residential and commercial development survived community opposition, it would have facilitated, with significant state and city incentives, development of a multibillion-dollar Amazon headquarters. Envisioned for the south side of the Queensborough Bridge, blocks away from the Queensbridge Houses and adjacent

12
See "Affordable Housing, Racial Isolation," editorial, *New York Times*, June 29, 2015; Jacqueline Rabe Thomas, "Separated by Design: Why Affordable Housing Is Built in Areas with High Crime, Few Jobs and Struggling Schools," *Connecticut Mirror*, Nov. 25, 2019. See also Ingrid Gould Ellen, "Spillovers and Subsidized Housing: The Impact of Subsidized Rental Housing on Neighborhoods," paper presented at Revisiting Rental Housing: A National Policy Summit, Joint Center for Housing Studies, Harvard University, Nov. 2006.

13
"High-density" in the zoning context refers to the height and massing of buildings rather than the use but enables higher intensity of uses because permitted floor areas are greater than in low-density districts.

14
Kilgannon, "Amazon's New Neighbor."

15
Alfred Bettman, "Housing Projects and City Planning," *Law and Contemporary*

to already prospering Long Island City, the facility would have employed 25,000 skilled tech-sector employees, many of whom would have resided in surrounding high-end housing. However, distance and natural separation enforced by the bridge anchorages and related facilities would to a large extent have prevented the headquarters from uplifting the quality of life or making opportunities available for the residents of the Queensbridge Houses.

It can be argued that the isolation of the Queensbridge Houses has protected the housing and its minority residents from the impact of the many rezonings and resulting gentrification of nearly all of Long Island City. My position, however, is that these efforts have isolated the development and its occupants from any chance for urban, economic, health, and educational success.

Dislocating Affordability: Urban Renewal Areas, Slum Clearance, and New "Affordable Housing" Projects

Disdain for the slum conditions of the tenement house neighborhoods and the belief that they were immune to improvement led city planners in the late 1920s to conclude that demolition was the only solution.[15] While these slum clearance efforts reflected the hopeful utopian visions of contemporary urban planners, they seemingly, and purposefully, ignored the plight of the poor who depended on the cheap housing the tenements offered, providing no alternatives. To construct the Williamsburg Houses in Brooklyn in the 1930s, for example, the city and the developers did not look to underutilized industrial land (as at the Queensbridge Houses) but instead cleared 12 blocks of tenement buildings to make way for 20 identical mid-rise apartment buildings on four superblocks that ignored the Brooklyn urban grid. Clearing the site displaced 1,300 tenement-dwelling families; 439 of them applied for relocation in the new development but only 341 were accepted.[16]

Subsequently, Title 1 of the National Housing Act of 1949 initiated urban renewal through eminent domain. In the 1950s, the program saw the citywide demolition of approximately 8,000 acres of slums housing almost 40,000 families in tenement buildings. The cleared areas made way for the construction of superblock housing projects for middle-income residents, many of them cooperative apartment buildings, supported by community-oriented cultural, educational, and commercial centers. These efforts were subsidized through various incentives, including significantly reduced land acquisition costs for developers and government-financed demolition. Although some of the displaced families were eventually housed in existing low-income public housing, it is unclear where the other ousted low-income slum dwellers were relocated. The program also ignored the impact of the clearance program on area businesses, making no provisions for their reestablishment in the new neighborhood of superblocks.[17]

Evidently, the planners lacked the imagination and probably the desire to envision the tenements renovated into desirable homes. But units in "old law" tenements (multifamily buildings built before 1901) can be renovated, some more stylishly than others, to be compliant with the New York City Building Code and the New York State Multiple Dwelling Law. These renovated one-, two-, and even three-bedroom apartments with natural ventilation in every room and modern bathrooms and kitchens can sell for more than half a million dollars on Manhattan's Upper East Side.

Similarly, single-family row houses and town houses of the mid-19th century, converted into multifamily tenements in the late 19th and early 20th centuries, or to multiple

Problems 1, no. 2 (1934): 206.

16
Nicholas Dagen Bloom and Mathew Gordon Lasner, eds., *Affordable Housing in New York* (Princeton, NJ: Princeton University Press, 2016), 97.

17
National Housing Act of 1949, Title I, "Slum Clearance and Community Development and Redevelopment," Pub. L. No. 171 (1949); Wayne Phillips, "Title I and Slum Clearance: A Decade of Controversy," *New York Times*, June 29, 1959; "I.L.G.W.U. to Take Title for Project," *New York Times*, June 29, 1959.

18
See "Report: Focus on Density," The Stoop, May 4, 2015, https:// furmancenter .org/thestoop /entry/the-state -of-new-york -citys-housing-and -neighborhoods -in-2014.

19
Such as the Upper East Side Historic District, desig- nated 1981, and the East Village/ Lower East Side Historic District, designated 2012.

20
2021 New York City Housing and Vacancy

dwellings after World War II, are in many cases converted back into single-family homes to appeal to the wealthy. The same applies to "new law" tenement buildings, built after 1901 and before 1929 along Park Avenue; opposite Central Park on Fifth Avenue and Central Park West; and on stretches of the Upper West Side, Brooklyn, and the Bronx: these buildings comply with then-new regulations for multifamily buildings, which required larger building lots and wide ventilating courtyards.

All of this to state (what is by now perhaps) the obvious: 19th- and early 20th-century building typologies and housing stock have proven that earlier building techniques, materials, and methods endure literally for centuries; meet the needs of changing economies; and are able to adjust, through repeated renovations, to meet new demands within the same building envelope or handle reasonable enlargements while retaining neighborhood character, variety in scale, and a sense of place. What they can- not do is live up to developers' demands to increase bulk (rather than density[18])—hence economic opportunity—as made newly possible on their properties by upzonings and related tax and public-financing incentives. These incentives encourage the removal of existing buildings, along with the businesses and residents who occupy them, except where the structures have been protected by historic district designations (which has happily been the case for many old and new law tenements).[19] New construction on the cleared sites rarely lives up to the quality of what it replaced, with design service lives calculated according to tax depreciation schedules of 30 to 50 years and the realities of poor material selection and installation.

But removal of New York City's old housing stock has had a costly impact on housing affordability. Nearly all the rental apartments in pre-1947 multifamily buildings became subject to rent control laws, and those built before 1974 to rent stabilization laws, both of which made housing affordable to middle- and low-income renters. These regulations still apply to over a million apartments in New York City. In 2021, there were 16,400 rent-controlled and approximately 1,006,000 rent-stabilized or rent-regulated units. Of these units, 773,200 are in buildings built prior to 1974, and the balance are in later buildings that enjoy statutory tax reduction incentives. There were also 174,400 units in public housing and 1,023,000 market-rate, unregulated rental units citywide.[20] These numbers represent a marked decline in affordable units. Between 1994 and 2021, 321,745 rent-stabilized units were removed from the market through various means, including statutory decontrols, conversions to cooperatives or condominiums, expiration of tax incentive regulatory periods, and demolition. During the same period, only 175,095 rent-stabilized units were added.

Each time an upzoning permits greater bulk in a formerly lower-bulk district or underbuilt building scale in high-bulk districts combined with market trends that encourage developers and property owners to replace existing housing stock with new buildings or to combine small units into larger ones, units that are actually affordable to lower- and middle-income renters are permanently lost. In Manhattan, for example, rows of tenement buildings, each containing between 8 and 15 small and modestly priced market or rent-regulated units, are demolished to make way for luxury high-rise apart- ment buildings with much larger units, considerably reducing the overall unit count on the site. Very few of these new units, if any, are the rent-stabilized, albeit higher-priced units that entitle the building to significant tax reductions.[21] Furthermore, New York City has not yet given up on its slum clearance efforts, famously evicting, through court-sanctioned eminent domain, businesses and lower- and middle-income residents

Survey Selected Initial Findings (New York: NYC Department of Housing Preservation and Development, May 16, 2022).

21
See Kim Velsey, "When a New High-Rise Means Less Housing," Curbed, July 21, 2022, https://www.curbed.com/2022/07/bigger-building-fewer-apartments-nyc.html; Stefanos Chen, "Taller Towers, Fewer Homes," *New York Times*, Sept. 23, 2022. See also "Info Brief: Net Change in Housing Units, 2010–2020," NYC Department of City Planning, Feb. 2021, https://www.nyc.gov/assets/planning/download/pdf/planning-level/housing-economy/info-brief-net-change-housing-units-2010-2020.pdf; and "Changes to the Rent Stabilized Housing Stock in NYC in 2021," NYC Rent Guidelines Board, May 26, 2022. Section 421-a tax incentive programs for affordable rental units in new construction were discontinued in 2022.

22
For instance, the Atlantic Yards area in downtown Brooklyn.

to satisfy private developers interested in high-rise, high-end, mega-block, upper-income housing projects, sports complexes, and office towers.[22]

Benjamin Flower would be disappointed still.

Conclusion

Planning for the future city, with its varied population and wide range of economic groups, businesses, and educational, health, and cultural needs, is complex, but it must be done, and it must be done regularly. The planners responsible for New York City's 1916 Zoning Resolution were probably the last ones to actually plan the city, starting as they did with a sparsely developed and easily altered canvas. By contrast, even before they began to rework the zoning maps, the planners of 1961 had largely abandoned any planning efforts and instead took on the role of "zoners." Zoning districts were designated reactively, just as they are today, to respond to the desires of property owners, developers, neighbors, and politicians. Some of these zoning efforts have led to improved results for the community, its residents and businesses, and the city as a whole; other designations have given way to private and political interests that are stronger than civic-minded ones.

Rezoning initiatives, coupled with legislation at every governmental level to regulate the city's finances, economy, building and neighborhood safety, environment, transportation, parkland, waterfront, housing, schooling, health, businesses, jobs, and unions, including the government's own operations, rarely consider the impact of one initiative on the other; indeed, consideration of the "other," i.e., members of the community with smaller, less politically powerful voices, is often purposefully omitted. Hence, no planning—or rather, no zoning and legislating—is pursued with a balanced, or even a well-informed, hand. Political structures force legislation that is rushed, short-sighted, and devoted to short-term "solutions."

It is essential to be open and honest about where the city has been and what it has been doing and not doing to accomplish the tasks it set out over 100 years ago. Infinite data gathering will not deliver solutions—it is a stalling tactic—and layers upon layers of laws upon laws only obfuscate the problem. Elected and government officials, urban planners, legislators, policymakers, urbanists, housing professionals, and civic associations, among so many others, must look around with open eyes and honesty, recognize the failures, concede the shortcomings, and start asking the questions in the right way.

Racial Bargaining for Housing in Newark

David Dante Troutt
is Distinguished Professor of Law and Justice John J. Francis Scholar at Rutgers Law School. He is the founding director of the Rutgers Center on Law, Inequality, and Metropolitan Equity. Troutt teaches and writes about the metropolitan dimensions of race, class and legal structure; intellectual property; torts; and critical legal theory.

Newark, New Jersey, has tried to be many things since the 1967 uprising, an event that defined it to the rest of the world as a city to be avoided at all costs. It has tried to be safe for its residents, to condone rampant police abuse, and then to condemn it by consent decree. It has tried to be a builder of mayoral empires, of corruption and anti-corruption. After generations as a magnet for Italian, Irish, Jewish, and Portuguese immigrants as well as Black and Puerto Rican migrants, it has tried to be a modern magnet for Latin American, West African, and Caribbean immigrants. It has tried to be an arts city but not a riverfront city, a transportation hub but not a destination city, a lab for educational experimentation and teacher villages, and most of all a "renaissance city" on the come up. Like all Black and Hispanic majority cities in America, it has done all these things while in the despised shadow of name-brand cities and wealthy suburbs, without a blueprint to follow or an economy to support it.

Now, Newark is trying to be an equitable city. For its majority poor and working-class residents, that means becoming an affordable place to live.

Equity is a complicated civic value in one of the most expensive metro areas of the country. The equity idea sits between two poles. On one hand, Newark needs economic growth; the investments in jobs, commercial development, and housing that bring more jobs; expanded amenities; a stronger tax base; and a public sector equal to the needs of a disproportionately vulnerable population. The tool kit for economic growth in postindustrial American cities tends to foster neoliberal relationships between public and private actors while giving due regard to market-rate returns. Nationally, this quid pro quo has contributed to an urban economic boom, widespread gentrification of urban neighborhoods, and mounting inequality. On the other hand, Newark needs to "hold the line" (a favorite phrase of its current mayor, Ras Baraka); to ensure "gentrification from within," that is, in which economic growth meets the dignitary needs of a population entitled to the same dreams of economic mobility, wealth creation, health, and safety as anyone else.

Equitable growth must also mean housing, because you can't share in the rising fortunes of a city if you can't afford to live there. Affordability is such a crisis in America now that it means radically different things to different people. Most people don't think of cities like Newark as experiencing such problems. Yet when my colleague and I studied the affordability gap in Newark, we found a city of cost-burdened renters.[1] Four out of five Newarkers rent their homes, with two-thirds paying over 30 percent of their household income on rent and about 40 percent paying over half. Median household incomes are low—only about $37,000 a year. The median affordable rent should be about $750 a month. Instead, renters pay closer to $1,100. How many affordable units would it take to bridge the gap? Over 16,000. How many were built in the last five years? About 3,500. Do the math, as they say.

Before we actually consider what it would take to do the math, however, another contradiction of housing economics arose: corporate house buyers.

Newark's habitable streets are spread thin across about 19 square miles and five wards. By big city standards, this land mass is but a pinch of the Earth. Yet these wards and their neighborhoods have distinctive feels. I know them not as a resident but as a student, an urbanist, and someone who's worked here for decades—in other words, a curious stranger who won't leave. In the Ironbound (the East Ward), narrow streets running off broad avenues entangle like those of Philadelphia, and the housing stock resembles that of blue-collar Boston, but neither of those cities has anything like the restaurants per square inch here, the sheer busy-ness of the commercial streets, the amount of Brazilian barbecue per capita, or the fact that so much of it is actually sold to neighborhood people themselves, still mostly Portuguese and Brazilian, but changing. Contrast the Central Ward, which includes a downtown built for proximity to commuter trains, the possibility of the next riot (few storefronts), and a couple of major universities (including my own), which have benefited from urban renewal programs that cleared Black people for public housing only to later clear the public housing. This is the heartland of economic hopes, the beginning of all bets on the city's future. A pipeline of sprawling new projects foretells a transformation that in five years will render the city unrecognizable. In the North Ward are mostly Latino hill neighborhoods. These start to look like their neighboring towns—places that should have been annexed when Newark was first outgrowing its footprint but weren't.

The same is true of the West and South Wards, where I want to linger for a minute. These are Newark's primarily Black wards and are adjacent to three smaller municipalities (Irvington, Orange, and East Orange); together, these make up a miniature metro of Black households in Essex County. Commercial street life is quieter and spottier in these wards. What walkability exists along the broad sidewalks is more purposeful, with fewer targets. Investment is overwhelmingly residential whether you're in the more working-class side streets or the more middle-class neighborhoods of Vailsburg and Weequahic. Beyond their African American character, the two wards are distinguishable from the rest of Newark by three facts:

1
Katherine Nelson and David D. Troutt, *Homes Beyond Reach: An Assessment and Gap Analysis of Newark's Affordable Rental Stock* (Newark: Rutgers CLiME, 2021), https://static1.squarespace.com/static/5b996f553917ee5e584ba742/t/602ee8e07a067a5f21fbd453/1613687010432/CLiME+Report+2021-02+v20210218+FINAL.pdf.

- They have seen the greatest number of foreclosures since the 2008 crash.
- They are home to the most rent-burdened households and the accompanying displacement risk that comes with financial insecurity.
- Institutional investors have come for them in droves.

The investors come by text message, robocalls, notes in your mailbox, and knocks on your door. They engage in campaigns staffed by call centers, using public and proprietary data on homeowners in distress, or on older homes needing repair, or simply on older homeowners tired of maintaining a two- or three-family home. They are relentless, intrusive, and, despite being ubiquitous, mostly anonymous. For years they've been showing up in the West and South Wards, buying up properties by the thousands and earning steadily increasing rental income.

Our research suggested a connection between increasing rents and the phenomenon of institutional buyer activity since 2010.[2] Wall Street firms, first incentivized by Freddie Mac to buy up vacant foreclosed homes, cautiously began buying in small tranches at auctions. HUD sold thousands of foreclosed properties to national firms like Blackstone in the early 2010s. Soon, single-family rentals became an established asset class for investors in a country that was moving precipitously from a nation of homeowners to a nation of renters. Across Southern cities like Atlanta and Jacksonville and Rust Belt cities like Cleveland and Detroit, large companies like Invitation Homes and Waypoint Starwood discovered that rents could deliver passive gains to their investors from the very tenants who used to be stable homeowners. Not coincidentally, the original model disproportionately relied on Black neighborhoods—often adjacent to growth areas—foreclosed Black homeowners, and soon-to-be Black renters.

These changes in a neighborhood—especially one dominated by renters—have a stealth occurrence; you sense it, but you can't quite put your finger on it. You get the calls and constant solicitations, you see the strange men knocking on doors and the construction crews that follow, but it's hard to fit those impressions into a big picture. Outside residential investors had always existed in Newark, but now they were transforming the market one private transaction at a time. Using deed data, we found a threefold increase in the number of property sales of 1–4-unit homes to large-scale limited liability companies between 2010 and 2020. In just the three years ending in 2020, these LLCs purchased about 2,000 1–4-unit properties in each of the West and South Wards, far more than in any other ward in Newark. We could trace the identities of only three or four LLCs—which together accounted for about a quarter of those deals—because the labyrinthine nature of the deal structure hides the identities behind holding and shell companies, general partners, and limited partners, all of them private. Newark neighborhoods had morphed into company towns, though neither tenants nor researchers knew which company. Even Newark government officials—like their counterparts across the country—were unaware of the changing landscape of ownership.

A young real estate agent—we'll call him "B"—read our study and let me know that we had revealed only the half of it. He had talked with some of the institutional investors we named in the report, and they were laughing. By relying only on deeded transactions, we had undercounted everything, he explained, because LLCs transfer tranches of properties within the parent company. One of the main investors reported that he was disappointed in his company's low reported property count; the man bought as many properties in a year as we had attributed to him over five. B said the investors weren't all

2
David D. Troutt and Katharine Nelson, *Who Owns Newark? Transferring Wealth from Newark Homeowners to Corporate Buyers* (Newark: Rutgers CLiME, 2022), https://static1 .squarespace .com/static /5b996f553917 ee5e584ba742/t /626fd98bb835 7d201cb8dcb5 /1651497359130 /Who+Owns +Newark+Final+1 .pdf.

the same, either. Some were rich family companies looking for a safe investment and committed to good property management. Some were regional investment companies—smaller versions of the national firms—with a mixed record of ownership, renting, and flipping. A third group would stop at nothing and, like so many investor buyers, would aggressively bully tenants, charge high fees, evict old ladies for a single missed rent check, and delay on necessary repairs.

"They could take *your* house, too," he declared with confidence.

Maybe they could or maybe they couldn't, but the threat B was communicating has to do with a constellation of factors related to what I call "racial bargaining." The whole business model for institutional buy-to-rent companies relies on finding places with low costs of entry and high rates of stable renters in a market with growth potential. B explained that many factors lowered the cost of entry in Newark—for starters, its low rates of homeownership and low house prices relative to its expensive region. These are factors that go to Newark's racial and economic history, particularly the practice of redlining that undercut residential investment once Blacks arrived in significant numbers, to segregated suburbs that subsidized White flight, to urban renewal that sucked the value out of privately owned homes, to public housing—what went up in towers and what eventually came down through implosion. By the time reverse redlining and predatory lending began tearing paths through these same neighborhoods in the 1990s and early 2000s, the subprime lending crash seemed inevitable. Newark had one of the highest foreclosure rates in the country. Though you might not know it to look at them today, these zip codes are a graveyard of broken American dreams.

The key point is that public and private policies that systematically destabilize or exploit Black housing consumers instill contractual vulnerability and invite further exploitation. Black people are not typically exploited in transactional terms because they're easy marks, they're easy marks because they're typically exploited in transactional terms by interests that have superior bargaining power and know they can capitalize on the imbalance.

Racial bargaining creates unstated contractual rules of the road. Sophisticated institutional buyers know that there are particular means to create low costs of entry among a population that has been buffeted by marginalized housing markets for generations: meet them in their desperation and offer them desperate terms. The investor buyer starts in 2010 with foreclosures, the lowest cost of entry. As time goes on, however, more purchases are made from private sellers—regular homeowners—who see a relative price boom going on around them. The institutional buyers find them, B explained. They know who is probably a "motivated seller." The buyers dazzle the owners with a price well below the property's worth, then make a cash offer considerably below that. The buyers may not even have the cash, but they can get it with a hard money loan of, say, 10 percent, because they're buying so low that they have instant equity of tens of thousands of dollars.

Why does this illustrate racial bargaining? Racial bargaining is the perversion of contractual norms because of disparities that result from the unique context of racism. African Americans have experienced a long history of real estate transactions where terms, benefits, and bargaining power have been defined differently because of race. For instance, redlining meant that Newark Blacks in the 1940s and 1950s leased homes at higher rents because of segregated neighborhoods and bought them through exorbitant

3
See Robert Curvin, *Inside Newark: Decline, Rebellion, and the Search for Transformation* (New Brunswick, NJ: Rutgers University Press, 2014), 17–18.

4
See Bernard J. Frieden and Lynne B. Sagalyn, *Downtown Inc.: How America Rebuilds Cities* (Cambridge, MA: MIT Press, 1989), 33–36.

5
See, e.g., Elora Lee Raymond et al., "From Foreclosure to Eviction: Housing Insecurity in Corporate-Owned Single-Family Rentals," *Cityscape: A Journal of Policy Development and Research*, Department of Housing and Urban Development 20, no. 3 (2018), https://www.huduser.gov/portal/periodicals/cityscpe/vol20num3/ch9.pdf. Depending on the firm, institutional investors were between 11 and 205 percent more likely to file for eviction than mom-and-pop firms, even after controlling for property, tenant, and neighborhood characteristics. See also Public Advocates, ACCE, and Americans for Financial Reform,

land contracts with default terms and interest rates that dramatically benefited White sellers. (The practice was perfected in Chicago.)[3] While many lower-income people were displaced by urban renewal programs, Black neighborhoods were disproportionately targeted, leaving many owners without just compensation and most renters without relocation assistance despite government leases and federal rules obligating such assistance.[4] Racial bargaining affects not only the terms of a single transaction in time, but the expectations surrounding similar transactions over time. Racial bargaining conditions Black people to expect less for their homes, to pay more in fees and interest rates, and to accept deals they know are inferior to deals others can make. In Newark, the campaign by institutional buyers to identify "motivated" Black sellers only to discount the price due to desperation, a lack of information or education, or both is racial bargaining.

The racial bargaining that subverts wealth creation in predominantly Black housing markets like Newark's West and South Wards affects more than the buyer and seller in an individual deal. We found that in these wards rents are rising fastest and burdening a greater number of tenants. These are also the wards where homeownership rates have declined by more than 5 percent. The institutional buyers are beating out first-time home buyers as well as local nonprofit developers of affordable housing for the smaller homes they used to buy. B says that most houses for sale are not even listed before they are bought up. Our research shows that a third of all sales of 1–4-unit homes in these neighborhoods are now from investor to investor. This means that investors have remade the residential real estate market in their own image, a market not of homeowners and wealth builders but of large-scale rent seekers and profit makers selling to each other.

The growing body of research on single-family rentals and the own-to-rent asset class shows that affordability and stability have fallen dramatically.[5] Landlords who owe fiduciary obligations to investors may or may not invest in their properties' upkeep, but they surely must keep the rents high in order to offer steady, passive returns. At the lower end of the market, this dynamic is strongly associated with more aggressive evictions, more fees, greater delays in repairs, and, yes, higher rents.

Of course, another characteristic of racial bargaining is the inability to compel transactional terms, even if they carry the force of law. In other words, just because a tenant knows she is being unfairly denied repairs, or asked to leave, or low-balled through fraudulent claims doesn't mean she can bring the law to bear in her defense. It requires resources—time, money, and confidence—to push back with expert representation in court. Large landlords know they've brought guns to a fistfight. Your rights are only as good as your ability to enforce them.

Which makes Newark a hard city to make equitable.

Victoria Pratt is the retired chief judge of Newark Municipal Court. Judge Pratt knows that housing is central to dignity as well as to equity, especially for the indigent people who came before her for misdemeanors and parole violations. Once you are in the system, you'd better have an address. Without an address, you can't receive mail notices from the court, like when to appear again or for your probation officer to check up on you. For a great many people, Judge Pratt explains, the only stable address to use is Grandma's—even if you don't live there, even if it is a crowded and tenuous place to be. Grandma is the primary source of housing for untold people in America who struggle to lead financially independent lives. If it's discovered that you don't actually live at Grandma's house, you may miss a court date and be in default or, worse, violate probation and be sent to jail.

Wall Street Landlords Turn American Dream into a Nightmare, Public Advocates (2018), 21–25, https://www .publicadvocates .org/our-work /housing-justice /wall-street -landlords-turn -american-dream -into-a-nightmare/; https://drive .google.com /file/d/0B50MO aXe7OI6UUJIR1 9iRkFTYzg/view.

This is a poor people problem, but Newark has a lot of poor people—almost a third of its residents. Maybe Grandma lives in public housing. If her live-in relative commits even a petty crime, everybody may lose housing. If she lives in senior housing, any live-in relative risks violating the lease. Not only does the system governing poor people's lives struggle to provide housing opportunities—even public housing is increasingly mixed-income these days—it's quick to take it away, which sends them into the streets.

This too is racial bargaining for housing—for a place to stay, for a way to stay out of jail, for a way to keep your children lest they be taken away by family courts. Some will win enough to have choices. Many will lose for failure of proof or for noncompliance with a demanding state apparatus whose rules are too powerful to overcome. The people affected are not all Black—just most of them. These systems of limited leverage and settling for less seem designed for Black people, but they also catch many other people— Latino, immigrant, low-income, disabled, in dangerous relationships—in their web of consequences.

So racial bargaining in the search for affordable homes leads to outcomes that make inequality common and equity rare. Because equity is rare, because it is a norm most Americans have never really seen in practice for long, it is even harder to agree on, let alone to achieve. At bottom, we can agree that the people who live in Newark now should be able to stay in Newark if they want to. This takes us back to some of the hard macroeconomic truths of the housing affordability crisis.

Housing is fundamentally a supply and demand industry, a capital-intensive business. Many factors determine supply, such as the price and availability of land, developer interest, financing rates and construction costs, labor and materials, and, especially when it comes to below-market-rate housing, the generosity of public subsidies. Newark does not do well by most of these market measures even though it has perhaps more subsidized housing than any city in New Jersey. A main reason for Newark's shortfall is that demand is so constrained by low incomes. If Newark consumers could pay more for housing, then the supply picture would probably brighten. Because they can't, we tend to focus on supply—preserving or producing deep affordability—which appears to be the only variable within our policy control. This simplistic helicopter view of housing economics reveals one important question: whose responsibility is it to create affordable housing options for the huge number of vulnerable housing consumers in an equitable city subject to racial bargaining?

This is a complicated issue for local elected officials, local advocacy organizations, and foundations that provide many of the basic supports for families who need them. Affordability problems in other American cities also involve supply, but the dynamics are different in Newark. First, demand for expensive homes in places like Austin, Texas, may be fueled by an influx of wealthier newcomers attracted to jobs. In Newark, newer residents aren't coming for jobs, but mainly for greater affordability relative to high regional housing prices. Second, development of new housing, such as the housing boom in Brooklyn, may be driven by the prospect of more economic growth. Newark's rising prices seem unattached to the city's ability to attract significant growth in jobs and new business. Third, supply of new housing in many cities is constrained by growth controls contained in zoning laws, a form of NIMBYism associated with cities like San Francisco. Newark doesn't have blocs of powerful property owners seeking regulatory protection for their property values.

While many cities (and their states) just don't make affordable housing a public policy priority, Newark does—and has for years. Why is the affordability gap so large, and who can close it?

The answer is complicated; the solution has escaped us all. One reason is that there is a very limited market for building deeply affordable housing. Developers have little reason to do it. Even if they did, factors like institutional buyer activity and COVID-induced relocations are increasing the value of land, materials, and property, making low-cost housing even further out of reach.

Second, government at all levels withdrew from direct housing production with passage of the Faircloth Amendment in 1998. Nearly every attempt to build housing with effective affordability restrictions has been created by incentive subsidy programs like federal tax credits that make up significant parts of the "capital stack" or direct-to-consumer benefits like housing choice vouchers, down payment assistance, and property tax relief. Cities like Newark can strengthen their rent control laws, but they do not build new homes. (They should.) The Faircloth Amendment prohibits the federal government from building more public housing.[6] And higher interest rates price more people out of the market.

Third, the organizations that grew up in the 1970s and 1980s with the goal of developing communities in the interest of their working-class residents have struggled with the bricks-and-mortar complexities of building affordable housing on a large scale.

One such organization is Newark's New Community Corporation, a storied community development corporation that rose from the ashes of Newark's 1967 rebellion. According to Richard Cammarieri, New Community's director of community engagement, the CDC maintains 1,700 units of housing for low-income seniors and families on a 50-acre footprint. Since the 1970s, it has been a functioning model, with wrap-around services, that defies the shibboleth that 100 percent affordable housing cannot succeed. Over the past 20 years, NCC has developed a 200-unit condominium complex, a third of which were low-income affordable, and also a 24-unit supportive housing facility for chronically homeless individuals. Nevertheless, Cammarieri concedes one truth: New Community hasn't built a single unit of permanently affordable low-income rental housing in over 30 years. It's not alone. Our research confirms that CDCs in Newark have produced only about 2,400 units since 2000.

This is how hard it is to create affordable housing in a grossly unequal nation. Financing and land acquisition costs have prevented New Community from doing more during the very period when everyone knew the affordability crunch was tightening. Community development corporations have had to service the rise in homelessness. CDCs are traffic cops at the intersections of food scarcity, workforce readiness, health care, early childhood education, and senior programs. They know all about Grandma and the generations her housing stability supports. Indeed, they are central to whatever it takes to become an equitable city, because the need to live with dignity is not only about affording your home. But building affordable housing is not their expertise.

The challenge for the equitable city is to align the right actors with the right resources toward truly equitable housing goals before the next wave of profit seeking yanks the opportunity further out of reach. Cities can change quickly. Decisions are being made. Real estate remains hot. Newark has a great many attributes—proud and resilient population, deep reservoir of creative talents and artistic institutions, long

6
According to the Department of Housing and Urban Development, "Section 9(g)(3) of the Housing Act of 1937 ('Faircloth Amendment') limits the construction of new public housing units," Guidance on Complying with the Maximum Number of Units Eligible for Operating Subsidy Pursuant to Section 9(g)(3)(A) of the Housing Act of 1937 (aka the Faircloth Limit), accessed Nov. 2, 2022, https://www.hud.gov/sites/documents/FRCLTH-LMT.pdf.

history of not bowing to efforts to isolate and subordinate it, experimental spirit. But it has limited time to institutionalize equity.

The equity challenge arises from an irony common to environments with racial bargaining. Cities like Newark have long sought the very investments that now risk displacing their residents. The history of disinvestment and racial bargaining that devalued Black homes and spaces facilitated the low costs of entry that investors and speculators have quietly exploited since the 2008 crash decimated household wealth. Institutional buyers wouldn't come if they didn't see the economic upside. They're betting on it with tens of millions of dollars. In a classic citywide case of gentrification, Newark's prospective success in finally attracting investment has put its residents at risk of being replaced.

Whatever the solution, the approach must address four interrelated issues: economic autonomy, regulatory protection, systemic disqualification, and information deficits.

First, economic autonomy focuses on the tenuous status of renters and homeowners in acquiring, holding, and growing permanent assets. Homeownership used to be called the American Dream. Many advocates continue to seek it as a way out of housing insecurity and negative wealth. I'm not so sure the old model scales. I imagine taking a page from the institutional investor playbook and financing shared-equity cooperatives, community land trusts, or some other form of partial communal ownership in a housing asset that carries long-term affordability restrictions. The point is to question the traditional mortgage as the best way to help moderate-income people control their own housing fate. Partial communal ownership might offer a far more cost-effective way to finance the production of more varied types of affordable housing—by private builders or CDCs working with the city for cheap land and with community development financial institutions for low-cost loans. Imagine a collection of Grandmas on a board together, family members watching and learning along the way.

Second, regulatory protection requires the intervention of public actors to enforce laws already enacted, like code enforcement for health violations. But protective regulation can also police markets against fraudulent activity, harassment, predatory practices, and speculation. A lot of everyday inequity would cease to exist if economic actors—be they real estate agents, institutional investors, or banks—knew that there might be serious consequences if they're caught. Crafting the right consumer protections is always good for economic fairness—middle-class people routinely count on them. But doing so in the context of racial bargaining, where it can have the greatest intergenerational impact, would be truly equitable.

Third, systemic disqualification goes back to Judge Pratt's courtroom and the rules that casually deny people their dignity. There is no good reason to insist on a defendant's address on pain of incarceration when it's clear that many are housing insecure or unhoused. That is a system that disqualifies poor people as of right—in effect criminalizing homelessness. There are many other examples that must be rooted out in an equitable city. Like how the lack of a lawyer disqualifies tenants facing eviction. Or how it's not possible to raise a habitability defense without posting bond. Or how parental rights are terminated because of the recurrent presence of mold.

Finally, information deficits—the first tool to fraud—run throughout. Living in the Information Age, you would think we would champion ways to ensure that residents and renters, homeowners and workers have trusted sources of critical information, like where to get COVID-19 testing, whether a purchase offer is fair, and how to find reliable counsel when tenant rights are at risk. Newark already does some of this. Cities can do more, but they have to have the capacity to put a system in place and they have to be trustworthy stewards of their residents' interests, which takes us back to the goal of an equitable city that started this essay.

Sometimes it's best to know what we all want, so I'll end with something else Richard Cammarieri told me: "Too often we're fixed on the logistics—the means—and we lose sight of the ends, which is a humane environment for people to live in, among residents, building owners, and others. It's to affirm the humanity of the people who live there and allow them self-determination over their lives. I know it's implicit, but saying it out loud wouldn't hurt."

Climate Disasters and Environmental Justice

Justin Steil is associate professor of law and urban planning at the Massachusetts Institute of Technology. Steil recently co-edited the books *Furthering Fair Housing: Prospects for Racial Justice in America's Neighborhoods* and *The Dream Revisited: Contemporary Debates about Housing, Segregation, and Opportunity*.

Recent hurricanes, floods, and wildfires across the United States highlight the devastating effect of climate change–related disasters on individuals and households. The impact on access to housing and housing stability is no less devastating. As a result of historic and contemporary racial and economic discrimination and inequality, households with low incomes and communities of color are disproportionately exposed to these disasters, are disproportionately harmed by these disasters, and benefit less over the long term than others from public disaster recovery programs.[1]

The effects of disasters on housing are an environmental justice issue, one intertwined with broader crises of housing affordability and global heating that have been building since the 1970s. Low- and moderate-income households simultaneously face crushing housing costs and increased exposure to more frequent and severe environmental events. Hurricanes, wildfires, coastal and riverine flooding, and other extreme climatic events between 2015 and 2017 extensively damaged more than 500,000 rental homes and displaced 324,000 renters.[2] The risks in the future are even greater: according to risk maps from the Federal Emergency Management Agency, roughly 40 percent of renters' homes across the United States are at moderate or greater risk of flooding, drought, earthquakes, and hurricanes.[3] Especially troubling, the long-term benefits of public funding for disaster recovery seem to aid homeowners more than renters and White households more than Black households.[4] Recent federal cases concerning fair housing and civil rights help identify why the benefits of disaster recovery programs are

1
Alice Fothergill
and Lori A. Peek,
"Poverty and
Disasters in the
United States: A
Review of Recent
Sociological
Findings," *Natural
Hazards* 32
(2004): 89–110;
NYU Furman
Center, *Population
in the U.S.
Floodplains*, data
brief, Dec. 2017,
https://furman
center.org/files
/Floodplain
_PopulationBrief
_12DEC2017.pdf;
US Government
Accountability
Office, *Disaster
Assistance: Greater
Coordination and
an Evaluation
of Programs'
Outcomes Could
Improve Disaster
Case Management*,
report, 2009,
https://www
.gao.gov/assets
/gao-09-561.pdf;
Junia Howell and
James R. Elliott,
"Damages Done:
The Longitudinal
Impacts of Natural
Hazards on Wealth
Inequality in the
United States,"
Social Problems
66, no. 3 (2019):
448–67; Jee
Young Lee and
Shannon Van
Zandt, "Housing
Tenure and Social
Vulnerability
to Disasters: A
Review of the
Evidence," *Journal
of Planning
Literature* 34, no. 2
(2019): 156–70.

felt unevenly and how environmental justice, civil rights, and affordable housing advocates can improve recovery programs and housing stability.

Affordable Housing after Climate Disasters

Race, socioeconomic status, gender, and age all powerfully shape both physical and social vulnerability to the effects of disasters.[5] Housing tenure occupies the intersection of these physical and social dimensions of vulnerability.[6] Extreme environmental events reinforce pre-disaster patterns of racial and class inequality, both in their effects on homes directly and in their effects on household financial stress.[7]

Exposure to extreme weather related to climate change has worsened the already severe crisis of housing affordability. For instance, Butte County, California, lost 13.9 percent of its homes in 2018 because of the Camp Fire.[8] In 2020, more than 100,000 people across the United States were forced from their homes due to disasters.[9] In 2021, the property data company CoreLogic estimated that nearly 15 million homes, or one out of 10, were affected by severe environmental events, causing $57 billion in property damage.[10] The National Oceanic and Atmospheric Administration estimated the total costs of major disasters in 2020, 2021, and 2022 at $88.5 billion, $128.2 billion, and $138.7 billion respectively.[11] This trend of increasing disaster effects on homes, and particularly the homes of renters with low incomes, will likely continue, given that roughly 39 percent of the 3.1 million rental homes supported by the Low-Income Housing Tax Credit program and 30 percent of the 2.3 million rental homes supported by HUD's project-based vouchers are located in what FEMA categorizes as high-risk locations.[12]

Weather disasters are not individual environmental events but long-term social processes in which exposure to hazards and the ability to recover are shaped through political processes of social and physical investment and disinvestment.[13] Vulnerability based on location and social location "encompasses both the probability of suffering the negative effects of hazards and disasters and the likelihood that some groups will be less able than others to navigate the recovery process successfully."[14]

Low-income renters are disproportionately physically vulnerable, that is, disproportionately exposed to the potential for loss from environmental hazards, for three main reasons. First, by economic imperative in our current housing markets, low-income renters are often exposed to riskier housing contexts. Areas vulnerable to environmental hazards often have lower land values *because* of their vulnerability and are thus more affordable to households with low incomes. Second, older homes are generally more affordable than newer ones. Older rental homes, however, because of both building codes at the time of construction, which did not take climate change–related disasters into account, and deterioration over time, are also more likely to have structural deficiencies and to be less resilient to disaster.[15] Third, because of the history of racial and economic discrimination in housing in the United States, low-income households and households of color are more likely to live in neighborhoods that have been redlined or otherwise systematically disinvested, leading to infrastructural neglect and locational or physical vulnerability.[16]

Occupants of rental housing are also disproportionately socially vulnerable, in part because of the restrictions that the current system of property rights places on renters' ability to control their physical environment and maintain housing stability. Renters face limitations on "their capacity to anticipate, cope with, resist and recover from the impacts of a natural hazard."[17] Socioeconomic status determines the financial and social

2

Harvard Joint
Center for Housing
Studies, *The State
of the Nation's
Housing*, report,
2020, https://www
.jchs.harvard.edu
/sites/default/files
/reports/files
/Harvard_JCHS
_The_State_of_the
_Nations_Housing
_2020_Report
_Revised_120720
.pdf; NOAA
National Centers
for Environmental
Information, "U.S.
Billion-Dollar
Weather and
Climate Disasters,"
2023, https://www
.ncei.noaa.gov
/access/billions/;
Hannah Perls,
"U.S. Disaster
Displacement
in the Era of
Climate Change:
Discrimination
& Consultation
Under the Stafford
Act," *Harvard
Environmental Law
Review* 44, no. 22
(2020): 512–52,
https://harvardelr
.com/wp-content
/uploads/sites
/12/2020/08/44
.2-Perls.pdf.

3

Harvard Joint
Center for Housing
Studies, *The State
of the Nation's
Housing*, report,
2022, https://www
.jchs.harvard.edu
/sites/default/files
/reports/files
/Harvard_JCHS
_State_Nations
_Housing_2022.pdf.

4

Howell and Elliott,
"Damages Done."

capital on which households can draw to access and make use of recovery assistance, as well as the political capital often necessary to successfully advocate for sufficient recovery resources.[18] The intersection of economic marginalization, racial discrimination, social isolation, and legal exclusion creates "cumulative vulnerability," meaning that both the immediate consequences of disasters and the long-term obstacles to recovery are particularly acute for low-income renters of color.[19]

After a disaster, housing costs may increase in the short term because of a simultaneous decrease in housing supply caused by damage to existing homes and increase in need from displaced residents, which can leave low-income renters homeless or displaced.[20] Recent research analyzing county-level data on evictions and disasters nationwide between 2000 and 2015 combined with qualitative interviews with survivors of Hurricane Michael, which devastated the Florida Panhandle in 2018, found that severe flooding in one year is associated with significant increases in evictions in that and the following years.[21] Further, higher county-level median rents are associated with higher rates of eviction, highlighting how high housing costs and disaster vulnerability intersect.

Disaster Housing Policy Context. The government response to major disasters generally entails collaboration among federal, state, territorial, tribal, and local agencies. Often conceptualized around four steps—mitigation, preparedness, response, and recovery—federal programs allow states, territories, or tribes and also households to apply for financial assistance for projects that support recovery from a disaster and reduce the risk of future damage.

Generally, states, tribes, and territories request a presidential disaster declaration and various forms of federal aid from FEMA. The Robert T. Stafford Relief and Emergency Assistance Act of 1998 (42 USC §§ 5121 et seq.) authorizes FEMA to provide up to $35,000 to families whose homes are rendered uninhabitable by a disaster to rent alternate housing for up to 18 months and to repair owner-occupied private residences (though not all federally declared disasters qualify households for housing assistance, and the specific forms of assistance vary by region and declared event). In situations where households are unable to take advantage of financial assistance because of either challenges securing an appropriate temporary home or limited inventory, the Stafford Act authorizes FEMA to provide for up to 18 months of temporary housing, often in the form of mobile homes or travel trailers. In 2021, FEMA provided more than $2 billion in rental assistance and support for home repairs to more than 850,000 households. However, recent research has found that the more aid an area receives from FEMA, the wider the post-disaster wealth inequality between renters and homeowners and between Black and White households.[22]

There is no established program that addresses the need for permanent rental housing after disasters.[23] The closest existing program is the periodic congressional appropriation of Community Development Block Grant Disaster Recovery funds, which affected states can use in various ways to fund rebuilding and recovery. If funds are appropriated by Congress, which is uncertain after any given disaster, each state designs its own recovery program in compliance with guidelines from the US Department of Housing and Urban Development.

The Low-Income Housing Tax Credit program also plays a significant role in providing permanent housing for low-income renters. The LIHTC program has become the primary federal tool for encouraging the development of affordable multifamily housing.

5
Betty Hearn
Morrow and Walter
Gillis Peacock,
"Disasters and
Social Change:
Hurricane Andrew
and the Reshaping
of Miami?," in
Hurricane Andrew:
Ethnicity, Gender
and the Sociology
of Disasters, ed.
Walter Gillis
Peacock, Betty
Hearn Morrow,
and Hugh
Gladwin (London:
Routledge,
1997); Bert
Bolin, *A History*
of the Science
and Politics of
Climate Change:
The Role of the
Intergovernmental
Panel on
Climate Change
(Cambridge:
Cambridge
University Press,
2007); Mariana
Arcaya, Ethan
J. Raker, and
Mary C. Waters,
"The Social
Consequences
of Disasters:
Individual and
Community
Change," *Annual*
Review of
Sociology 46
(2020): 671–91.

6
Lee and Van Zandt,
"Housing Tenure."

Recent research has found that, on average, the number of LIHTC units per million people allocated to flood-affected counties in the year following a severe flood increases by 57 percent.[24] It is important to note, however, that severe floods had a positive and significant effect on the number of LIHTC allocations *outside* the 500-year floodplain in a disaster-affected county for three years following the flood, but no significant effect on allocations inside the floodplain. The LIHTC program, which was not designed with disaster response in mind, is being repurposed by states and housing developers both to increase subsidized rental options in disaster-struck counties and to reduce risk for low-income renters by locating units outside of floodplains.[25]

Though extreme weather disproportionately affects low-income renters, current federal and state disaster assistance programs disproportionately benefit homeowners.[26] For instance, a Government Accountability Office study found that after Hurricane Katrina, 62 percent of damaged homeowner units but only 18 percent of damaged rental units received federal assistance.[27] The substantial divergence by race and income in homeownership rates, combined with the fact that housing in lower-income areas tends to sustain more damage and recover more slowly than housing in higher-income areas, means that recovery processes that disproportionately assist homeowners reinforce historic racial and economic disparities.[28] How can affordable housing advocates and environmental justice organizers intervene?

Climate Disasters, Environmental Justice, and Fair Housing

Four recent legal actions illuminate how federal aid can contribute to widening inequality and suggest ways to change the allocation of aid to support renters, communities of color, and the creation of more durable, more affordable housing.

Greater New Orleans Fair Housing Action Center v. US Department of Housing and Urban Development.[29] In 2010, five years after Hurricane Katrina devastated New Orleans, a local nonprofit fair-housing organization sued HUD and the Louisiana Recovery Authority for the racially disparate impact caused by the state's design of the Hurricane Katrina recovery program. More than 123,000 owner-occupied homes were destroyed or severely damaged by Hurricanes Katrina and Rita in 2005. To support recovery, Congress allocated funds to Louisiana through the block grant program, supervised by HUD. The Louisiana Recovery Authority used these CDBG-DR funds to create the Road Home Homeowner Assistance Program to provide $8 billion in rebuilding grants to 117,744 Louisiana homeowners. The state calculated grants by taking the lesser of either the pre-storm value of the home or the cost to rebuild and subtracting the value of any FEMA assistance or insurance payments or, if the homeowner had no insurance, applying a 30 percent penalty (i.e., decreasing by 30 percent the value or the cost to rebuild). Assistance was capped at $150,000.

The Greater New Orleans Fair Housing Action Center argued that using pre-storm values as a grant ceiling had a disparate impact on African American homeowners because homes in predominantly Black neighborhoods were valued lower than homes of comparable size and quality in predominantly White neighborhoods. Using the pre-storm value of the home as a ceiling violated the Fair Housing Act and the Housing and Community Development Act of 1974, the Greater New Orleans Fair Housing Action Center contended, because it led to a wider gap for Black homeowners relative to White homeowners between the total resources available for rebuilding and the total cost of rebuilding. As a result of the case, the parties reached a settlement with HUD and the

7
Andrew Rumbach and Carrie Makarewicz, "Affordable Housing and Disaster Recovery: A Case Study of the 2013 Colorado Floods," in *Coming Home after Disaster: Multiple Dimensions of Housing Recovery*, ed. Alka Sapat and Ann-Margaret Esnard (Boca Raton, FL: CRC Press, 2016), 99–112; Lee and Van Zandt, "Housing Tenure."

8
Lauren Medina and David Armstrong, "New Census Housing Unit Estimates Use FEMA Data to Capture Impact of Disasters in Every State," US Census Bureau, May 21, 2020, https://www.census.gov/library/stories/2020/05/how-disasters-affect-the-nations-housing.html.

9
Harvard Joint Center for Housing Studies, *The State of the Nation's Housing*, report, 2021, https://www.jchs.harvard.edu/sites/default/files/reports/files/Harvard_JCHS_State_Nations_Housing_2021.pdf.

Louisiana Recovery Authority to change the grant formula—basing awards on cost of damage rather than on pre-storm market value of the home—and to provide supplemental grant awards to low- and moderate-income homeowners. The arguments made by the Greater New Orleans Fair Housing Action Center highlight how disaster recovery programs with metrics that may appear neutral can nevertheless be shaped by historic and continuing discrimination and reinforce and exacerbate racial inequality in recovery.

Greater New Orleans Fair Housing Action Center v. St. Bernard Parish.[30] In a long-running set of cases against St. Bernard Parish, which neighbors New Orleans but has a much smaller share of Black residents than New Orleans, the same fair-housing organization highlighted various discriminatory local laws and policies that limited the creation of and access to affordable housing after disasters. First, the organization successfully sued to enjoin the "blood relative ordinance" enacted by St. Bernard Parish after Hurricane Katrina, which prohibited individuals from renting, leasing, loaning, or otherwise allowing occupancy or use of any single-family residence other than by family members related by blood without first obtaining a special permit from the St. Bernard Parish Council. The Greater New Orleans Fair Housing Action Center argued that the ordinance was designed to keep Black residents from New Orleans affected by Katrina from renting homes in St. Bernard Parish. In response, the parish replaced the blood relative ordinance with an ordinance that required homeowners to obtain a Permissive Use Permit from the parish council before renting out single-family residences. Given that this policy would have had a similar discriminatory effect as the blood relative ordinance, the Greater New Orleans Fair Housing Action Center sued once again. The parish council withdrew the ordinance and signed a consent decree.

After the second ruling, a builder, with support from low-income housing tax credits, initiated work on a housing development with 70 percent of the units designated as affordable. To block the construction, the St. Bernard Parish Council issued a moratorium on the construction of all multifamily buildings. The fair-housing organization sued the parish again, arguing that the parish had violated both the consent decree and the Fair Housing Act. The district court found that the moratorium would have had a disparate impact on the basis of race in denying homes to Black households and, further, that the ordinance was intended to be racially discriminatory, as revealed by legislative history, contemporaneous statements, and the inadequacy of alternative goals asserted by the parish council.

The cases against St. Bernard Parish identify two types of common obstacles that limit the ability of low-income households to find affordable housing after a disaster. First, wealthier communities often seek to block access to disaster survivors through ordinances like the ones put in place by St. Bernard Parish that limit residence by non-relatives or limit the rental of single-family homes, or by restricting the ability of FEMA or state agencies to site temporary housing. Second, wealthier communities often already have, or enact post-disaster, land-use regulations that severely limit or completely prohibit the construction of new multifamily housing that can enable the production of units affordable to low- and moderate-income households.[31]

Latino Action Network, New Jersey State Conference of the NAACP, and Fair Share Housing Center v. New Jersey.[32] After Superstorm Sandy hit New York and New Jersey in October 2012, Congress appropriated nearly $3 billion in CDBG funds to New Jersey to assist in recovery efforts. The State of New Jersey submitted an action plan to HUD to describe how it would use the funding. Three statewide advocacy groups—the

10
CoreLogic Hazard HQ Team, "2021 Climate Change Catastrophe Report," 2022, https://www.corelogic.com/intelligence/2021-climate-change-catastrophe-report/.

11
NOAA, "U.S. Billion-Dollar Weather."

12
Harvard Joint Center for Housing Studies, *State of the Nation's Housing*, 2022.

13
Chris Benner and Manuel Pastor, "Just Growth: Inclusion and Prosperity in America's Metropolitan Regions," *Berkeley Planning Journal* 25, no. 1 (2012), https://doi.org/10.5070/bp325112311; Rumbach and Makarewicz, "Affordable Housing"; Lee and Van Zandt, "Housing Tenure"; Arcaya et al., "Social Consequences."

14
Kathleen Tierney, *Disasters: A Sociological Approach* (Cambridge: Polity, 2019), 72. See also Susan L. Cutter, Jerry T. Mitchell, and Michael S. Scott, "Revealing the Vulnerability of People and Places:

Latino Action Network, the New Jersey State Conference of the NAACP, and the Fair Share Housing Center—organized community forums and collected data to assess the extent to which the state's disaster recovery programs were serving renters and low-income households of color.

The information gathered in the community forums and the analysis of data regarding the recovery efforts indicated that New Jersey's plan would benefit high-income homeowners disproportionately relative to the harm they had suffered. The advocacy groups also realized that the state was not complying with regulations meant to ensure that non-English speakers would have an equal opportunity to benefit from federally funded programs. The organizations identified thousands of applicants who had lost the opportunity to participate because of violations of language access rules as well as several thousand applications that were erroneously denied by a private contractor. The three organizations filed an administrative complaint with HUD in April 2013, alleging violations of Title VI of the Civil Rights Act of 1964, prohibiting racial discrimination in federal programs, the Fair Housing Act, and the state's obligation under the Fair Housing Act to affirmatively further fair housing.[33]

After the complaint was filed, New Jersey agreed to a settlement that required it to direct $240 million in additional funds to the communities hardest hit by the storm, with an emphasis on meeting the needs of low-income renters. The settlement also set out steps to redress language barriers that had prevented storm survivors from accessing recovery programs. The agreement governed the state's administration of nearly $2.8 billion in HUD disaster recovery funding and required the state to add $215 million in supplemental funding to its principal program to build replacement units for households displaced by the storm. It also established an additional $15 million for immediate help for renters who were still displaced from Sandy that could be used for up to two years while replacement homes were being built, as well as $10 million for mobile homeowners.

The Latino Action Network, New Jersey NAACP, and Fair Share Housing Center case identified other common paths through which disaster recovery programs fail to benefit low- and moderate-income households equally relative to wealthier households. As in this case, state disaster recovery programs funded through CDBG-DR programs often disproportionately benefit homeowners relative to the damage suffered. Further, outreach efforts often do not effectively reach some communities of color because of insufficient language and cultural proficiency.

Texas Housers v. State of Texas and Texas General Land Office.[34] After Hurricane Harvey in 2017, Congress appropriated more than $5 billion to Texas through the CDBG program to support recovery. In 2019, Congress appropriated another $4.3 billion to carry out "strategic and high-impact activities to mitigate disaster risks and reduce future losses." More than $4 billion of those funds were administered through the Texas General Land Office, which created the Hurricane Harvey State Mitigation Competition to allocate $2.1 billion of the funds. Cities, counties, tribes, and other government entities could apply for funding for flood control and drainage improvements, infrastructure improvements, green infrastructure construction, public facility resilience, and buyouts of homeowners in high-risk locations.

Texas Housers, a nonprofit organization dedicated to empowering low-income individuals and families by supporting their community goals through coordinated action, together with the Northeast Action Collective, a community group formed by

A Case Study of Georgetown County, South Carolina," in Susan L. Cutter, *Hazards, Vulnerability and Environmental Justice* (London: Earthscan/Routledge, 2012), and Ben Wisner, Piers Blaikie, Terry Cannon, and Ian Davis, *At Risk: Natural Hazards, People's Vulnerability and Disasters* (London: Routledge, 1994), https://doi.org/10.4324/9780203428764.

15
Fothergill and Peek, "Poverty and Disasters"; Betty Hearn Morrow, "Identifying and Mapping Community Vulnerability," *Disasters* 23, no. 1 (1999): 1–18; Lee and Van Zandt, "Housing Tenure."

16
Arcaya et al., "Social Consequences"; David Robinson and Justin Steil, "Eviction Dynamics in Market-Rate Multifamily Rental Housing," *Housing Policy Debate* 31, nos. 3–5 (2021): 647–69; Ingrid Ellen and Justin Steil, eds., *The Dream Revisited: Contemporary Debates About Housing, Segregation, and Opportunity* (New York: Columbia University Press, 2019); Yang Zhang, "Residential

residents and flood survivors in Houston after the hurricane, filed an administrative complaint with HUD alleging that the General Land Office's criteria for selecting recipients of mitigation funding violated Title VI of the 1964 Civil Rights Act and the Fair Housing Act. In 2022, HUD found that the design and operation of the mitigation competition discriminated on the basis of race and national origin. HUD identified one cause of the discrimination as the competition's exclusion of areas designated as the most impacted from competing for half of the funds, even though nearly 90 percent of the population eligible for assistance resided in those areas. The second cause was the point system used by the General Land Office to score applicants. Points were based on the jurisdiction population, with more points given to a smaller jurisdiction than to a larger jurisdiction for an equivalent project. Both of these policies disadvantaged areas that the General Land Office itself had identified as having the greatest mitigation needs and directed funds disproportionately away from low- and moderate-income households.

The two jurisdictions in Texas with the largest numbers of residents affected by Hurricane Harvey—Harris County and the City of Houston—received no funds from the mitigation competition. The policies enacted show how state-designed criteria for the allocation of disaster recovery or mitigation funds can end up benefiting smaller, wealthier, Whiter, and more politically influential communities, and also disadvantage areas that have the greatest mitigation needs.

Conclusion

Households with low and moderate incomes face a worsening crisis of housing unaffordability and are also at disproportionate risk of physical, economic, and social harm from increasingly frequent and severe climate change–related environmental disasters. These disasters exacerbate the crisis of housing unaffordability because of their negative effects on affordable units and housing supply in the disaster-affected area. The result is an increase in evictions and a loss of housing stability.

Actions by local and state governments frequently have disproportionate adverse impacts on communities of color, especially low-income renters. As seen in the cases against St. Bernard Parish, local governments in areas near communities affected by disaster frequently block the construction of multifamily and affordable housing and sometimes seek to limit access to existing rental housing. State disaster recovery programs are sometimes designed with criteria that disproportionately disfavor low-income households, as seen in the litigation regarding the Road Home Program; that disproportionately favor homeowners over renters, as in the New Jersey litigation; or that favor wealthier, Whiter communities, as seen in the Texas mitigation funding administrative complaint. Continued advocacy by civil rights organizations, proponents of affordable housing, and fair housing advocates is essential to future disaster preparedness and recovery programs that reduce rather than augment racial inequality and create more environmentally just communities.

Housing Choice in a Multihazard Environment: Implications for Natural Hazards Mitigation and Community Environmental Justice," *Journal of Planning Education and Research* 30, no. 2 (2010): 117–31.

17
Wisner et al., *At Risk*, 9.

18
Lee and Van Zandt, "Housing Tenure."

19
Shannon Van Zandt et al., "Mapping Social Vulnerability to Enhance Housing and Neighborhood Resilience," *Housing Policy Debate* 22, no. 1 (2012): 29–55, https://doi.org /10.1080/10511 482.2011.624 528; Fothergill and Peek, "Poverty and Disasters"; Arcaya et al., "Social Consequences."

20
Fothergill and Peek, "Poverty and Disasters"; Robert Bolin and Lois Stanford, "Shelter, Housing and Recovery: A Comparison of US Disasters," *Disasters* 15, no. 1 (1991): 24–34; Rumbach and Makarewicz, "Affordable Housing"; Lee and Van Zandt, "Housing Tenure"; Jacob Vigdor, "The Economic

Aftermath of Hurricane Katrina," *Journal of Economic Perspectives* 22, no. 4 (2008): 135–54.

21
Mark Brennan, Aditi Mehta, and Justin Steil, "In Harm's Way? The Effect of Disasters on the Magnitude and Location of Low-Income Housing Tax Credit Allocations," *Journal of Policy Analysis and Management* 41, no. 2 (2022): 486–514.

22
Howell and Elliott, "Damages Done."

23
See X. de Sousa Briggs, Carlos Martin, Vincent Reina, and Justin Steil, "Seeing More, Learning More: Equity in Housing and Community Development," *Cityscape: A Journal of Policy Development and Research* 24, no. 2 (2002).

24
Mark Brennan et al., "A Perfect Storm? Disasters and Evictions," *Housing Policy Debate* 32, no. 1 (2022): 52–83.

25
Brennan et al., "In Harm's Way?"; Aditi Mehta, Mark Brennan, and Justin Steil, "Affordable Housing,

Disasters, and Social Equity: LIHTC as a Tool for Preparedness and Recovery," *Journal of the American Planning Association* 86, no. 1 (2020): 75–88.

26
Fothergill and Peek, "Poverty and Disasters."

27
US Government Accountability Office, *Disaster Housing: Federal Assistance for Permanent Housing Primarily Benefited Homeowners; Opportunities Exist to Better Target Rental Housing Needs*, report, 2010, https://www .gao.gov/products /gao-10-17.

28
Lisa K. Bates, "Post-Katrina Housing: Problems, Policies, and Prospects for African-Americans in New Orleans," *Black Scholar* 36, no. 4 (2006): 13–31; Howell and Elliott, "Damages Done."

29
Greater New Orleans Fair Hous. Action Ctr. v. United States Hud, 723 F. Supp. 2d 11 (DC 2010); Greater New Orleans Fair Housing Action Center v. United States Hud, 639 F.3d 1078 (DC Cir. 2010).

30
Greater New Orleans Fair Hous. Action Ctr. v. St. Bernard Parish, 641 F. Supp. 2d 563 (D.La. 2009); Greater New Orleans Fair Hous. Action Ctr. v. St. Bernard Parish, 648 F. Supp. 2d 805 (D.La. 2009); Greater New Orleans Fair Hous. Action Ctr. v. St. Bernard Parish, 2011 US Dist. LEXIS 119630 (D.La. 2011).

31
See also Yonah Freemark, Justin Steil, and Kathleen Thelen, "Varieties of Urbanism: A Comparative View of Inequality and the Dual Dimensions of Metropolitan Fragmentation," *Politics & Society* 48, no. 2 (2020): 235–74; Yonah Freemark and Justin Steil, "Local Power and the Location of Subsidized Renters in Comparative Perspective: Public Support for Low- and Moderate-Income Households in the United States, France, and the United Kingdom," *Housing Studies* 37, no. 10 (2022): 1753–81.

32
See Voluntary Compliance Agreement and Conciliation Agreement Between the

Department of Housing and Urban Development, the Latino Action Network, the New Jersey State Conference of the NAACP, the Fair Share Housing Center, the State of New Jersey, and the New Jersey Department of Community Affairs, May 30, 2014, https://clearing house.net /doc/70100/.

33
See Justin Steil, Nicholas Kelly, Lawrence Vale, and Maia Woluchem, eds., *Furthering Fair Housing: Prospects for Racial Justice in America's Neighborhoods* (Philadelphia: Temple University Press, 2021), for a description of the affirmatively fur-thering fair housing requirement.

34
See Letter Finding Noncompliance with Title VI and Section 109, from HUD Region VI Director Office of Fair Housing and Equal Opportunity to Texas General Land Office Commissioner George P. Bush, Mar. 4, 2022, https://www .relmanlaw.com /media/cases /1258_Title%20IV %20Determination .pdf.

Points of View

The View from City Hall: Architecture, Planning, and the Housing Crisis in Los Angeles

Christopher Hawthorne is senior critic at the Yale School of Architecture and lecturer in English at Yale College. From 2018 to 2022, Hawthorne served as the first chief design officer for the City of Los Angeles. From 2004 to 2018, he was the architecture critic for the *Los Angeles Times*.

One morning in 2018, a few months after I joined the administration of Los Angeles mayor Eric Garcetti as the city's first chief design officer, a position in which I provided design oversight for everything from street furniture to new residential towers, there was a knock on the door of my office in City Hall. I opened it to see a colleague steadying a pile of bulging cardboard boxes stacked on a hand truck. These were the responses from teams of affordable housing developers and architecture firms, nearly two dozen in all, to a request for proposals for innovative approaches to permanent supportive housing in Los Angeles. The RFP was issued by the city's Housing and Community Investment Department (today the Los Angeles Housing Department), the city administrative officer (who oversees the city budget), and the mayor's office, and it was part of a larger housing initiative called Measure HHH, which had been approved by city voters in 2016 and included $1.2 billion in dedicated bond funding. The City Council ultimately earmarked 10 percent of that amount, or $120 million, for 1,000 new permanent supportive housing units. "In particular," the RFP noted, "this program seeks to fund innovative housing typologies that clearly respond to the urgency of the city's homeless crisis."

The text of the RFP had largely been drafted by the time I arrived in my City Hall job. The phrase "innovative housing typologies" was not meant to refer to design per se. Instead, the focus was on inventive approaches to the *approval*, *financing*, and *construction* of HHH units, in line with HCID's paramount challenge of devising ways to make permanent supportive housing cheaper and quicker to build. Yet I also felt that it was important to make the units as effective as possible in their architecture and urban design, primarily in an effort to ensure that they would be welcoming and livable for their residents (including residents who would be moving in directly from tent encampments along the city's sidewalks and in other public spaces) and also as a means of expanding public support for affordable housing across the city.

Housing for the formerly homeless in Los Angeles was at that moment balanced, politically speaking, on a knife's edge. Large majorities of voters at the city and county level continued to favor significant public spending on emergency and supportive housing; Measure HHH, for instance, passed in November 2016 with a vote of 77 percent to 23 percent. At the same time, however, opposition to the prospect of new temporary "emergency" shelters (which in Los Angeles were part of a program called A Bridge Home) and permanent supportive housing complexes was often loud and combative. In fall 2018, Mayor Garcetti joined Mike Bonin, a City Council member representing sections of the west side of Los Angeles, in the beachside neighborhood of Venice for a town hall focusing on the Bridge Home program. Much of the meeting was concerned with a proposal to build a 154-bed shelter on an empty three-acre lot owned by the county transit agency and located about 300 feet from the Venice Boardwalk, where the number of homeless encampments had been on the rise. Garcetti pledged at the start of the meeting that he would not leave until he had heard from every resident who wanted to share an opinion on the planned shelter.

"Frustration bubbled over as locals took turns at the microphone, talking about feces and drug needles in the alleys and beaches," the *Los Angeles Times* reported. "After shushing the audience repeatedly [and] then fielding dozens of questions that devolved into angry rants, Garcetti sat and listened."

That meeting, in retrospect, was the beginning of the end of Bonin's tenure in public service. Opposition to his support of the Bridge Home shelter—and to his policies on homelessness in general, which tended to focus on supportive services rather than on more aggressive cleanups, or "sweeps," of tent encampments—led to a formal recall measure in 2021. Though the effort failed, it took a toll, and after nearly a decade on the City Council, Bonin announced in early 2022 that he wouldn't seek a third term. He cited his dismay over the rising vitriol of the homelessness debate as a key reason, along with his own deteriorating mental health. (His office's private polling numbers were reportedly not particularly positive, either, suggesting he might have had trouble winning even if he'd chosen to run.) The Bridge Home shelter in Venice, which opened in early 2020 after construction costs of $8 million, is still in operation in 2023.

In was in that context—with much of the Los Angeles public desperate for the city to provide new housing options to address homelessness, but with many of those options facing heated and sustained opposition, especially in the neighborhoods where they would be located—that I took up the question of the role architecture should play in the Measure HHH Innovation RFP. I began working with colleagues overseeing the RFP to strengthen the requirements and refine the language related to design, which ultimately made up 15 percent of the score for each response. And I invited a panel of experts in residential architecture—including the dean of the USC School of Architecture, Milton Curry, and the Los Angeles architects Sharon Johnston and Julie Eizenberg—to score the design features of each proposal.

As I began reading the binders containing the RFP responses, I saw both the results of the added emphasis on good design and the constraints of the HHH permanent-supportive housing initiative as a whole. The submissions ranged widely in their scale and architecture, from towers made of stacked modular units to empty church facilities reimagined as residential compounds to two-story wood-frame apartment buildings meant to blend agreeably into existing residential neighborhoods. The architecture was at once hopeful and attuned, sometimes depressingly so, to the need to spend not a penny more than necessary on each lobby, handrail, facade detail, front garden, or kitchen. After all, the RFP had been launched in part to address surging costs for the first batch of projects funded by Measure HHH; in some cases, the cost per unit for these projects had soared past $700,000, generating disdainful headlines in the local and national press. In the end, we recommended that the City Council approve funding for six of the proposals, comprising 975 new units, at an average estimated per-unit cost of $352,000. In the process I gained a whole new appreciation for the complexity, architecturally and otherwise, of building publicly funded affordable housing in Los Angeles and other major cities.

Much of that complexity—indeed, much of the high cost of affordable housing in Los Angeles—can be explained by the fact that the city does not build (and has essentially never built) public housing or social housing as those terms are generally understood by the public and the press. Instead, as is the case in many American cities, affordable-housing programs like Measure HHH fund new units by bringing together public subsidy (from city, county, or state sources) with private investment, much of it incentivized with tax credits; the result is a tall and sometimes teetering "capital stack" stuffed with contributions from a number of private and nonprofit companies and public agencies. Each of those contributors, no matter how efficiently they are operated, adds overhead costs and layers of bureaucracy to the ultimate price of each unit of affordable housing. The sites for new affordable developments, even if they are owned by the city or another public agency, tend also to be less than ideal: they are often eccentrically shaped, steeply sloped, environmentally compromised, or located next to a busy freeway. There is a reason they have been passed over for earlier development. These characteristics, too, make them more expensive to build on.

    The history that gives rise to this state of affairs is a long and fascinating one that reaches back nearly 75 years and involves a contentious race for mayor, the modernist architects Richard Neutra and Robert Alexander, and the relocation of a major-league baseball team, the Dodgers, from Brooklyn to Los Angeles. Southern California faced a severe housing crunch immediately following World War II, with a population boom driven in part by veterans who had been stationed in the region during the war deciding to put down permanent stakes. Meanwhile Congress, beginning in the late 1930s and accelerating a decade later with the National Housing Act of 1949, was making significant funds for new affordable housing available to the states. In fall 1949, Los Angeles mayor Fletcher Bowron, who had been in office for 11 years and was a strong supporter of social housing programs, launched a major campaign to take advantage of this new funding by building 10,000 affordable units, paid for entirely by the federal government, across the city. More than 3,300 of those units were planned for a large site in Chavez Ravine, just north of downtown Los Angeles. The City Housing Authority hired Neutra and Alexander, whose proposal for the site included housing for roughly 17,000 people as well as schools, churches, and shops.

    In the plan for what the architects called New Elysian Heights, "new and old streets would complement each other, major roads would skirt rather than bisect the area, [and] most interior streets would be traffic-free cul de sacs," architectural historian Thomas Hines has written in the *Los Angeles Times*. "Housing would face inward, toward garden plots or finger parks. The buildings would be modernist in massing and detail, with the crisp elegance of Neutra's minimalist aesthetic."

This proposal has become an example of the abuses of urban renewal in postwar America. The Neutra/Alexander proposal gave attractive architectural cover to an aggressive version of what planners in those days, without embarrassment, called "slum clearance." Even Neutra admitted to feeling at least a degree of ambivalence about the plan, Hines has noted, pointing out that Chavez Ravine, long home to a community of Mexican immigrant families living in a series of largely low-rise neighborhoods, some of them low-density enough to feel quasi-rural, was remarkable for "a certain human warmth and pleasantness ... The trees of the lovely mountain park have grown high around the strangest 'blightlocked' area that can be found in any city of America."

That part of the story, and the tale of how many of those residents resisted the forced sale of their houses, has been well documented by historians and journalists. But if the Chavez Ravine plan was a fork in the road for urban renewal in Los Angeles, an example of how often cities flush with federal funding slapped a "blighted" tag on a vital low-income community as a precursor to razing a whole neighborhood, it also had profound implications for the future of affordable housing in the region.

Mayor Bowron's support for public housing, and the way that support was by the early 1950s turbocharged by new federal funding, had begun to worry many of the more conservative members of the Los Angeles elite. Bowron's decision to champion the Chavez Ravine project was for many of those well-connected Angelenos the final straw. Especially aggrieved was the powerful publisher of the *Los Angeles Times*, Norman Chandler, whose political philosophy was based on a pair of unshakable faiths: his fierce opposition to labor unions, among his own employees foremost but also in industries across the city, and his deep skepticism of ambitious social-welfare programs, including those focused on public housing—the appearance of which he, like many wealthy residents in Los Angeles, understood as a sign of creeping socialism.

Near the end of 1952, Chandler convened a lunch meeting of Los Angeles power brokers to discuss Bowron's public housing plan and the Chavez Ravine proposal in particular. The latter site was, after all, just a short distance from the Times headquarters, at the corner of First and Broadway, and even closer to Bunker Hill, where Chandler's wife, Dorothy, known to friends as Buff, would soon spearhead the urban-renewal-driven evolution of Grand Avenue into a new cultural center for Los Angeles. (The centerpiece of the first postwar Grand Avenue development, a gilded opera house seating 3,100 and designed by the office of prolific Los Angeles architect Welton Becket, is still called Dorothy Chandler Pavilion.) The lunch group, after some discussion, decided that Bowron needed to go, and that little-known Republican congressman Norris Paulson should be the man to oppose him in the mayoral race of 1953.

Chandler, as author and Occidental College professor Robert Gottlieb has documented, volunteered to write to Poulson. Typed on Times letterhead, his letter was dated December 26, 1952. "Dear Norrie," it began, before informing Poulson that the lunch group had unanimously agreed that he should challenge Mayor Bowron. "'Why did we not think of Norris in the first place?' was what went through all of our minds," Chandler explained.

According to Gottlieb, "The L.A. group promised to provide ample campaign funds if Poulson would run for mayor . . . and would make sure the mayor's salary was increased. To top it off, Chandler wrote, the group would provide Poulson with other perks, including a Cadillac 'to strut around in' as well as a 'chauffeur supplied by the city.'"

"Looking forward with great anticipation to receiving the 'right answer,'" the letter concluded.

Paulson agreed to run. Scare tactics in relation to the Chavez Ravine proposal, which he labeled a Communist plot, were a key element of his campaign. His victory over Bowron in May 1953—by 53 percent to 47 percent—was a death sentence for the Neutra/Alexander plan. The site, already mostly cleared, went on to become the location for Dodger Stadium, which opened in 1962. Paulson's win also spelled the end of the prospect of truly public housing in Los Angeles for the remainder of the 20th century.

Many big American cities never broke with public housing as definitely as Los Angeles did. The New York City Housing Authority, created by Mayor Fiorello La Guardia in 1934 to produce publicly funded alternatives to low-quality tenements in the depths of the Depression, continues to own and operate more than 300 buildings across the city. NYCHA has a complicated history. (See David Burney, "What Happened to NYCHA and How Can We Fix It?," in this volume for a detailed account.) For many years, the agency excluded the lowest-income New Yorkers, including those on welfare, from public housing, concentrating instead on serving working-class and middle-class residents. Single motherhood or a lack of furniture, among other perceived shortcomings, could be grounds for rejection from NYCHA. Many of its buildings initially accepted only White residents. In recent years, NYCHA complexes have become notorious for run-down and sometimes unsafe conditions; in 2018, the agency agreed to federal oversight by a court-appointed monitor after a damning complaint issued by the US attorney in Manhattan called out its "management dysfunction and organizational failure."

All the same, the consistent size of the NYCHA portfolio across many decades provided a housing backstop for New York that did not exist in other cities. Chicago, St. Louis, and other urban areas infamously razed many postwar housing projects in the 1970s, reducing the supply of affordable housing just as Reaganomics, the crack-cocaine epidemic, and other forces were ravaging low-income communities. Other cities, such as Los Angeles, never built up such a portfolio. The first four or five decades of NYCHA's existence, by contrast, were successful enough to earn the agency a reputation as the most successful big-city housing authority in the country. At the height of its reach, the author Gregory Umbach has noted, and even as other social programs began to wither, "The housing authority's projects were anchors of stability and safety. They were places that you wanted to get into as the neighborhoods were deteriorating around you." By the 1960s, as eligibility requirements loosened and the agency kept building, the number of residents in its buildings exceeded 500,000.

New York City also takes an approach to addressing the homelessness crisis that differs from that of Los Angeles. The so-called Calahan Consent Decree, issued in 1981 by the New York State Supreme Court, essentially established a legal right to housing in the city. Extended by a pair of additional rulings, the consent decree requires New York City (one of just three American cities with such a mandate) to build enough shelter beds each year to house its unsheltered population. Like NYCHA, the so-called Shelter Industrial Complex has received its own set of withering legal and press critiques in recent years.

Yet however much bloat and excess it may contain, the NYC Department of Homeless Services, with an annual budget of $2 billion, does add another layer of support to the city's comparatively robust housing safety net. In Los Angeles, despite a sustained effort to add emergency housing and permanent supportive programs over Garcetti's 2013–22 term, the homeless population on a typical night exceeds by a significant margin the number of shelter beds.

The 500,000 residents that NYCHA housed at the peak of its reach is a figure that looks all the more remarkable after my experience serving in the Garcetti administration. Measure HHH's goal of using public money to subsidize, rather than fully fund, 10,000 units was seen as an unusually large goal in the context of Los Angeles housing politics and has taxed the capacity of the agencies overseeing the effort, starting with HCID. The Innovation RFP was, of course, just 10 percent of that total. In that context, building publicly funded and publicly owned housing for half a million people seems almost unfathomably ambitious. The 2022 Greater Los Angeles Homeless Count found that there are 48,548 people living unsheltered each night in Los Angeles County. Building even 10 percent of the NYCHA high-water mark would provide housing for that entire population.

In the absence of a shelter mandate or a public agency like NYCHA, Los Angeles's approach to low-income housing has been necessarily piecemeal, driven in part by emergency shelter programs like A Bridge Home, which build shelters, and in larger part by policies that provide incentives to the private market to develop new affordable units as part of larger, for-profit apartment complexes. Yet even as Los Angeles remains comparatively lacking in social housing infrastructure, the city had and still has the ability to take advantage of opportunities that do not exist in other US metropolitan regions. Chief among these are the major boulevards that form a loose megagrid across the city and the extensive collection of neighborhoods of single-family homes—two land-use categories that retain the capacity for significant additional density with no or limited changes to the basic land-use patterns or largely horizontal character of Los Angeles.

The city has made notable progress in adding new housing to both areas, especially compared to other cities in California. Along the boulevards, the Transit Oriented Communities policy, which was approved by voters in 2016 as part of a ballot measure called JJJ, has incentivized the production of affordable units within larger complexes. The Department of City Planning released guidelines for TOC projects in May 2017. They allow developers to increase the density of their projects by up to 80 percent and the floor-area ratio by up to 55 percent depending on factors including distance to a major transit station and in exchange for providing a quantity of restricted low-income units or paying an in-lieu fee. So far, a total of 36,762 units, 7,398 of them affordable, have been permitted through the TOC program. And in some recent years, TOC units have made up more than a third of the total permitted apartments in Los Angeles; in 2019, the figure reached 42 percent.

Los Angeles, meanwhile, has seen far more success than any other California city in supporting the construction of accessory dwelling units in single-family neighborhoods. The State of California loosened restrictions in 2017 on the production of these backyard apartments, also known as granny flats or *casitas*, and in the years since, ADUs have consistently accounted for between 20 and 25 percent of new housing units built each year. In late 2021, the city issued its 10,000th certificate of occupancy for an ADU—a truly remarkable number.

Yet there is more capacity to tap into at the low-rise scale. Far more, by some estimates. Single-family neighborhoods still make up more than three-quarters of residential land in Los Angeles. If low-rise multifamily neighborhoods, where there is a mixture of one- and two-story single-family and multifamily buildings, are included, the figure approaches 85 percent. Encouraged by the success of ADU streamlining across California, legislators in Sacramento passed two laws in 2021, Senate Bills 9 and 10, to open up single-family neighborhoods to additional density. They were signed by Governor Gavin Newsom in fall 2021 and went into effect on New Year's Day, 2022. SB9 is essentially a fourplex bill: it allows the subdivision of single-family lots in most areas and a duplex to be built on each of the parcels. SB10 enables streamlined approvals for up to 10 units on a single residential parcel, although unlike SB9 it does so not automatically ("by right," in the language of urban planners); rather, SB10 projects must be affirmatively approved by individual cities.

This one feature of SB10 threatens to significantly limit its impact. Why? Because denser development in single-family neighborhoods, much like Bridge Home shelters, remains a political lightning rod. In polling, large majorities supported both SB9 and SB10, but the opposition, where it did emerge, was loud and angry. It also came from a variety of perspectives. Wealthy and often White homeowners in high-end neighborhoods opposed the bills—no surprise—but so did many housing advocates and leaders of communities of color, who worry about real estate developers taking advantage of the new legislation to finance the kind of housing construction that might accelerate displacement and gentrification in their neighborhoods. As a result, many elected officials at the city and county levels continue to steer clear of debate on zoning reform and density levels in single-family neighborhoods, seeing only political downside in venturing into such territory.

SB9, for its part, has produced relatively little new housing since the beginning of 2022. According to a report from the Terner Center for Housing Innovation at the University of California, Berkeley, examining that law's first year on the books, "The impact of SB9 has been limited so far. Some of the state's largest cities reported that they have received just a handful of applications for either lot splits or new units, while other cities reported none." One explanation is that the protections against displacement and eviction that were added to the bill as amendments, helping secure its passage in Sacramento, have blunted its impact; these include a requirement that any homeowner applying for an SB9 lot split pledge to live on the property for at least the next three years. Another explanation is that, as was the case with ADU legislation, it will take some time for Californians to fully understand what the bill allows and for the legislature to tinker with the language of the law until it begins to produce a significant volume of new housing units.

What became clear to me early in my tenure in City Hall was that there was a role for architects to play in making the debate over zoning reform safer for elected officials to explore in good faith—and, more broadly, in clarifying the benefits that more housing options could bring to single-family neighborhoods. To a large degree, debates over zoning changes in those neighborhoods had focused—both in community meetings and in the press—on the potential damage those changes might cause. In addition to the danger of displacement, these potential downsides primarily include increased traffic, strain on infrastructure, and threats to what preservationists and other opponents to new construction often refer to as "neighborhood character," a reference to the scale and design of the existing urban fabric.

The benefits of adding housing options in low-rise neighborhoods, though extensive and quantifiable, were often buried in these debates. The advantages include affordability, to begin with, but also support for multigenerational households and the prospects of local retail outlets serving customers who arrive on foot or by bike. What's more, there is no way Los Angeles will meet its ambitious climate goals or reduce dependency on private automobiles without opening significant sections of single-family neighborhoods to denser housing and allowing new apartments to be located closer to shops, jobs, and transit lines. There is also the complex history of residential zoning in many parts of the country, including Los Angeles, to contend with; the racist system of redlining, for instance, made it impossible for would-be homeowners of color to be approved for mortgage loans in the most desirable residential neighborhoods, thus severely limiting their ability to build generational wealth through rising home values.

Both of the major housing initiatives I helped launch as chief design officer were aimed at expanding the constituency—and making clear that the support was already substantial—for adding more housing options to single-family and other low-density neighborhoods. Low-Rise: Housing Ideas for Los Angeles was a design challenge I organized in 2020 with the goal of producing new prototypes for residential architecture in the range of three to ten units, a sort of Case Study program for the post-single-family-zoning age in Los Angeles. With a design brief shaped by extensive community-engagement programs, it ultimately attracted more than 370 submissions by firms large and small, emerging and established, from around the world. At the same time, I worked with colleagues in the mayor's office and the Department of Building and Safety to start the Standard Plan Program, a design preapproval system for ADUs. It allows any architecture firm to submit plans for accessory structures to vetting by city engineers; when approved, the plans are added to a DBS website of designs. Once homeowners find a design they like, they contact the architects directly to arrange fees and access to the plans. The result is a budget-neutral program for the city that has become the most frequently used of any of the nation's half-dozen ADU-preapproval measures, which are also in operation in Seattle, San Jose, and other cities.

I discovered not long after joining City Hall, as I mentioned earlier, that there was a role for architecture to play in changing the tenor of debates about affordable housing and zoning reform. I still believe that. Yet the political role remains the most crucial. The support for adding density and new housing options to single-family neighborhoods remains broad among Angelenos and is growing broader. Yet elected officials remain gun-shy about throwing their support behind such changes because the groups opposed to them, whether the leaders of homeowners associations or community-based advocacy organizations, are well-connected and influential and come from both the conservative and progressive ends of the political spectrum in Los Angeles.

For proof of that gun-shyness, look no further than the 2022 race to replace Mayor Eric Garcetti. In many respects, the two candidates who faced each other in a December 2022 runoff, longtime congresswoman Karen Bass and high-end, open-air mall developer Rick Caruso, could not have been more different. Bass is a veteran of mainstream Democratic politics, a national player who showed up on Joe Biden's vice-presidential shortlist in 2020. Caruso is a lifelong Republican and supporter of abortion restrictions who registered first as an independent and then as a Democrat to give himself a chance to win the race in heavily blue Los Angeles.

Yet the candidates did find common ground in their opposition to zoning reform in single-family neighborhoods. Asked by Liam Dillon, the housing reporter for the *Los Angeles Times*, how they would deal with housing and homelessness, both politicians endorsed the idea that limits on the production of new apartments should be loosened across the board. When it came to the future of single-family neighborhoods specifically, however, both demurred. Noting that she didn't want to "force things on people," Bass said she had reservations about whether low-rise areas were the appropriate setting for denser housing. Similarly, Caruso told Dillon, "Leave the single-family neighborhoods … We've got an enormous amount of commercial, industrial—great areas."

The changes that new housing policies have brought to single-family neighborhoods in Los Angeles—ADUs in particular—have so far proved hugely popular. It is worth remembering that when they were first proposed, they produced a level of anxiety and opposition from familiar quarters that is similar to what has greeted SB9 and SB10. The same dynamic is likely to play out in making the leap from the second unit in the single-family zone to the third, fourth, fifth, and beyond: lots of *sturm und drang* when reforms are proposed, or go into effect, followed by a general acceptance that on balance they turn out to be positive forces for neighborhoods. We need more elected officials willing to endorse that leap unequivocally.

A recent shift in the makeup of the Los Angeles City Council, with a growing minority of young, progressive council members taking office in 2023, may presage more fundamental change. These council members and others have begun speaking, albeit in nascent terms, about developing a new system of fully public housing. This discussion is worth heeding. The point in building such a system would not be to avenge the results of the 1953 mayor's race, since the Neutra/Alexander plan for Chavez Ravine, while architecturally innovative, was freighted with damaging and outdated notions about urban progress and slum clearance. Yet the other choice—leaving progress almost entirely in the hands of state legislators, private developers, and politically influential community-based organizations and homeowners groups—has left us with the unaffordable, inequitable, and environmentally wasteful status quo we struggle with today.

What Happened to NYCHA and How Can We Fix It?

David Burney
is the co-founder
and director
of the Urban
Placemaking and
Management pro-
gram at the Pratt
Institute School
of Architecture.
Burney was
a member of
the New York
City Planning
Commission from
2019 to 2022,
commissioner
of the New York
City Department
of Design and
Construction from
2004 to 2014, and
chief architect of
the New York City
Housing Authority
from 1990 to 2004.

The United States has a long tradition of republicanism and laissez-faire capitalism that has not favored strong federal housing policy or intervention in the housing market. Policymakers have believed that private enterprise could best provide sufficient housing and that, as with health care and education,[1] government involvement would bring in "socialism" and undesirable control of the free market. There are two major exceptions to this tradition: the 1937 US Housing Act, a result of the devastation of the Great Depression, and the "war on poverty," initiated by the Johnson administration in the mid-1960s.[2] Successful as these programs were, subsequent federal housing policy has mostly been aimed at undermining them, through either malice or neglect. Instead, federal policy has mainly sought to promote homeownership—the American dream—but that approach was eviscerated by the collapse of financing due to the subprime loan crisis and its aftermath. The result is that there is currently virtually no cogent federal housing policy. Thirty-five million Americans live in substandard housing; a much larger number devote 50 percent of their income to a roof over their heads. Housing construction is at a historic low, and construction costs have risen so high that they are well beyond the means of the average citizen.

The New York City Housing Authority has always been an exception to this picture. Galvanized by Jacob Riis's reporting on unsanitary and congested conditions in the city's tenements as well as pressure from social reformers, New York City created NYCHA in 1934. Using funds from the Public Works Administration, at least in part, NYCHA produced several iconic developments: First Houses in 1934 (the selective demolition

1

In the aftermath of the Depression, and later after World War II, most European countries included in their reconstruction plans large government programs for health care, education, and housing. These social programs, requiring large capital outlays, could not be left to the free market. The United States, having not suffered the devastation of the wars in Europe, developed no such policy.

2

Other federal initiatives included housing for "war workers" engaged in production for World War II and postwar housing under the GI Bill.

3

Ingersoll Houses close to the Brooklyn Navy Yard, Clason Point in the Bronx, and Markham Gardens (since demolished) on Staten Island were all built to accommodate war workers and later became part of the NYCHA portfolio.

and renovation of tenement buildings), Williamsburg Houses in 1935, and Harlem River Houses in 1937. Between 1934 and the end of the century, NYCHA grew to manage more than 180,000 units, becoming by far the largest housing authority in the nation.

But NYCHA's portfolio was not the result of one consistent program; instead, it worked within several different programs motivated by changing policies over the decades. After the Depression and the end of the PWA program, NYCHA would have struggled to finance more construction. But World War II intervened, and the housing authority undertook several developments to house workers engaged in the war effort.[3] After the war, federal funding of public housing authorities continued as the demand for housing for returning veterans became a priority. Ironically, this period of renewed government support sowed the seeds for NYCHA's eventual demise.

The US Congress saw public housing primarily as a program to address poverty. Officials declared that taxpayer dollars were to be spent sparingly and only to serve those who could not afford housing. Public housing was not to compete with the private-sector housing market. NYCHA was not allowed to build anything but the minimum. So gone were the retail stores, day care centers, health centers, and branch libraries that were included in its early developments.[4]

The distinction between early and later subsidized developments can be felt viscerally on the Lower East Side of Manhattan. At Peter Cooper Village and Stuyvesant Town, ground-floor retail enlivens the street; Wald and Baruch Houses, on the other hand, provide only bare-bones apartments with none of the commercial activity that could enhance streets and sidewalks. To make matters worse, influence from Europe, advocating the modernist "tower in the park" typology, resulted in buildings that were set back from the street wall, breaking the Manhattan grid with anonymous towers of plain, minimal design. And worse still, Congress decided in 1969 to restrict eligibility for public housing to families earning less than 30 percent of the area median income. Despite fierce resistance from housing advocates and professionals, the Brooke Amendment to the Housing and Urban Development Act of 1969 succeeded in concentrating large numbers of very poor families in public housing at the expense of working families. The resulting rise in social problems and crime in public housing is widely known and often erroneously blamed on the architecture.[5] But it was the Brooke Amendment that precipitated the social problems that came to plague public housing in the decades that followed.

As disenchantment with the housing program increased in Congress (the fact that the problems were of their own making seemed to escape the legislators), the federal government slowly abandoned it. When the Nixon administration terminated the capital construction program, new public housing across the nation was effectively ended.[6] This policy continued during all subsequent presidential administrations. Even when Democrats controlled Congress, they saw no future for public housing. Neoliberal economic policies held the private sector to be the solution to housing production, and whatever taxpayer dollars were allocated to the matter were funneled through programs such as the Low-Income Housing Tax Credit or the Section 8 Housing Choice Voucher program.

NYCHA became the largest recipient of Section 8 program assistance,[7] which allowed many families access to private-sector rental apartments. However, the Section 8 program worked only when private-sector apartments were available. It was never a catalyst for housing production, and in New York City's tight rental market, many Section 8 vouchers went unused.

Harlem River Houses still includes a branch of the New York Public Library, giving working-class autodidacts access to knowledge.

5

It is often claimed that high-rise apartment living is the cause of social problems in public housing. However, this assumption is contradicted on the one hand by the success of so much high-rise residential in, for example, New York City and on the other hand by the desperate social conditions of much low-rise public housing in, for example, the notorious Taylor Homes in Chicago.

6

NYCHA was able to retain some of its capital development funds but had difficulty finding sites on which to build. In the years between 1990 and 2000, NYCHA succeeded in building on a number of small "infill" properties, bringing public housing seamlessly into New York City in a way that housing professionals had long advocated.

Meanwhile, the federal government continued a quiet war of attrition on public housing programs. The HOPE VI program offered capital grants to public housing authorities to renovate but preferably demolish their public housing. Many cities participated, for the most part choosing to demolish their housing, although NYCHA used the program only sparingly.[8] The federal operating subsidy that bridged the gap between PHA rent receipts and the cost of operations was slowly reduced until it was below the actual cost of maintenance and operations. Unable to raise rents, and with a high proportion of welfare families and low proportion of working families (a result of the Brooke Amendment), PHAs fell further into financial difficulty. Neither states nor cities, which had largely ended their support for public housing once the federal government stepped in, were willing or able to fill the gap. At NYCHA, these circumstances resulted in staffing cuts and a backlog of preventive maintenance. One initiative—the Comprehensive Grant program, which allocated capital funds to PHAs for renovation of existing housing stock (but could not be used for new housing construction)—did continue after the Nixon administration. NYCHA received significant Comp Grant funds in the 1980s and 1990s that allowed it to rehabilitate several of its older developments. The terms of the funding also allowed NYCHA to renovate or build community centers and senior centers to serve the youth and senior populations in NYCHA housing, making up to some extent for the lack of such provisions in the postwar development program. But eventually, even the Comp Grant program was cut back.

Where does all of this leave us in 2023? With more than 170,000 units, NYCHA is still by far the largest PHA in the nation. Vacancy rates remain extremely low, and the waiting list for NYCHA housing is decades long. Among its strengths, NYCHA counts a population of active residents, many of whom remain in public housing for decades, often for life. For the most part, NYCHA did not site its housing in ghettos of poverty far from the city center, and many NYCHA developments stand cheek by jowl with market-rate housing in desirable neighborhoods.

But the underlying financial crisis continues, and it is probably reasonable to assume that no federal supply-side housing program is likely in the foreseeable future. Federal policy is reluctant to launch into any form of housing production—a position that seems to be true regardless of political affiliation. The only extant federal subsidy is the LIHTC:[9] notoriously inefficient in terms of return on the dollar, the program nevertheless remains popular with both political parties. Direct government involvement in housing production is even less likely at the city or state level. Efforts in New York City to incentivize private developers to build "affordable" housing—the current Mandatory Inclusionary Housing requirements—have had limited success but also unforeseen adverse consequences.[10] Equally improbable is the provision of sufficient demand-side subsidy, such as the Section 8 voucher system, which would allow all Americans to participate in the free market for housing, regardless of income. Even if adequate subsidy was provided, there would not be enough available stock to satisfy demand.

In the mid-1990s, the Department of Housing and Urban Development—the federal oversight agency for all public housing authorities—relaxed the Brooke Amendment to allow PHAs to set aside up to 50 percent of vacancies for families earning up to 50 percent of median income. This welcome change will go some way toward restoring the economic balance among public housing residents so that it more accurately reflects the demographics of the wider community. It would also, theoretically, increase the rental income to PHAs, with higher-income tenants coming back to public housing. However,

7

Section 8 vouchers were allocated to both NYCHA and the City Department of Housing Preservation and Development.

8

Notably at HOPE Gardens in Brooklyn, where several towers were demolished on the spurious grounds of "poor foundations" and replaced by row houses.

9

Created under the Tax Reform Act of 1986, the LIHTC gives incentives to use private equity in the development of affordable housing aimed at low-income Americans. The tax credits, which provide a dollar-for-dollar reduction in a taxpayer's federal income tax, are more attractive than tax deductions, which provide only a reduction in taxable income. To qualify for the LIHTC program, at least 20 percent of the residential units in a development must be both rent-restricted and occupied by individuals whose income is 50 percent or less of the area median gross income. At least 40 percent of the residential units must be both rent-restricted

the very low turnover rate for NYCHA housing means that it will take many decades to produce any significant change.

So there appear to be two main problems facing NYCHA—how to stimulate (i.e., subsidize) production of housing at a level affordable for the thousands of families on its waiting list, and how to sustain the current public housing program and steer it out of its current fiscal crisis. Since any solution to either of these problems will involve significant capital investment, finding the source of that capital presents the first challenge.

A third problem, perhaps shorter in duration than the first two, is that NYCHA's aging housing stock has suffered from years of underfunding and, as a consequence, delayed maintenance. Estimates of current needs to bring the portfolio into a state of good repair have grown to around $78 billion. Policymakers seem to be ignoring this predicament. If NYCHA housing ultimately fails, then the problem will become one of housing 400,000 families—a crisis far more serious than the current ones.

It is tempting to point out that if the United States did not devote a substantial part of its budget to massive defense spending and even more to tax breaks for the wealthy, all funded by deficit financing, there would be ample capital for housing subsidies. But it is probably more realistic to look at redistributing the federal funds already allocated to housing and also at other regulatory changes that might support low-income housing production and subsidize NYCHA operations.

Other than the LIHTC, federal support for housing currently comes in the form of mortgage tax relief. Mortgage tax relief cost the treasury $70–$100 billion in 2019, and the estimated cost of the LIHTC was $8 billion in fiscal year 2019. In the mid-2000s, a presidential advisory panel, headed by former Senator Connie Mack, recommended limiting the mortgage tax deduction to loans of up to $313,000 instead of the then ceiling of $1 million, which benefits wealthy homeowners far more than low-income ones. The limit was subsequently reduced to $500,000.

The panel also recommended eliminating any tax deduction for local property taxes. Some redistribution of the current mortgage tax relief, combined with a more efficient use of LIHTC funds, would be progressive and could free up significant capital for other subsidies. Most European countries (the United Kingdom included) have eliminated any mortgage tax credit for homeowners. While it is probably politically unrealistic to expect the United States to follow suit, it may be possible to free up as much as $30 billion annually simply by restricting the mortgage tax credit to those most in need and/or to first-time home buyers. With redistributed mortgage tax relief and LIHTC funds, it would be possible to use supply-side subsidies more effectively. Rather than providing tax cuts for the wealthy, the federal government could repurpose that money for housing production. Funds from the subsidy could be allocated to the states instead of continuing with the inefficient LIHTC program. For developer-led housing, the government could avoid or mitigate three costs: the cost of land (in cases where municipalities can contribute the land, as in NYCHA giving up unused parking lots for new development); the cost of borrowing (the government can borrow at much lower rates than private developers); and the cost of developer profit. When people say "Government can't build efficiently," I simply point to NYCHA and the 180,000-plus units of housing it has developed—more than any private developer in New York City.

For NYCHA's immediate problem of declining operating subsidy, the European example once again proves helpful. The countries that ran large government housing programs after World War II—the United Kingdom and the Netherlands—have since

and occupied by
individuals whose
income is 60 per-
cent or less of the
area median gross
income.

10
Neighborhoods
that have been
upzoned under
the MIH program
have seen real
estate speculation
that may lead to
a net *reduction*
in affordable
units. Subsidized
rents (tied to area
median income
rates) have not
been low enough
to meet the
income levels of
many residents of
the neighborhoods
in which the zoning
tool has been used.

11
By 1968, 41 per-
cent of all housing
built in the United
Kingdom was pub-
lic housing. It is
interesting to note
that during the
Thatcher adminis-
tration, the United
Kingdom sold
much of its public
housing stock
(Council housing)
to residents on
preferential terms.
Residents were
encouraged to
take out mortgage
loans, but in a
small mirror of
the subprime loan
crisis that swept
the United States,
those loans saw a
high rate of default.

ended those programs and worked to privatize the housing stock.[11] In those two coun-tries, the main responsibility for low-income rental housing was given over to housing associations that could both manage an existing portfolio and develop new housing. They were given access to very low-interest loans, the main constraint being that the units be rented to income-qualified tenants. HAs, particularly in the Netherlands, were given broad authority in managing the government housing stock they inherited. They were allowed to sell part of the portfolio and use those funds to develop new housing and also to develop mixed-income projects that would generate higher income levels. As a result, many HAs were able to significantly expand their portfolios at a time when government programs were being phased out.

So it may be possible in the United States to convert PHAs to not-for-profit housing associations freed from the constraints of HUD and thus operating more freely in the marketplace. With access to low-interest loans or direct grants (making more efficient use of LIHTC funds), PHAs would be free to act as the HAs in Europe have done. Mixed-income developments would move new development away from the current "warehous-ing" of very poor families and toward a model with a broader range of incomes that would more closely reflect the demographics of the community. The current dearth of affordable rental housing would be addressed, and capital would be available to improve and preserve the existing public housing stock. These revisions might just become a cogent and successful federal housing program.

At the local level, NYCHA has begun its own program to escape, Houdini-like, its current financial straitjacket. The Rental Assistance Demonstration program invites property managers to take over the administration and operations—but not ownership—of selected NYCHA developments. Repairs are funded by project-based Section 8 funds. So far, NYCHA properties in the RAD program seem to be doing well, and residents are satisfied. In addition to the influx of funding for repairs, the RAD program divests NYCHA's staff of some of the management burden. While there might be concerns that using Section 8 funds is simply robbing Peter to pay Paul, since presumably there are now fewer Section 8 dollars available for their original purpose, Congress may see fit to raise the Section 8 budget to compensate. As solutions are applied to NYCHA's deep-seated crises, NYCHA may now be transitioning from the old era under HUD to a new model that more closely resembles the HAs prominent in Europe. It may be imperfect, but it may also be NYCHA's only hope.

Affordable Housing: View from a For-Profit Developer

Jon McMillan is senior vice president and director of planning at the real estate development firm TF Cornerstone in New York City. He was previously director of planning for Battery Park City.

Real estate developers build our cities. They put up our skyscrapers, our office and apartment buildings, and our neighborhoods of town houses and brownstones. They also build our affordable housing, which comes primarily in the form of multifamily rental buildings. Developing affordable housing in expensive, dense, urban settings like New York City is especially challenging.

Affordable housing is built by both for-profit and not-for-profit real estate developers. For-profit developers are like most businesses—they invest private capital, make a product, then try to sell that product for more than it cost to make. They need the rents from their buildings to pay back the equity and loans used for construction, ideally with a return. (These days, 5–6 percent looks pretty good.) Not-for-profit developers use public grants and subsidies to construct their buildings. Since grants and subsidies usually do not need to be paid back, these developers have far lower costs to recoup and can set rents at more affordable levels.

I work for a for-profit developer, but I started my career in government as a planner and eventually became the head of planning for New York's Battery Park City in the 1990s. The company I now work for builds very large-scale rental housing: we have built about 10,000 units over my two decades with the firm. Currently, 70 percent of our apartments rent at market rates and 30 percent are set aside as affordable apartments. I oversee the design of the buildings and obtain community and government approvals for them. Long, contentious reviews bring me into close contact with politicians, community boards, civic organizations, and activists—some of whom may even organize protest rallies on the steps of City Hall.

The question I hear most often is simple: why don't developers lower rents and build more affordable housing so that more people can afford to live in New York City? The answer is equally simple: affordable rents do not cover the cost of building and operating apartments. Someone, somehow, has to make up that difference. Who steps in and how the gap is covered are the critical issues for any developer of affordable housing, whether for-profit or not-for-profit.

Subsidies vs. Developer Incentives

Two basic models are used to address the gap (or rent shortfall) in affordable housing. The first, which I call the "subsidy" model, is used by not-for-profit developers. It deploys public subsidies (cash or loans from cities or states) to construct buildings where all the apartments are affordable or, more accurately, "income-restricted." There are no market-rate apartments in these buildings. The subsidies from government cover the gap from the affordable apartments by reducing the costs of construction, which allows the developers to charge lower, more affordable rents.

The packages of grants and subsidized loans assembled by not-for-profit developers to construct these buildings (the "capital stack") are complicated, diverse, and time-consuming to arrange. Cash or equity for the project is often raised by the sale of syndicated tax credits, meaning that corporations buy the tax benefits generated by low-income housing projects to offset their own taxes. The subsidy model can take on many forms and involve many players; by its nature, it is plagued by myriad and lengthy procedural requirements and regulations. The pool of developers with the knowledge, expertise, and patience to survive in this environment is not large. Further, not-for-profit developers are themselves typically small, because the size of their companies is tied to the size of their projects, which are in turn limited by a scarcity of public subsidies and a shortage of public or institutional land (since projects built under the subsidy model cannot compete on the open market for land). All this puts severe constraints on how much affordable housing is produced using this model.

Not-for-profit developers pay themselves not from profits, obviously, but rather by way of a fee from the capital stack, as if the developer was an expense of the project, like the boiler or the hallway carpet. For-profit developers, on the other hand, have to wait until project revenues exceed project expenses, generating income, in order to realize any return on their endeavors.

Which brings us to the second model used to cover the shortfall in rent from affordable housing: the "developer-incentive" model. This method is how government gets everyday, profit-driven companies to take on the losses from affordable housing, which they are not at all keen to do. In this model, private capital pays for the entire construction and development costs of residential buildings that are mostly market-rate but include a percentage of affordable apartments. The most recent developer-incentive program in New York was 421-a (its legislative nomenclature), which required developers to make 30 percent of their units affordable. The idea is that the income from the other 70 percent of the units—the market-rate apartments—helps to cover the losses from the affordable apartments (which are substantial) in a sort of profit-capture scheme generally known as cross-subsidization. But cross-subsidization is not enough to cover the losses from affordable units, so government steps in with an "incentive" to lure the profit-driven developer to accept these losses. The incentive is not cash or loans to lower construction costs but instead some kind of non-cash assistance—like property tax relief—to lower long-term operating costs. The combination of market-rate cross-subsidy and tax relief is intended to cover the losses from the affordable apartments, allowing the developer to pay back the lenders and investors who provided capital for the project. In this way, the government and the private developer share the losses from the affordable apartments, whereas in the subsidized, not-for-profit model, the government covers the entire loss.

The 421-a program in New York, which provided relief from New York City's notoriously high real estate taxes, was introduced in the 1970s to get more market-rate housing built at a time when rents were not high enough to support new construction *and* pay full real estate taxes. As the city's housing market became stronger in subsequent decades, developers no longer needed help to build housing. The program was retained but modified to require that affordable housing be included for buildings to qualify for tax relief. This revision, the direct result of the withdrawal of federal support for affordable housing production in the 1970s, allowed cities to get affordable housing built without federal help and without any of their own capital. The obvious strength of a program like this is that it mainstreams affordable housing production, making it a part of the development industry's standard practices—in other words, what many big developers do on a daily basis for most of their projects. Between 2016 and 2022 in New York City, the latest iteration of 421-a assisted the production of approximately 40,000 rental apartments, of which about 12,000 were affordable.[1] Given the enormous need for affordable housing, both types of developers and both models are needed.

Developer Incentives at Work

The basic costs to develop an apartment building include construction, which consists of labor and materials (about one-half of the total cost), land acquisition (about one-third), and the "cost of capital," or interest, plus soft costs and fees (about one-sixth). Soft costs can include insurance, legal services, environmental clean-up, demolition, construction security, marketing, leasing commissions, and carrying vacancies. Each unit of housing is assigned a production cost, or development cost, that consists of a weighted percentage (based on square footage of the unit) of the overall cost. Each unit is also assigned an operating cost—a weighted percentage of salaries for those who maintain the building, real estate taxes (which, when unabated, consume a third of gross rents), utilities, insurance, and so on. Unit rents need to cover both production/development costs and operating costs; otherwise, the developer loses money.

Let's look at the costs and revenues of an 850-square-foot, two-bedroom apartment built in Queens or Brooklyn in the early 2020s. The production cost is at least $700,000, including land. For simplicity's sake, let's assume the entire project is financed by bank loans, which means that about $3,500 in monthly rent is required to pay the interest on that $700,000. The same unit also has operating costs of approximately $1,500 per month. So the rent needs to be at least $5,000 per month to cover the basic costs of constructing and operating the two-bedroom apartment. In New York City, renters are typically expected to have an annual income of 40 times the monthly rent. In this scenario, the $5,000-per-month rent requires a household income of $200,000. In a city where the median household income is $67,046, well over half the households cannot afford this 850-square-foot apartment.

Conversely, let's assume that the affordable rent in a particular community is deemed to be $2,000 per month. Renters would need an income of $80,000—still higher than New York City's median household income. And leasing the two-bedroom

1
New York City Independent Budget Office, "How Many Units of Affordable Housing Were Built or Are Underway Through the 421-a Affordable New York Tax Exemption Program?" *New York by the Numbers*, June 2022, https://ibo
.nyc.ny.us
/iboreports/how
-many-units-of
-affordable-housing
-were-built-or-are
-underway-through
-the-421-a
-affordable-new
-york-tax
-exemption
-program-nycbtn
-june-2022.html.

apartment at the affordable rate would result in a loss to the developer of $3,000 per month. How is the developer to cover this gap? Well, perhaps the market-rate apartments can be rented for more than the break-even rent of $5,000. If the developer charges $6,000, a portion of that $1,000 profit can be applied toward the $3,000 loss from the affordable unit. But with a program like 421-a, the building's real estate taxes are reduced, lowering the break-even cost of the market-rate unit to, say, $4,500. The $6,000 rent would free up $1,500 rather than $1,000 to be used to cover losses from the affordable apartment. Since there are just over twice as many market-rate apartments as affordable apartments, it becomes possible to cover the total gap. Such cross-subsidization is one of the major benefits of a developer-incentive program. Combining profit with reduced operating expenses resulting from the tax exemption will ideally close the $3,000 gap for each affordable unit.

Criticisms of Developer-Incentive Models

Currently, New York is without a developer-incentive program. Since the late 2010s, housing activists and progressive politicians have argued that the 421-a program was too beneficial to developers, and in June 2022, the New York State legislature terminated the program. But why? There are many variables that affect a developer's profitability—land and construction costs, market rents, interest rates—and all of these exert influence on the value of and need for a program offering an incentive like tax relief. The specific requirements of developer-incentive programs, such as the percentage of affordable units in a building or the level of affordability (how deeply the units are subsidized), need to be adjusted over time (as they were in 1985, 2006, and 2017) to account for the changing variables so that projects can get built but without too much profit, since there is a loss to the public of future tax revenue. Requiring a higher percentage of affordable units or lowering the rent of affordable units are two ways to reduce the compensation to developers.

Since the 1970s, cities have become increasingly reliant on private developers for the production of affordable housing, especially since the federal government provides no direct support. Cities on their own have never really had the funds required for housing production. But activists who see housing as a public good, even a human right—something that should be provided by government—claim that there is an overreliance on private developers. Housing, they say, should not depend either on the capitalist system or on private developers, who are "corrupted" by the profit motive. Progressives would prefer to see developer-incentive programs replaced by a new paradigm that removes profit from the equation and relies less on the private sector. More housing should be built by government, or by community land trusts, or by not-for-profit developers—all of which would presumably eliminate profit and lead to greater affordability.

But all builders of affordable housing, for-profit, not-for-profit, or governmental, face the same economic landscape, the same costs, and the same shortfalls in revenue—that same $3,000 monthly gap. In affordable housing there is no profit to eliminate, only losses to be recovered. For-profit developers capture profit from market-rate apartments and direct it to the revenue gap. Without that contribution from the private sector, the responsibility of covering the revenue shortfalls is shifted entirely to the public sector. Private capital markets would have no reason to participate in the construction of affordable housing, leaving other sources to provide the huge investments needed for housing construction, which would have draconian effects on municipal budgets.

These criticisms of profit as a corrupting influence might be better levied against our country's choice of a capitalist economic system. Under capitalism, the means of production are private but regulated by the state, as in health care. The system allows providers of public goods to realize gains.

Another reason 421-a was terminated stems from community attitudes. Many communities object to the basic formula of the developer-incentive model: two or three market-rate units for every one affordable unit. Local residents often do not want new market-rate housing in their communities, believing that it causes surrounding rents to rise, leading to gentrification, inequality, and displacement of long-term locals. They do not understand why they are forced to swallow "luxury" units in order to get desperately needed affordable apartments, holding the opinion that the paltry amounts of affordable housing gained from these programs are "crumbs" left by market-rate developers and that fewer affordable apartments are gained in a neighborhood than are lost to the resulting gentrification.

Displacement and gentrification are legitimate policy concerns. But without new housing, more people compete for existing housing. Where do people who would have lived in the new housing go when it doesn't get built? Furthermore, New York City has strong tenant protection laws that, among other purposes, prevent unreasonable rent increases in more than 1 million rental apartments. Displacement should be addressed with better tenant protection rules, not by stopping the production of new housing.

Less ideological, more practical criticisms of 421-a may also have contributed to the program's demise. The first is that the affordable housing is not affordable enough. Lowering rent on an affordable unit means that the developer's loss on that unit increases. The developer cannot afford to subsidize as many apartments. If the tax break the developer receives under 421-a is equivalent to, say, $1,000 per year, that subsidy can be allocated to ten units at $100 each or to five units at $200 each. If the subsidy is used to make five units more affordable, then the other five units can't be subsidized, tossing those five families out of the building. If the goal is deeper affordability without loss of affordable units, then public assistance needs to increase. What this requires is a recalibration of the terms of developer incentives according to public priorities. Some municipal administrations push for more units at higher moderate-income levels (often to provide housing that allows public servants like teachers, police and court officers, and health-care workers to live locally), and some push for fewer, more deeply affordable units.

A second problem with 421-a, and with developer-incentive programs in general, is that of the "leaky subsidy." The most efficient way to provide a benefit payment or subsidy is cash, in the form of a rent voucher, for example. But the 421-a program gives its operating subsidy—real estate tax relief—to the developer rather than to the tenant. Some of that subsidy may make its way through the developer to a landowner rather than to the tenant.

Here's how that happens. Developers need land to build on. The price of land is determined by a competitive bidding process. Bidders determine how much they can pay for the land by comparing projected revenues from a potential development to projected expenses. If revenue projections increase or expense projections decrease, then more capital can be devoted to land acquisition. Adding a 421-a tax break to the development model lowers expenses, freeing up the projected income that had been dedicated to those taxes and thereby increasing the price that can be paid for the land. Developers of 421-a affordable housing projects compete neck and neck with developers who do not provide affordable housing, usually condominium developers. This competitive process drives up the price of land, which increases the development cost of all units, including affordable apartments. So while 421-a allows developers of affordable housing to compete for land, it also probably increases those land costs.

Perhaps the most serious objection to the 421-a developer-incentive program is the actual construction and operating costs of the affordable apartments. Market-rate housing in high-rise buildings on valuable, sought-after land with deluxe, top-of-the-line services is the most expensive housing to build. The 421-a program takes costly housing in costly neighborhoods with costly services and deems it "affordable," which it simply is not. It is cheaper to build affordable housing in less expensive areas of the city and in less expensive low-rise buildings. But market rents in those neighborhoods and those buildings are not high enough to provide cross-subsidization, which means that the program only works in expensive, high-rent areas.

These are some of the reasons that developer-incentive programs have recently become so unpopular in progressive circles. However, if you take our capitalist system as a given, and then look for ways to turn it into a tool for the production of affordable housing, most of the other criticisms of the program can be dealt with by making modest adjustments to the requirements of the program or to the duration of the tax relief. These are all dials that are easily turned. It is especially notable that in New York, no alternative to 421-a has been proposed.

The Cost of Developer Incentives

Cities bear a theoretical cost for affordable housing built by programs like 421-a, but calculating that cost is virtually impossible, which has made understanding and assessing such programs confusing and difficult. This situation exists because the program was designed to provide all rental housing with operating subsidies, not just affordable housing. The basic problem is that real estate taxes on rental housing in New York City are so high (the tax rate for rental units is twice as high as that for condominium units) that even fully market-rate buildings require some kind of tax break.[2] So a portion of the 421-a tax benefit flows through to reduce the operating costs on market-rate apartments. Where and how the subsidy lands and who benefits from it is hard to define or quantify. In 2021, the program amounted to tax exemptions of $1.7 billion[3] and probably covered around 200,000 affordable and market-rate rental apartments (my best estimate). The cost of the tax exemption would be $8,500 per apartment. Ideally, the full $1.7 billion is devoted to reducing rents for income-restricted apartments. But it also allows developers to set rents for market units at levels that the market will actually bear, which is why rental housing typically does not get built without 421-a.

So there is another devilishly complicated factor in determining the cost of 421-a. Yes, the city is giving up future tax revenue (to the tune of $1.7 billion per year), but without that tax break, these buildings probably wouldn't have been built. Future tax revenue is only a true cost if the building would have been built without the tax break and thus would have paid full real estate taxes. Since almost no rental buildings can be built without a tax break, the appropriate comparison is between a building with affordable units paying abated taxes (and eventually full taxes) and an unbuilt building paying no taxes. It turns out that the cost of the 421-a program is hard to quantify because 421-a helps in the delivery of all rental housing in New York, market and affordable, and because the lost tax revenue is mostly theoretical and would probably never have materialized.

2
A Better Way Than 421-a: The High-Rising Costs of New York City's Most Unaffordable Tax Exemption Program, report (New York: Office of the New York City Comptroller, Mar. 2022); *Amend It, Don't End It: Improve 421-a to Spur Rental and Affordable Housing Development*, report (New York: Citizens Budget Commission, Mar. 15, 2022), https://cbcny.org/research/amend-it-dont-end-it.

3
"No Windfall: Ending 421-a Today Won't Free Up $1.8 Billion for Decades," blog post, Citizens Budget Commission, May 5, 2022, https://cbcny.org/research/no-windfall.

Benefits of Mixing Affordable and Market-Rate Housing

Aside from the economics of housing, there are also social dimensions of housing programs and policies. One of the main benefits of the developer-incentive model is that it results in "mixed-income" housing, that is, it brings together different income groups within buildings and within neighborhoods. Affordable apartments are integrated into buildings without causing marketing, operational, or social issues—at least, not in the experience of my company.

Integration has not always been the goal of housing policies. When I was at Battery Park City in the 1990s, for example, the master plan did not include affordable housing (although it had been incorporated into plans from the 1960s and 1970s). As a result, we were able to charge developers much more for the land, maximizing the value of each site. We funneled these land proceeds into a bond issue used to construct affordable housing in Harlem and the Bronx. The rationale was that more units of affordable housing could be built where land costs were lower. But we worried about the implied economic segregation. The well-off got to live in Battery Park City; the less well-off, farther out in what were seen at the time as less desirable areas of the city—though these neighborhoods may not be seen that way today.

Another positive feature of the developer-incentive model is the profit motive, this time a force for good rather than a corrupting influence. In any competitive market, developers work hard to keep their properties shined up. Building exteriors and interiors are well-maintained; lobbies and hallways are renovated regularly. In buildings consisting entirely of affordable housing, both the motivations and the funds for this level of care are less likely to be present. New York's public housing and its tenants have suffered greatly from avoided maintenance, which compounds over time to the extent that repairing these units may be more expensive than replacing them.

Finally, developer-incentive affordable housing simply means more affordable housing across the board. The 421-a program allows affordable housing to be built, without capital from government, in areas where market rents are high enough to allow cross-subsidization. Consequently, whatever capital resources government does have can be used for not-for-profit affordable housing in communities where private developers can't make market-rate housing work.

Affordable Housing and the Cost of Land

Most successful affordable housing programs, either historically in the United States or currently around the world, have been accompanied by attempts to rein in the cost of land. Perhaps land that is designated for affordable housing is kept off the market so that its price is not bid up by developers who aren't building affordable housing. Or perhaps the land is secured, as used to occur in the United States, through heavy-handed federal- and state-backed condemnation and eminent domain.

In Asia, particularly Singapore, the government is willing to condemn private land for affordable housing. In European cities, most notably Vienna, public housing agencies are a little more subtle, using a less authoritarian, semi-open-market model: the government process of purchasing land for public housing has advantages that private buyers vying for the same land do not. In both cases, the goal is to remove developers who are not building affordable housing from competition for the land.

In New York City, perhaps a division of the Department of Housing Preservation and Development could be the bridge between landowners and developers of affordable housing. HPD could, for example, approach owners of properties zoned only for manufacturing uses (abundant throughout the city, much of it unproductive) and purchase it for affordable housing. The price paid by the city would be more than its value for manufacturing but less than its value for private developers hoping to create market-rate housing. Once in possession of the land, HPD would turn to the NYC Department of City Planning and the New York City Council to rezone it for affordable housing. HPD would then put the rezoned parcels out for bid (thereby recouping its costs)—but only to developers building affordable housing using 421-a or other programs. This imaginary course of action could drastically cut land costs for affordable housing developments (nearly in half, I estimate), lowering the development cost of each unit substantially.

Since about 2010, New York City has been conducting a somewhat similar process at Hunters Point South in Long Island City. The land was acquired through condemnation around 2000 and is currently being made available to developers only for affordable housing. My company just completed almost 1,200 units at Hunters Point South, over 700 of which are affordable. We were able to change the usual proportion of 70 percent market/30 percent affordable to roughly 34 percent market/66 percent affordable because we had no land cost—the city contributed the land.

It is essential that government, using whatever means and tools it can bring to the table, return to a more engaged role in facilitating affordable housing—including affordable housing built by for-profit developers—by finding ways to bring land costs down. This approach would bring the strength and resources of both the private and the public sectors to bear on the problem of affordable housing. Unfortunately, in the United States, federal housing policies since the early 1970s have been directed at pushing the production of affordable housing out of the public sector and into the private sector. The Faircloth Amendment of 1998 actually prohibits federal funds from being used to increase the number of public housing units. The result has been the attenuation of public housing agencies across the country, which increases the reliance on the private sector, and also a loss of vision for the role of the public sector and how it can leverage its strengths to contribute to solutions.

Conclusion

The US housing market is so riddled with distortions that it cannot function normally. For one thing, it does not respond to the forces that usually bring supply and demand into equilibrium. Zoning restrictions severely limit the availability of land, pushing its costs higher and higher. Rent stabilization and rent control effectively keep more than 1 million units off the market, further limiting supply and pushing up rents on all other apartments. These big picture issues must be confronted.

But we must also establish the most effective role for for-profit developers of affordable housing. A housing policy that produces housing via standard business processes is probably sensible. A housing policy that attempts to capture market value and use it for affordable housing is probably wise. A housing policy that gets affordable units produced without any capital outlay from government sounds pretty good to me.

If a housing policy does not produce enough affordable units, or units that are affordable enough, or if the policy overbenefits (or even underbenefits) developers, the program parameters should be adjusted. Incremental adaptation rather than radical change—that is how society, and housing policies, do best.

Bookending Affordability: Notes on New York City Housing

Viren Brahmbhatt
is adjunct professor at the Spitzer School of Architecture, City College of New York. He is an architect and urban designer and founder of de.Sign Studio in New York City.

Richard Plunz
is emeritus professor, Graduate School of Architecture, Planning and Preservation, Columbia University. His most recent book is *New York Global: Critical Writings and Proposals, 1970–2020.*

Despite 140 years of progressive experiments, production of affordable housing in New York City remains a challenge. The city's housing landscape has been marred by a history of inequitable planning practices, including exclusionary zoning and weaponized "bulk" regulations. Years of discriminatory financing have exacerbated the problem of housing affordability. Additional complications include the lack of a critical conversation regarding the spatial design of housing; the increased complexities of the contemporary urban experience, particularly in the post-pandemic era with its redefined needs for health, hygiene, and personal space; funding that continues to decline, making it increasingly difficult for individuals or families to qualify for housing, despite the subsidies embedded in both government-owned and/or -operated buildings and privately owned rent-controlled and -stabilized apartments; and a developer-friendly real estate sector that favors private, for-profit developers.

Notwithstanding these circumstances, New York City has the nation's most extensive social housing system, and its housing developments have been at the forefront of housing policy innovation. Two architectural competitions—the 1879 Tenement House Competition and the 2013 adAPT NYC Design Competition—bookend more than a century of efforts to improve the design and production of affordable housing.

1879 Tenement House Competition

In many ways, 1879 was a watershed moment for housing reform in New York City. The city economy was evolving to include a vastly expanding industrial base. Employment

1

Richard Plunz and Andrés Alvarez-Dávila, "Density, Equity, and the History of Epidemics in New York City," State of the Planet, Columbia Climate School, June 30, 2020, https://news .climate.columbia .edu/2020/06/30 /density-equity -history-epidemics -nyc/; John H. Griscom, M.D., *Annual Report of the Interments in the City and County of New York, for the Year 1842, with Remarks Thereon, and a Brief View of the Sanitary Condition of the City* (New York: James van Norden, 1843), 166. See also "On the Uses of Air: Perfecting the New York Tenement, 1850–1901," in *Berlin/New York: Like and Unlike*, ed. Josef Paul Kleihues and Christina Rathberger (New York: Rizzoli, 1993), 159–79.

2

Ira Rosenwaike, *Population History of New York City* (Syracuse, NY: Syracuse University Press, 1972), 39, 42, tables 19, 63; Citizen's Association of New York, Council of Hygiene and Public Health, *Report upon the Sanitary Condition of the City* (New York: D. Appleton, 1865).

was robust, and workers were able to afford higher rents. Attracting and maintaining a workforce required improved housing conditions, and the 1879 Tenement House Competition was a starting point in setting minimum space standards and required amenities for housing.

The previous half-century had seen scientific documentation of the relationship between poverty, race, health, and housing type. In many ways, those studies mirror conditions that are endemic to today. For example, early on, a study of the cholera epidemic of 1819 showed that "out of 48 blacks, living in ten cellars, 33 were sick, of whom 14 died; while out of 120 whites living immediately over their heads in the apartments of the same house, not one even had the fever." History reveals that the social justice issues present in housing in 1819 share certain similarities with those of the COVID-19 pandemic two centuries later.[1] The most definitive study on housing pathologies in New York City was completed by the Council on Hygiene in 1865 as the city's population approached 1 million and the question of inadequate production of housing for the poor had reached pervasive proportions.[2]

Between the 1865 study and 1879, pressure for tenement housing reform grew, but the marketplace produced no breakthroughs. The ubiquitous "railroad flat" (a series of rooms in a line) dominated tenement production. The worst versions typically had no indoor toilets, and only 2 of 16 or more rooms per floor had windows with outdoor exposure. In 1879, the impasse was broken by a competition for the "ideal tenement" organized by the New York City trade journal *Plumbing and Sanitary Engineer*. The growing sanitation industry understood the financial advantage that would derive from legislating improved housing, which would create a large new market for production—including plumbing infrastructure and fixtures.

While there were numerous innovative design submissions to the competition, the winning entry was the "dumbbell" tenement, a form resulting from an internal airshaft. Though it was substandard even then, the dumbbell organization was immediately adopted by New York City in the Tenement House Act of 1879 (the "Old Law"), which for the first time established hygiene and spatial design standards in New York City. The Tenement House Act mandated lot coverage limitations, normatively enforced to 80 percent. Common wet areas and toilets were required for each floor, replacing outdoor "slop sink" toilets. Despite the internal airshafts, there could still be rooms with no outdoor exposures. Yet in spite of such obvious deficiencies, the dumbbell was an improvement over the railroad flat.

By 1900, some 60,000 Old Law tenement buildings had been constructed. Continuing reform pressure and an enhanced affordable housing marketplace led to passage of the Tenement House Act of 1901.[3] The dumbbell became illegal, replaced by "New Law" tenements with more generous spatial design standards that remain a metric for housing design today. Every apartment was required to have a toilet and kitchen. Every room was to have direct outdoor exposure. Airshafts required minimum outside exposure, while larger internal courtyards were incentivized. Minimum dimensions, including lot coverage and room dimensions, were strictly enforced.

The Inter-Competition Era

The Old and New Laws launched a century of innovation in improved housing design in New York City. Essentially, the New Law standards, with modification, still prevail. During the two decades immediately following 1901, several housing design

Points of View

3
For a detailed overview of the evolution of tenement house legislation in New York City, see Richard Plunz, *A History of Housing in New York City: Dwelling Type and Social Change in the American Metropolis* (New York: Columbia University Press, 1990; rev. ed., 2016), ch. 2.

4
For the history of housing design competitions, see "Strange Fruit: The Legacy of the Design Competition in New York Housing," in *Reweaving the Urban Fabric*, ed. Maria Gutman, Ghislaine Hermanuz, and Richard Plunz (New York: Princeton Architectural Press, 1988), 99–119, 126–29.

5
NYC Department of Housing Preservation and Development, *New Housing Marketplace Plan: Creating a More Affordable, Viable, and Sustainable City for All New Yorkers*, 2013, https://courseworks2.columbia.edu/files/661867/download?download_frd=1.

competitions incubated design experimentation and also continued a dialogue with Western European cities on housing design innovation.[4] Perhaps the most notable new legislation was in 1929. Prior to 1929, the tenement laws applied only to housing characterized as "tenements," that is, high-density, low-rise, low-cost housing. But already in the early 20th century, upscale 12-story buildings were constructed using plans that would be illegal under tenement law spatial requirements. No spatial design requirements held for the upper-middle-class and luxury market, the assumption being that the demands of an upscale market would provide acceptable minimum standards without legal mandates. This was not the case, however, with the incorporation of elevators and proliferation of high-rise apartment buildings for middle-income tenants.

The Multiple Dwelling Law of 1929 placed all housing typologies under the same spatial standards, addressing the large number of new high-rise technologies. Other technological innovation governed spatial design: for example, forced-air ventilation systems led to the legalization of internal corridors without windows to the exterior, in effect a reduction of the design standards from 1901. Substantial discussion of reducing spatial standards, however, did not happen until the recent micro-unit discourse, which bookends the affordability question.

The 21st Century

The 21st century has seen substantial concern over increasing demand for affordable housing. Beginning in 2002, Mayor Michael Bloomberg's administration pioneered numerous attempts to provide more and better housing, but for the most part these initiatives did not result in measurable improvement. One of his initial efforts, the New Housing Marketplace Plan,[5] may even have worsened the crisis, in that many of the units created under NHMP required income thresholds that would exclude the New Yorkers who most needed affordable housing. According to a 2013 Association for Neighborhood and Housing Development report, "About two-thirds of the city's recently developed affordable housing required occupants to have minimum income levels that were higher than the median household income in the areas where the housing was built."[6]

A major rezoning implemented by the Bloomberg administration affected close to 40 percent of the city with ramifications for housing.[7] According to Amanda M. Burden, New York City's planning commissioner at the time, the rezoning was characterized by a "finely grained" approach that took into account the needs of different communities and neighborhoods. It was designed to preserve neighborhood fabric where it was deemed necessary and upzone where "it's sustainable, and where reinvestment is needed."[8] Upzoning was reserved for neighborhoods like Williamsburg, Hudson Yards, and Long Island City driven by pressure from affluent, vocal communities; real estate developers; and the Bloomberg administration itself. By contrast, neighborhoods with demands for affordable housing and higher density were targeted for downzoning, making it harder to build more housing where it was needed.[9]

According to a report by NYU's Furman Center for Real Estate and Urban Policy, "contextual-only" upzoning was intended to preserve neighborhoods by ensuring that new development would not be at a scale much larger or denser than the existing context.[10] This protective methodology likely contributed to uneven distribution of residential density. In the end, rezoning of almost half of New York City between 2003 and 2007 increased the capacity for residential development only 1.7 percent.[11] A subsequent program, put forth by the Bloomberg administration in 2005, was based on inclusionary

6
Winnie Hu, "Some 'Affordable' Units Too Costly, Report Says," *New York Times*, Feb. 13, 2013, https://www .nytimes.com/2013 /02/14/nyregion /report-cites -shortcomings -of-affordable -housing-plan.html.

7
Richard Florida, "Dan Doctoroff on Rebuilding New York after 9/11," City Lab, Sept. 19, 2017, https://www .bloomberg.com /news/articles /2017-09-19/dan -doctoroff-on-the -dramatic-growth -of-nyc-under -bloomberg.

8
Kareem Fahim, "Despite Much Rezoning, Scant Change in Residential Capacity," *New York Times*, Mar. 21, 2010, https:// www.nytimes .com/2010/03/22 /nyregion /22zoning.html.

9
Fahim, "Despite Much Rezoning."

10
Furman Center for Real Estate and Urban Policy, New York University, *Policy Brief: How Have Recent Rezonings Affected the City's Ability to Grow?* 2013, https:// furmancenter.org /files/publications /Rezonings _Furman_Center

zoning. Inclusionary zoning policies allow developers to increase density (in neighborhoods where density limits can be increased) in return for a certain percentage (usually) of affordable units. However, according to a 2015 report from the Association for Neighborhood and Housing Development, this effort too "fundamentally failed," with fewer than 3,000 affordable apartments created in the years after it was implemented.[12]

In general, the consequences of these efforts were palpable. The deficit in affordable housing increased, as did homelessness. Both New York City (2004) and New York State (1998) cut NYCHA's operational subsidies, leaving the agency crippled. High vacancy rates in luxury housing and the addition of significant amounts of new office space did not help. Remaining at the end of Bloomberg's tenure were large questions about the inequality and displacement that followed new density as well as the idea that development and prosperity for some increased housing unaffordability for many.

2013 adAPT NYC Competition

Between 2011 and 2012 alone, the poverty rate in New York City increased from 20.9 to 21.2 percent.[13] Workers, especially service workers essential to the day-to-day functioning of the city, could not keep up with increasing rents. In response, Mayor Bloomberg proposed the adAPT NYC Competition. The competition called for innovative design prototypes with smaller living spaces that would translate into higher densities and lower rents, especially in the face of scarce developable land. The "living small" phenomenon has been around for over a century and a half, especially in large global cities. In New York City, micro-typologies have included studio apartments and single-room-occupancy units. AdAPT represented a new condition, however, in that the targeted market was associated with young technology workers and others unable to afford high rents but deemed essential to growing the new IT economy. Bloomberg characterized the city's housing stock as "misaligned with the changing demographics of its population." In response, reduced apartment square footages, presumably for reduced rents, would be allowed for prioritized tenant groups.

The competition was an offshoot of the 2011 Citizen Housing Planning Council initiative "Making Room," which was based on demographic changes affecting household size in New York City.[14] In 1950, 78 percent of households were married couples with children. In 1989, that number was 56 percent, and in 2013, 46 percent.[15] At the time of the competition, the city had at least 1.8 million one- and two-person households but only 1 million studios and one-bedroom apartments.[16] The competition was hosted by the New York City Department of Housing Preservation and Development, which allowed a special exception to the 400-square-foot minimum space mandated by New York City's building code. HPD would reduce the minimum space requirement to 300 square feet for an experimental micro-housing unit, the first time since 1879 that minimum space standards were reduced rather than increased.[17] Because micro-units are not allowed in affordable housing, the competition was directed to market-rate housing.

The immediate result of the competition was the Carmel Place housing on East 27th Street in the Kips Bay neighborhood, designed by nArchitects. The 55 units were smaller than legal minimums, between 260 and 360 square feet in size. They demonstrated the efficacy of micro-unit design, not necessarily as a planning model for affordable housing but as one potential alternative for future housing production in New York City. This successful implementation of micro-units introduced a form of "living small" that previously had not been considered viable. The competition showed that for

_Policy_Brief
_March_2010.pdf.

11
Furman Center,
*How Have Recent
Rezonings.*

12
Association for
Neighborhood
and Housing
Development,
*NYC Inclusionary
Zoning: A
District-by-District
Analysis of What
Was Lost, Gained,
and What Remains,*
July 2015, https://
anhd.org/wp
-content/uploads
/2015/07/ANHD
-Inclusionary
-Zoning-Rpt-7-15
.pdf.

13
Sam Roberts,
"Poverty Rate Is Up
in New York City,
and Income Gap Is
Wide, Census Data
Show," *New York
Times,* Sept. 19,
2013, https://www
.nytimes.com/2013
/09/19/nyregion
/poverty-rate-in
-city-rises-to-21-2
.html.

14
Citizen Housing
Planning Council,
"Making Room,"
CHPC, accessed
June 5, 2023,
https://chpcny.org
/making-room/.

15
US Census
Bureau, "Families
and Households,"
accessed June 5,
2023, https://www
.census.gov/topics
/families/families
-and-households
.html; Gretchen
Livingston, "Fewer

one-person households, reduced minimum space requirements would not automatically lead to reduced quality of living.

The Future of Housing in New York

In both 1879 and 2013, technological innovation—whether advances in domestic hygiene or shifts in demographics and work practices—drove discussion around affordable housing. While the 1879 competition led to the 1901 Tenement House Act, what if anything might the 2013 competition bring about? Though minimum space standards remain unchanged, the requirement for minimum unit size was removed from the New York City Zoning Resolution, so perhaps micro-living will eventually trigger an adjustment to how the city regulates housing design and development. Micro-typologies may hold promise for a higher-density urban future that is focused more on affordability than on lifestyle; for a new model of affordable housing, possibly along with shared units and alternative typologies.

Other questions remain. How small is too small, and how small is enough? Can a revision of zoning and land-use regulations align with new building codes and bulk regulations to increase affordable housing production in neighborhoods with high rents? At what point does the higher density permitted by smaller unit size offset rising land prices and construction costs, particularly for affordable rental housing relative to income? Is the micro-unit market to be limited to young professionals or are there creative solutions that will appeal to a wider group? And will the micro-unit strategies represent a new phase in the evolution of housing legislation, returning to the era before 1929 and risking a reinforcement of negative social equity issues with two sets of design standards?

The current housing crisis is the culmination of a shortage of affordable housing that has lasted for more than a century, with increasingly complex associated problems: soaring rents, lack of building maintenance, homelessness, limited availability of land, high costs of labor and materials, financing restrictions. Yet there are also opportunities unique to this moment in the history of New York City, with micro-living strategies representing only one aspect. While micro-typologies do not address the larger affordable housing questions, they may, if managed well, achieve a new moment in providing lower-cost shelter for some New Yorkers as we come to understand the changing meaning of home and home-less within our collective lifeworlds.[18]

Than Half of U.S. Kids Today Live in a 'Traditional' Family," Pew Research Center, Dec. 22, 2014, https://www.pewresearch.org/short-reads/2014/12/22/less-than-half-of-u-s-kids-today-live-in-a-traditional-family/.

16
"Mayor Bloomberg Announces Winner of adAPT NYC Competition to Develop Innovative Micro-Unit Apartment Housing Model," NYC.gov, Jan. 22, 2013, https://www.nyc.gov/office-of-the-mayor/news/032-13/mayor-bloomberg-winner-em-adapt-nyc-em-competition-develop-innovative-micro-unit#/2.

17
NYC Department of Housing Preservation and Development, *Design Guidelines for Supportive Housing*, Feb. 2012, https://www1.nyc.gov/assets/hpd/downloads/pdfs/services/sro-constr-guidelines.pdf, 9.

18
In recent years, homelessness in New York City has reached the highest levels since the Great Depression. See "Basic Facts about Homelessness: New York City Data and Charts," accessed June 5, 2023, https://www.coalitionforthehomeless.org/basic-facts-about-homelessness-new-york-city-data-and-charts/. There are approximately 250,000 single-parent households in New York City, and approximately 580,000 (or 32 percent of) New York City children live in a single-parent home. See "Vulnerabilities and Service Needs of Single-Parent Households in New York City," Center on Poverty and Social Policy, Columbia University, accessed June 5, 2023, https://www.povertycenter.columbia.edu/nyc-poverty-tracker/2017/single-parent-households.

The Death and Life of Marcus Garvey Village: A Case Study

Marcus Garvey Village in Brownsville, Brooklyn, was an early attempt at rectifying the sins of modernist planning with traditional street wall and courtyard urbanism. But the development was less than successful due to several factors. Modernist planning did away with the street, which Le Corbusier called a place "where death threatens us at every step...and is a sea of lusts and faces," and replaced it with freestanding linear blocks of apartments and towers set in a park. These isolated buildings, divorced from the life of the city, became centers of crime.

Named after the early 20th-century Black leader Marcus Garvey, the development was meant as an antidote to alienating modern spaces. Designed by the Institute for Architecture and Urban Studies with Kenneth Frampton,[1] it was a prototype for low-rise, high-density housing that reinterpreted both the traditional New York town house and the principles of modern architecture according to urban concepts championed by Oscar Newman in *Defensible Space: Crime Prevention through Urban Design* and Jane Jacobs in *The Death and Life of Great American Cities*. Their ideas of urban density and "eyes on the street" were essential to safe public spaces. Indeed, Frampton et al.'s design brought back the street front by means of a modern interpretation of stoops as a place of community interaction.

Unfortunately, the development became a focal point for street gangs and violence. As Frampton points out, the plan was compromised because it was not built exactly as per the design. The main problems were the cul-de-sac courtyards where drug dealers

1
Architectural design of Marcus Garvey Village prototype: New York State Urban Development Corporation (Theodore Liebman, Anthony Pangaro, Michael Kirkland). Architectural design of Marcus

Garvey Village application: Institute for Architecture and Urban Studies (Kenneth Frampton, Peter Wolf, Arthur Baker, Lee Taliaferro). Associate architect: David Todd and Associates.

met and the numerous hiding places for criminals along the street front. In addition, the neighborhood of Brownsville where Marcus Garvey Village was located continued to deteriorate after the development was built.

Eventually Marcus Garvey Village was sold to L+M Developers, which hired Curtis + Ginsberg Architects to renovate the complex and ameliorate specific problems: the open mews courtyards, the too numerous (99) entries, the lack of security systems, and the unclear signage. While it was not demolished like the Pruitt-Igoe complex in St. Louis, the changes to some degree recall another Le Corbusier housing development in Pessac, France, of 1922. The residents resented the abstract, modernist vocabulary and personalized the exteriors with pitched roofs and flowerpots. Asked about these changes, which were at odds with his architecture, Le Corbusier responded, "You know, it is always life that is right and the architect who is wrong." **—AG**

UDC/IAUS Prototype

Kenneth Frampton trained as an architect at the AA School of Architecture in London. From 1967 to 1972, he taught at Princeton University, and from 1972 to 2020, he served as Ware Professor of Architecture at Columbia University. His books include *Modern Architecture: A Critical History*; *Studies in Tectonic Culture*; *Labor, Work & Architecture*; and *A Genealogy of Modern Architecture*.

Low-rise, high-density housing first came to the fore in the 1960s. The relatively unprecedented residential paradigm was initiated by the realization of Siedlung Halen, built outside Bern, Switzerland, in 1960 to the designs of Atelier 5. This canonical achievement was inspired by Le Corbusier's Roq et Rob low-rise housing projected for a site at Roquebrune-Cap-Martin in the south of France in 1948. Derived like Roq et Rob from the coastal vernacular of the Mediterranean, Halen would anticipate Bernard Rudofsky's reevaluation of this vernacular in his *Architecture Without Architects* exhibition, staged at the Museum of Modern Art in 1964.

The first attempt to design low-rise, high-density housing for the United States took the form of an "alternative suburbia" projected by Serge Chermayeff and Christopher Alexander in their book *Community and Privacy: Toward a New Architecture of Humanism* of 1964. In this prototype, both the typical house and the overall land settlement pattern were predicated on the iteration of a flat-roofed single-story unit. The exemplar was set between party walls and, rather eccentrically, had entrances at both ends. The house was thus conceived as a family dwelling in which adults would enter from one end and children from the other. The dialectic of community and privacy was evident in the sequence of living spaces, where full-height, floor-to-ceiling glazed rooms alternated with small courtyards: entry patio–adult living space (i.e., primary bedroom)–courtyard–family living space–courtyard–children's living space (i.e., children's bedrooms)–entry patio.

Chermayeff built a house along these lines for his own occupation in New Haven during the time he was teaching at the Yale School of Architecture. The students in his studio designed more complex versions of a similar single-story type—one that could accommodate the automobile in close proximity to the house, a convenience that the original Chermayeff/Alexander prototype failed to provide. In Siedlung Halen, Atelier 5 met this essential requirement by incorporating a large collective garage into the form of the stepped housing; most residents of Halen were able to access it via covered walkways.

The crucial issue of being able to integrate convenient parking into low-rise residential fabric resurfaced in the design and realization of the New York State Urban Development Corporation and Institute for Architecture and Urban Studies low-rise, high-density housing prototype, exhibited at the Museum of Modern Art in 1973 in *Another Chance for Housing: Low-Rise Alternatives*. Both the UDC, founded by New York State governor Nelson Rockefeller in 1968, and the IAUS, established in 1967 as an urban "think tank" by Arthur Drexler, curator of architecture at MoMA, and Peter Eisenman, an architect and the director of the organization, were supported to some degree by Rockefeller patronage. Much the same applied to Edward Logue. Appointed by Rockefeller to the directorship of the UDC, he became interested in low-rise, high-density housing as a result of his dissatisfaction with the freestanding, mid-rise housing blocks designed and realized by a number of young New York practices in the Twin Parks district of the Bronx during the early years of his directorship. As Logue wrote in his introduction to *Another Chance for Housing*:

> These high-rise "projects," as they are usually called, house a great many families on a relatively small amount of land, and they do provide decent living space in quantities which would be difficult to achieve at lower densities. However, their design and landscaping often remain quite sterile. The scale of such projects seems frequently to be way beyond any human dimension, and families, particularly young children, miss the feeling of a familiar, homelike atmosphere. Furthermore, such housing projects often seem not to fit in with the surrounding neighborhood, but rather stand apart from it.

Drexler, having been trained as an architect, was interested in having the museum play a more active role in influencing public policy in the fields of architecture and urban design, as is evident as early as his exhibition of 1966 *The New City: Architecture and Urban Renewal*. This exhibition, coordinated with the City of New York, was the first exhibition on which Drexler collaborated with Eisenman. It consisted of four demonstration projects designed by four teams of young architects, at the time members of the architecture faculties of Cornell, Columbia, Princeton, and the Massachusetts Institute of Technology. MoMA commissioned these projects to illustrate the role of architectural planning in relation to certain problems confronting American cities: waterfront development, focusing on new housing without relocation, modifications of the existing grid street system, and creation of new land and new neighborhoods.

Thus the subsequent collaboration between Logue and Drexler may be seen as a marriage of convenience between two prestigious New York institutions that ultimately resulted in a low-rise, high-density housing prototype being sponsored by the UDC and designed jointly by architectural teams drawn from the architect's section of the UDC (led by Theodore Liebman in collaboration with his colleagues Anthony Pangaro and Michael Kirkland) and the IAUS (Eisenman, Peter Wolf, and myself, with Arthur Baker serving as the executive architect). This prototype would not only be exhibited at the Museum of Modern Art but also subsequently realized by the UDC as a trial run in Brownsville, Brooklyn, between 1972 and 1975.

Two polemical texts of the moment exercised a powerful influence on the design of the UDC/IAUS housing prototype: Jane Jacobs's renowned *Death and Life of Great American Cities* of 1961 and Oscar Newman's influential *Defensible Space: Crime Prevention through Urban Design* of 1972. As a result, the low-rise, high-density prototype was as much influenced by the traditional five-to-eight-story, walk-up, brick-faced residential fabric of New York as it was by Newman's categoric critique of "undesignated public space," invariably found at the time in the access corridors and galleries of medium- to high-rise public housing.

The prototype consisted of two variations of the same basic type: the street type and the mews type. Both were four-story units comprising duplexes stacked on top of duplexes. And both were accessed in pairs from a central stair—except where they were accessed directly from the stoop on either side of the stair. In the street units, the stoop, elevated half-a-story above grade, served, alternately, two up-going and two down-going duplexes, while in the mews type, it served either two- or three-bedroom units on the ground floor, with one three- and one four-bedroom unit in the up-going duplexes above. The stoops of the prototype offered spontaneous surveillance of the street or the mews space beneath.

The upper duplexes were furnished with ample balconies to compensate for lack of access to the garden on the lower ground floor. The prototype integrated off-street parking, so that no dwelling would be more than 200 feet from its parked automobile. Parking was organized in two different modes, either parallel to the sidewalk or at an angle to the sidewalk, in chevron formation. Alternating between parallel and chevron parking throughout would have made every other street a narrower one-way street. At a density of between 70 and 90 units per acre, this every-other arrangement would yield 50 percent of the required parking within the grid.

Unfortunately, this number proved impossible to achieve in the realization of the prototype. The site was adversely affected by the noise of an IRT elevated line, which cut through the virtual center of the available multiblock site, and the plan stipulated that residential fabric had to be set back a minimum of 100 feet from such a noise source. This disposition meant that the blocks on either side of the elevated train could be used only for parking lots; the rest of the parking was distributed evenly in lots throughout the site. Moreover, the fragmentary nature of the site in many instances consisted of half-blocks, 100 feet deep, which were uneconomical to occupy with street units. As a result, these blocks had to be developed as mews units running directly off the street at right angles to the grid.

Other factors made it difficult to varying degrees to apply the prototype as it had been originally designed. The first of these was the bedrooms of the lower down-going duplexes. These bedrooms had been conceived from the onset as being half-a-level below the rear garden. Although this placement did not compromise the units in terms of light or ventilation, it was psychologically unsatisfactory for the occupants that they were unable to gain access to the garden immediately adjacent. Although a modification could have been introduced, such as a threshold and short stair giving access to the rear yard, Herbert Tessler, who as director of construction at the UDC had the authority to overrule the design team, declared, "Where I live people go upstairs to sleep." On the basis of this convention, he resisted applying the prototype as it had been designed. The ensuing dispute was resolved by Tessler insisting that because the whole exercise was an experiment, half of the housing would be built as designed and half would be built in a modified form—with all the down-going units eliminated. This draconian decision not only compromised the exercise but also entailed the preparation, at considerable expense, of another set of executive drawings.

One of the key principles of the design was that all the duplexes had to be either a half or one and a half floors above grade, and the living spaces had to have access to a back garden via a stair from the main living level or, in the case of the upper duplexes, to a balcony. In the site layout, the street units formed a continuous frontal terrace that together with the mews units enclosed the rear gardens as a continuous fabric. In the prototype, these gardens were divided from one another by brick walls, thereby assuring lateral visual privacy to each unit despite overlook from above. But this feature proved to be unrealizable due to budget restrictions, and the result was that the rear gardens were separated only by chain-link fences. Where the same UDC/IAUS prototype was projected at a lower density—38 rather than 70 units per acre—as in a planned application for Fox Hills, Staten Island, the stoop was raised two-thirds of a floor height above the general datum, while the rear garden was situated only one-third of a floor height below the same datum. This arrangement would have meant that, with careful grading of the site, the bedrooms of the lower duplexes would have had ready access to the rear garden. It is to be regretted that a more open, less dense application of the prototype was not attempted.

The built-in limitations of the prototype as applied to the fragmented site in Brownsville returns us to the fundamental dilemma confronting the provision of public housing in the United States: namely, that it is invariably underfunded or projected for compromised sites or both. Moreover, society cannot begin to evolve successive generations of public housing prototypes without a long-term political commitment to address the issue of homelessness that today prevails in every major city.

What this state of affairs suggests is that the cultivation of socio-ecologically viable patterns of land settlement—as opposed to continual suburbanization with its built-in waste in terms of both land and energy—will only be possible through a determined, enduring pursuit of environmentally sustainable housing policies on the part of both federal and state governments. In its relatively short existence, from 1968 to 1975, the New York State Urban Development Corporation realized some 33,000 housing units, most of which were not low-rise, high-density. But the UDC has moved away from its role as a housing developer. At a public inquiry coinciding with the fiscal crisis of New York in the mid-1970s, the UDC was depicted as an example of governmental overreach, and Edward Logue was duly compelled to resign. The UDC was also accused of financial mismanagement, and its mandate to sponsor public housing was withdrawn.

For all its shortcomings, the low-rise, high-density housing as realized in Brownsville helped to stem the deterioration of the neighborhood in terms of street crime and drug use. At the same time, although the prototype was designed in accordance with Oscar Newman's concept of "defensible space," as manifest in our provision of spontaneous surveillance, no architectural arrangement can in and of itself be effective in the face of dire urban poverty and mass unemployment. If Brownsville is a safer place to live today than it was in the 1970s, it is partly due to the fact that the UDC/IAUS prototype in all its variations remains largely as it was built, amounting to a continuous urban fabric capable of bestowing on the community a unique sense of sociocultural continuity.

Renovation

Mark Ginsberg is a partner at Curtis + Ginsberg Architects, New York City. His firm's work is community and policy focused and includes developments of over 20,000 units of housing, much of it designated low-income and affordable.

n 1984, as part of the research for my master's thesis on affordable housing in New York City, I was introduced to Theodore Liebman, formerly the chief of architecture for the New York State Urban Development Corporation. Ted had been responsible for the development of Marcus Garvey Village in Brownsville, Brooklyn, in the early 1970s. It was, at the time, a radical project to create low-rise housing in a modernist style at a density close to the 60 to 100 units per acre achieved by "towers in the park."

Then the predominant form for housing, particularly for affordable housing, towers in the park were high-rise buildings in an open landscape. The tall buildings required elevators, meaning that, to a large degree, residents were disconnected from the ground plane. Poorly defined open space was a no-man's-land open to all and controlled by none.

Marcus Garvey Village represented a new model for affordable housing. Instead of towers, the project consisted of 99 four-story buildings containing 625 units. The resulting density was approximately 73 units per acre. The buildings defined the street edge, and numerous entrances created activity along the street, which aligned with the principles presented in Oscar Newman's 1972 book *Defensible Space: Crime Prevention through Urban Design*.

All units are within three and a half stories of the street—that is, better connected to the ground than the tower model. Entry doors were at the top of half-flight modern "stoops" and arranged in three configurations: along the street, along one of eight mews, and within one larger interior courtyard. In a nod to early 1970s car culture, entrances were located near parking lots. The original design included terraces for upper units, but this feature was removed sometime before construction, depriving upper units of private exterior space.

The buildings of Marcus Garvey Village could not be built today. Stair access (for all units except 13 studio units off the courtyard) does not meet current accessibility codes. New York City zoning laws were overridden by the UDC, resulting in a disregard for specified distances between buildings and requirements for rear yards. Further, the buildings do not conform to modern energy codes.

Once occupied, the site and the area were characterized by a high crime rate, in some cases because of the buildings' design. Crime was concentrated in the mews, which had no security. When my firm was commissioned to renovate the project, I was told that the police would not get out of their cars to enter these areas. Lighting levels were poor and uneven; high-pressure sodium fixtures gave the area an institutional feel. Monitoring the 99 entrances was hard, and there were few security cameras. (One of the advantages of towers in the park—an advantage not realized at the time—is that limited access points enable better control for large numbers of people.) The Brownsville buildings were located on seven blocks, and the similar appearance of these blocks across the development made navigation difficult. Addresses in small type were located on the doors that stood half a flight off the street. While a mature tree canopy shelters the complex, the landscaped areas in the mews and courtyard were mostly hardscape or fenced off.

Because the buildings were completed after the UDC went bankrupt in 1975, significant corners were cut during construction. Most electric panels were manufactured by a company that went out of business because the panels tended to burst into flames. Building systems included inefficient electric resistance heating and gas-fired hot water boilers. Below-window, through-wall air conditioner sleeves were installed but not used because more efficient, less expensive units could be mounted in the windows, leaving the sleeves as uninsulated holes in the walls.

There was no town center and very little retail to support the development and the neighborhood. Livonia Avenue and an elevated subway line (the subway stop is half a block east at Rockaway Avenue) bisect the site. The subway is separated from the Marcus Garvey blocks by a series of parking lots. These lots were mostly empty since residents had a very low rate of car ownership and tended to park for free on the street.

Curtis + Ginsberg Architects was retained to renovate the buildings in 2014 after forty years of wear and tear. Central to our work was the creation of new identity and placemaking elements that made security the highest priority. New decorative fences at the mews and courtyard are accessed by residents' key fobs; modern intercom systems facilitate guest entry. LED lighting fixtures provide more coverage with vastly improved color rendition. To improve wayfinding, addresses are identified with large aluminum numbers; backlit metal panels visually mark the entrances and foster a visual hierarchy along the street. Along with the new lighting, upgraded security cameras—and more of them—aid in crime deterrence and protection. These physical improvements, combined with increased security and greater coordination with the NYPD, have led to an almost 50 percent reduction in criminal incidents at Marcus Garvey.

We removed the fences around planted areas as well as areas of hardscape and installed new plantings and a new playground. Other important community investments include a renovated youth center and a half-acre urban farm that provides fresh produce to the community at discounted prices. These enhancements generate activity within the complex and on the adjacent streets.

To maintain long-term affordability, we instituted a number of energy efficiencies. New windows and roofs provide better insulation and air tightness. We repaired the facades and installed insulation behind the AC louvers. A new energy management system increases the efficiency of the electric baseboard heating. One significant advantage of low-rise over high-rise buildings is the larger ratio of roof to building area. The roof expanses provided an ideal opportunity for photovoltaic systems, which are installed where permitted by code. The PV system, along with one of the first fuel cells in Brooklyn, is located outside the buildings and significantly lowered the operational carbon footprint of the buildings.

In addition to correcting the original shortcomings of both design and execution, we developed a master plan and, with our client, applied for rezoning in order to permit new seven- and eight-story buildings on the empty parking lots. These structures bring commercial and community spaces to a widened sidewalk along Livonia Avenue and additional affordable housing to the upper levels. The new buildings generate a town center between the subway station and Betsy Head Park, at the west side of Marcus Garvey Village. The new mid-rise buildings increase the density of the development to 108 units per acre.

The concept of the low-rise, high-density development was revolutionary and over time has led to better affordable housing. Such projects work particularly well as infill housing. Architects benefit greatly from resident and client feedback, when available. So far, our clients have not reported on any design issues, and the lessons we have learned from Marcus Garvey Village are applied in the affordable housing we are building and will continue to build across New York City.

**Opposite,
from top**
Marcus Garvey
street type and
mews type before
renovation

**This page,
from top**
Marcus Garvey
street type (facade
design by GDSNY)
and green after
renovation

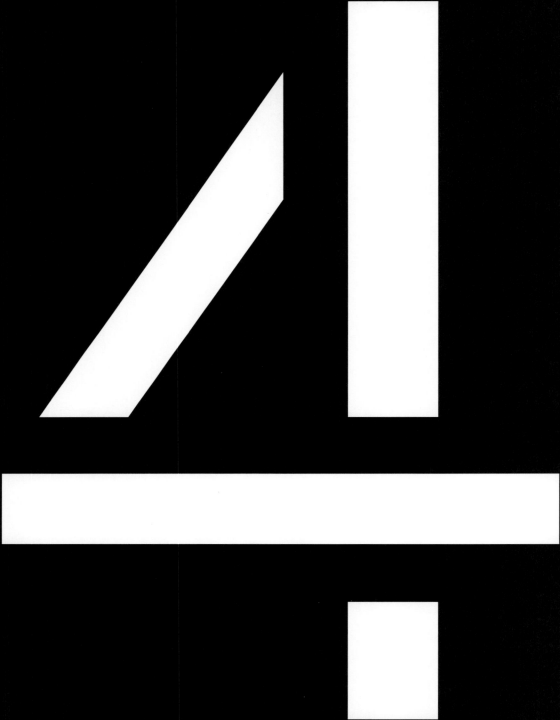

In Search of Solutions

Wheel Estate

Andrés Duany
is an architect, planner, and urbanist. He is co-founder of DPZ CoDesign (formerly Duany Plater-Zyberk & Co.) and the Congress for New Urbanism. Duany's No-Nonsense Housing Company was formed in 2020.

Fernando Pagés Ruiz
is project manager with the No-Nonsense Housing Company and has written widely on affordable housing and construction.

ntil the Great Depression, the United States had enough housing for tens of millions of poor Americans and immigrants. Much of this housing was considered substandard, and in 1937, the US Housing Act sought to improve accommodation for the poor through public housing subsidies. These programs raised standards but provided—and continue to provide—housing for only a small minority of those in need. According to the National Low-Income Housing Coalition, such programs supply only 36 affordable units for every 100 low-income families. Another, larger gap exists for those with incomes too high for subsidized rent and too low for conventional homeownership.

In the mid- to late 1920s, a new industry emerged to fill the affordability gap: prefabricated and inexpensive factory-made housing. Its genesis was the touring trailer, which glamorized automobile luxury camping. With the onset of the Great Depression, workers followed job opportunities around the country, moving via homemade trailers that evoked the days of covered wagons. The trailer parks that once received upper-middle-class campers became home to less well-off, itinerant laborers. Manufacturers responded by first designing small, portable houses and then larger ones more suitable for long-term living. The mobile home industry gradually became one of the fastest-growing sectors in America.

By the 1940s, mobile homes were large enough to house entire families, and ad hoc "trailer park" communities sprouted in open fields across every state. By the 1950s, the trailers had evolved from temporary to permanent use. The industry began to specify axles suitable for only a single transfer. Once the mobile homes were shipped from the factory to the lot, the wheels would be removed, and the trailer would become a permanent fixture.

Mobile homes continued to add size and amenities during the 1950s through the 1970s. At the time, site-built homes were selling for $40,000, and three-bedroom trailers were available for $6,000. By the 1970s, factory-made homes supplied 37 percent of the nation's housing, and the industry had transitioned from an unregulated business with a reputation for shoddy products to a federally chartered industry with a uniform code and strict quality control. As part of this transition, for reasons of marketing and regulatory distinction, the "mobile home" moniker was abandoned in favor of "manufactured housing." The name change did little to shift the perception of factory-made housing as substandard. A get-what-you-pay-for mentality hamstrings an industry that still over-delivers in a price-to-value ratio.

Today, a three-bedroom, federally regulated, new-from-the-factory manufactured home costs about $85 a square foot. The site-built version of the same three-bedroom house would run $250 per square foot, if not more. Yet cultural contempt—a problem that can be addressed with design—remains a significant hurdle to the industry. There is great prejudice against "trailer homes" despite evidence that they are safe and comfortable and that mobile home parks are often highly sociable. This problem is to an extent self-inflicted by the industry, which resists new designs with higher aesthetic qualities. But in reality, the manufactured home offers great potential in providing large quantities of affordable housing.

Mobile, Manufactured, or Modular?

The terms *mobile home*, *manufactured home*, and *modular housing* require clarification. *Mobile homes* existed until June 15, 1976, when the industry adopted the federal Manufactured Housing Construction and Safety Standards Act, 42 USC 5403 (HUD Code). HUD-code *manufactured housing* is the modern version of "mobile home." By contrast, *modular homes* follow state building codes rather than federal standards. In fact, the regulations that govern the construction of a modular home are the same as those that govern a site-built home. A modular unit has no chassis or wheels. The components, or modules, are made at a factory and then shipped to the site for assembly, finishing, and permanent installation.

Modular homes lack the cost advantages of factory-made and -finished manufactured homes. The former must have a rigid structure to withstand highway transportation and crane installation. Precise and time-consuming assembly is another characteristic of modular home construction. In addition, the industry offers extensive—and expensive—customization. Some modular companies are now attempting to offer more affordable units, such as HiFAB, a collaboration between Lake|Flato Architects and Oaxaca Interests. HiFAB's residences are smaller than 2,000 square feet yet still require on-site finishing and command prices above the limits of housing affordability, let alone within the means of those below the area median income.

HUD-code manufactured homes, intentionally designed for low cost, start under $45,000 and average $90,000 installed; these prices are widely accessible. Other financial advantages attach to the installation of manufactured housing, which can cost as little as $1,500 to $3,000. Wheeled units unhitch from a tractor and roll onto a lot. The foundation is constructed right underneath the unit, which means that no crane is required to lift and place it. Instead of the weeks required to finish a modular residence on site, a manufactured home can be move-in ready in a day or two.

Both modular housing and manufactured housing require a comparatively low level of investment in plant and operational setup. A primary facility, excluding the cost of real estate, runs between $5 and $10 million. The cost of HUD's review and approval process, though high, is amortized over hundreds, if not thousands, of units. The relatively small shipping radius, typically around 500 miles, means that manufacturing can occur in areas with a low labor cost while shipping can reach areas with a high sales value. This radius would enable, for example, fabrication in Nevada and installation in California—say, San Francisco or San Jose in the Bay Area, which has the second-highest median home price in the nation (if California zoning allowed manufactured homes, that is).

The Challenge of Manufactured Homes

The HUD-code manufactured housing industry provides affordability without taxpayer subsidy. The industry is efficient because it has collectively protected its prerogatives so that the applicable codes allow it to build less expensively. The largest challenge facing manufacturers is that many municipalities do not allow communities of manufactured homes. These restrictions have to do with the cultural associations hanging around unattractive, outmoded mobile home parks, in other words, have to do with design and construction quality.

Aesthetically, manufactured homes have not emphasized architectural coherence but instead implemented utilitarian, inexpensive expression. At the same time, many modular builders target unlimited, expensive custom options. Between these two extremes exists an untapped market: employed millennials, retired singles, empty nesters, grandfamilies, and other arrangements of one or more people.

The Modern House

In the past, architect-designed manufactured housing—from Vernon D. Swaback in Dallas (1970) to Paul Rudolph in New Haven (1968) to Marmol Radziner in Los Angeles (2011)—has, for the most part, failed. In some cases, the design was poorly matched to the building technology that makes manufactured housing cost-effective. In other cases, notably Rudolph's, union opposition and substandard construction were responsible for the lack of success.

The manufactured house designed by Miami-based DPZ CoDesign, dubbed the Modern House, attempts to leverage the cost advantages of mass production while reimagining the unit designs and community planning of this housing type. We learned the factory-building methods and applicable HUD codes and specified only preapproved materials, construction methods, and dimensions. We also took care to design within standard manufacturing specifications and with conventional products. Manufacturers are typically reluctant to introduce a new design, secure its approval, and retool a production line for an unproven market. By adhering to existing codes, materials, and methods, we limited manufacturers' risk.

We took the evergreen midcentury modern residence as our starting point. The plan is based on a rectangle of 54 by 17 feet (the standard HUD-code module is 16 feet wide and 60 feet long); two rectangles together form a double-wide home of 1,650 square feet with three bedrooms, three bathrooms, plus guest bath, dining room, living room,

This page, from top
Rendering of Modern House. Site plan. Plan. Modern House as installed at NAHB International Builders' Show, 2020.

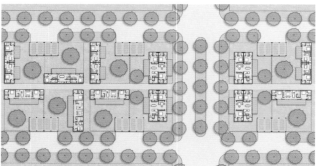

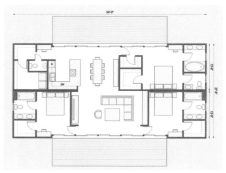

kitchen, and laundry room. Just under half of the long sides consists of standard sliding glass doors, which admit ample light and expand the interior.

The HUD-code height limit—13 feet 6 inches high from road to roof, a dimension that responds to state transportation guidelines and clearance restrictions—encourages low-pitched roofs and interior ceilings that start at 7 feet 6 inches and vault to the center. We instead designed a flat roof that permits an 11-foot internal volume. HVAC ductwork, along with fixtures for indirect lighting, occupies a center plenum. This configuration ensures a small opening at the "marriage line" where the two units meet.

The Modern House was exhibited as a model unit at the 2020 NAHB International Builders' Show and proved to be one of the most visited exhibits. It met the zero net energy code in place in California at the time, a standard not necessary for manufactured homes given that they are inherently energy efficient. Exterior materials included vinyl siding, which emulates the grooves of a shipping container; EPDM roof; aluminum gutters; and standard-width sliding glass doors. For the temporary display, we left the wheels on the unit; in an actual installation, the wheels would be removed, the floor height would be lower, and fewer steps would be required. The IBS sponsor selected high-end materials and finishes that increased the manufacturing price; had we followed the original specifications, the house could have sold for $150,000.

The New Urbanist Mobile Home Park

Traditional mobile home parks—often labeled "manufactured housing parks" or "manufactured housing communities"—offer ready-developed lots, including off-street parking and a level concrete pad with utility hook-ups. The efficient and economic infrastructure runs utilities along the rear of the lots, does away with curb-and-gutter requirements, and calls for a lower development cost than a conventional single-family subdivision. A particular benefit of mobile home parks is the social environment fostered, sometimes with amenities like trails, sports facilities, clubhouses, and swimming pools.

However, the planning of communities of manufactured homes has focused almost entirely on mechanistic geometries that minimize engineering costs. The units are sited on narrow slips with their short sides facing front. This orientation creates tiny front and back yards and long side yards. Parking is located along the street. The one positive aspect of this disposition is that many residences have street frontage.

The plans we have developed improve the design of neighborhoods by making use of repeating geometries that generate public spaces such as open areas shared by a small group of residences or public squares available to all inhabitants. Some configurations keep the short side facing the street due to existing park platting; we typically compensate with a Charleston side yard approach, where the outdoor living area is screened. Other arrangements place residences with the long side facing the street, affording private rear yards. In all cases, we aim to preserve mobile home parks' camaraderie and neighborly character.

Financial Considerations

Both manufactured houses and the plots on which they sit can be secured in various ways. As of 2018, Fannie Mae and Freddie Mac began offering conventional financing for manufactured housing, permitting appraisers to use traditional site-built houses to establish comparable values. This change facilitates conventional ownership of manufactured housing, although the units financed in this way must stand on a permanent foundation and an owned, not a leased, lot.

The land on which the manufactured home rests does not necessarily have to be purchased. Many lots are leased. In this situation, the financial arrangement involves a loan on the unit and the rental of the lot. This hybrid package, which limits the cost of land borne by the unit owner, reduces the monthly costs, benefiting lower-income residents. A subset of leased lots is long-term leased land, in the vein of a land trust, where residents run the community of manufactured homes as a collaborative.

Conclusion

Our manufactured housing initiative has involved research into all aspects of the industry, from construction techniques to code hurdles, financing, and aesthetics. Among the guidelines we have developed are:

- Code leads to economy. Keep wheels, dimensions, and accepted materials. Design standards can be raised with better fenestration and more robust siding.
- Embrace the container aesthetic. Use a vinyl siding profile, such as batten and board or channel, that is similar to a shipping container. Take advantage of the standard module with flat roof that boosts interior ceiling clearance to a lofty 11 feet.
- Take advantage of the sliding glass door. Current models have attractive profiles and hardware. These doors can serve as glass walls.
- Rethink the urban plan. Instead of the endwise orientation of typical mobile home parks, presenting the broad side to the front provides maximum privacy to the rear yard.

The success of the Modern House at the IBS is perhaps the best evidence that the manufactured home has transcended the cultural curse of the mobile home. As architects begin to take manufactured housing seriously, in regard to cost and aesthetic presentation, this American housing type may prove a potent remedy to the American affordable housing crisis.

Rural Housing: Learning by Doing

Jessica Holmes

is research manager for the College of Architecture, Design and Construction, Auburn University.

Rusty Smith

is a professor at the School of Architecture, Planning and Landscape Architecture, Auburn University, and associate director of Rural Studio, Auburn University's design-build architecture program.

f the 353 persistently impoverished counties in the United States—counties in which 20 percent or more residents are poor—over 85 percent are rural.[1] These counties are culturally, geographically, and geologically distinct from one another, but historically they are all landscapes of extraction, where material resources like oil, coal, iron, and minerals are taken out and few financial resources are put back. Access to safe and healthy housing is a particular need in these rural communities. Many low-wealth homeowners must opt for substandard housing in order to reduce the cost burden of homeownership and make ends meet. Housing solutions that help rural residents and communities thrive will preserve those communities and their traditions and also allow urban, suburban, and exurban communities to continue to benefit from the resources they provide.

The challenges of equitable and affordable access to homeownership cannot be addressed with bricks and mortar alone, however. Complex systems-based problems impact the availability of housing and the ability to purchase, protect, and maintain a safe, healthy, and beautiful home. For instance, the Southeast has environmental challenges that include heat, humidity, and extreme weather conditions (tornadoes, hurricanes, flooding). Systemic policy and infrastructure issues encompass affordable access to utilities (wastewater treatment, access to reliable electricity, internet availability), access to community fire protection, exclusionary zoning laws, heirs' property, and lack of a skilled workforce. These difficulties can directly affect the ability to secure homeowners' insurance and mortgage products or to access federal programs like disaster

The chapter is adapted in part from a presentation and interview given by Andrew Freear and Rusty Smith to the Architectural League of New York, Sept. 2022.

1
USDA, "Rural Poverty and Well-Being," Nov. 29, 2022, accessed Feb. 5, 2023, https://www.ers.usda.gov/topics/rural-economy/rural-population/rural-poverty-well-being/#geography.

2
USDA, "Heirs' Property," accessed Feb. 5, 2023, https://www.nal.usda.gov/farms-and-agricultural-production-systems/heirs-property.

3
Rural Studio, "About," "Our Story," accessed Feb. 5, 2023, http://ruralstudio.org/about/.

relief funding. For individuals, employment and health can impact not just the initial purchase of a home but the ability to maintain and retain it when unexpected costs push a family beyond their means.

For example, heirs' property practices and access to federal funding affect homeownership in the Alabama Black Belt. This region, located at the meeting of the southwest tail of the Appalachian Mountains and the eastern portion of the Mississippi Delta and originally named for its fertile black soil, did not allow Black families in the late 1800s and early 1900s to access the legal system. Thus Black landowners often did not develop wills. If a landowner died intestate, that person's land became owned in kind by a whole family (owned in the same way by all family members, that is, all family members own all the land).[2] When one of those family members passes away, that person's percentage of land gets divided equally among their heirs, and on and on and on. It is almost impossible to determine who owns which property in this region. Federal entities— the Federal Emergency Management Agency for distribution of disaster relief funding, the Department of Housing and Urban Development for housing subsidies, the Department of Agriculture for farm grant loans, funds, or resources—cannot distribute funds if it is not known who owns the property.

Even those without barriers to homeownership sometimes occupy substandard housing. It is often thought that people live in substandard housing because they are impoverished, but it is really the other way around: people tend to find themselves impoverished because they live in substandard housing, trapped in circumstances that negatively impact health, safety, and wealth creation. One element in addressing the housing crisis is recognizing that current conditions are partly an intentional outcome of historic policies and programs.

The built environment is a tool for making invisible systems visible. It is on this platform that designers, partners, and communities can work together to imagine alternative futures.

Rural Studio

Rural Studio is an undergraduate design-build architecture program, founded by Auburn University's architecture faculty members Samuel Mockbee and D. K. Ruth in 1993. It is located in Hale County, Alabama, one of the persistently impoverished counties in the Black Belt. Rural Studio's first projects were single-family homes; by the end of the 1990s, the program began adding community-focused projects. More than 200 built projects have emerged from Rural Studio, from the Bryant House in Mason's Bend to the Newbern Library to the Greensboro Boys & Girls Club.[3]

Rural Studio prioritizes community engagement—listening to neighbors, meeting local needs, seeking local approval for all projects, and taking responsibility for the results. While at Rural Studio, architecture students work collaboratively with faculty and other experts on design and construction, learning to participate as a member of a team. The students use a mutual-aid model, where they design and build houses for homeowners who cannot obtain a home via more traditional means. The homeowners are real-life clients, playing an invaluable role in the students' architectural education. The design process focuses on responding to the environment, functionality, attention to materials, feasibility of construction, and beauty of the final product.

In 2004, faculty and students decided to address substandard housing and rural poverty in a more comprehensive way. The 20K Program had a bold goal: to design

4
Rural Studio, 20K Projects, accessed Feb. 5, 2023, http://ruralstudio .org/project_tags /20k/.

and build a home for anyone for $20,000. Almost everybody can afford a house for that price, which equates to a $100 monthly payment on a 30-year mortgage.[4] As the program continued, the Rural Studio team collected feedback from homeowners and data on the structural and energy performance of buildings over time. This critical information allowed the teams to rethink design and materials and begin to consider the full cost of homeownership. Materials testing in the years since the COVID-19 pandemic started has allowed the teams to further consider what elements are truly essential to providing a healthy and safe home.

Expanding Reach with the Front Porch Initiative

In 2019, Rural Studio created the Front Porch Initiative to extend the impact of its applied research. Front Porch offers prototype house designs (including instruction, construction documents, and technical assistance) to housing providers outside the Rural Studio service area, which deliver homes in their own, often under-resourced communities. Along with the designs, Rural Studio shares the knowledge and products developed through its work in West Alabama. These external housing providers use their own procurement models to provide the same energy-efficient, resilient, and healthy homes to their clients. Thanks to research sponsorship, Front Porch Initiative services are available to partners at no cost.

Front Porch Initiative currently has a product line of five houses. The designs were initiated as part of the 20K Program and developed by Rural Studio on the ground in Hale County. Each is named after the initial client (Dave's House, MacArthur's House, Joanne's House, Sylvia's House, and Buster's House). These one- and two-bedroom houses are small but not tiny (an average of 655 square feet). They are efficient and durable, meet conventional code and lending requirements, can be titled as real property, and are occupied conventionally. Provider partners adapt the houses based on client needs, environment, and local conditions.

Our partners—currently at 15 providers in 8 southeastern states and increasing regularly—deliver the houses in a variety of ways. Some use volunteers for construction (e.g., Habitat for Humanity affiliates), others local tradespeople; some are focused on rural locations, others on urban sites. The strategic alliances developed between Front Porch, regional housing partners, and national housing policy stakeholders are based on both application and implementation. The regional partners report back to Front Porch regarding every project, particularly the opportunities and challenges that are applicable to varying geographies and the elements that are specific to location, community, and context. Our goal is to continue to refine the products and communication tools so that Front Porch can offer this research to a wider network of housing partners.

This collaborative, iterative approach allows Front Porch to build multiple versions of each home, evaluating performance in different climatic conditions and with various objectives necessitated by the circumstances of the housing partners or clients. The built projects become test-and-learn laboratories to consider different issues of efficiency, resilience, wellness, and community-building. The iterative process and the repeated evaluations of both the cost and value of building performance criteria lend themselves to highly customizable processes and yield multiple variations.

One of the most important research questions focuses on finding the balance between the front-end construction cost of improved performance and the associated back-end performance consequences. A survey of the pluses and the minuses of different building standards and their delivery includes the testing of detailed energy modes and scenarios during construction to ensure that the house is meeting or exceeding expectations. Post-occupancy energy monitoring yields the data to compare energy consumption to predicted energy use. Collection and analysis of this data allow Front Porch to construct better predictive models as well as to help our housing partners make better decisions about the up-front costs of construction and the collateral total costs of homeownership.

Adaptable, Variable, and Predictive

The extremes of the subtropical West Alabama environment are tough on buildings. Structures in the region do everything they can to separate themselves from their natural surroundings: they pick themselves up off the ground to get away from water and animals and insects; they extend large roofs to provide protection from rain and sun. The Rural Studio houses included in the Front Porch product line reflect that vernacular.

Functional elements have made the Front Porch houses adaptable in unexpected ways. Two sites in Chattahoochee Hills, Georgia, where the first two partner-built houses are located, were characterized by heavily wooded, rugged, rocky, and steeply sloping terrain. Building on piers similar to those used to lift houses off the ground in West Alabama ensured that the sites remained relatively undisturbed. A partner in Jean Lafitte, Louisiana, used piles to raise a Front Porch house even higher in an effort to mitigate the flood risks in the region. The building components developed for Hale County thus operate in Georgia and Louisiana even though the sites are very different.

The scale of the houses also promotes adaptability. The compact footprints of the product line houses lend themselves to working in areas where the cost to get foundations into the ground is high, report our partners in Appalachia and the Mississippi Delta. In both rural and urban environments, our partners often build on lots that are challenging due to size, zoning, and setback requirements. Sylvia's House in particular has a narrow footprint and can be successful on a site that might otherwise be considered unbuildable.

The Front Porch findings on energy efficiency show that deep roof overhangs really matter. Housing partners often need to change the roof due to fire code, setback issues, or consistency with surrounding residences. But altering the roof overhangs has a huge impact on the performance of the houses: a change of just a few inches necessitates a revised performance model relative to the shading. Part of our work with partners involves helping them to understand which elements of a house can or cannot be easily modified and to gauge the implications of those modifications in the short and long terms.

To be successful, a project with the scope of the Front Porch Initiative requires a range of partnerships working together and a comprehensive system of housing procurement. Rural Studio and Front Porch are distinguished by a remarkable feedback loop that encompasses students working in Hale County, faculty and staff, community members, and construction partners. As those relationships strengthen and grow, they improve the ability of everyone in the loop to tackle these critical issues. Affordable housing in rural areas, just like affordable housing in urban areas, is extraordinarily complex, but the three decades of Rural Studio show that designers, by extending their sphere of operations beyond design, have an important role in ensuring universal access to safe, affordable, and healthy homes.

What We Must Afford (Some Thoughts on System Change in Global Housing)

Elizabeth Gray and Alan Organschi are the founding partners and principals of Gray Organschi Architecture in New Haven, Connecticut. Organschi is also senior critic, Yale School of Architecture, and director of the school's Building Lab.

Andrew Ruff is the research director at Gray Organschi Architecture and runs GOA's Timber City Research Initiative.

Betwen now and 2050, humanity will add 2.5 billion new inhabitants to the planet's cities. In addition to straining existing housing stocks and associated urban infrastructures, upending current approaches to housing finance, and challenging local, regional, national, and even transnational governance, this massive global demographic trend will call for a construction boom of unprecedented scale.

First, a Word about the Planet...

By the end of the 21st century, cities will be in need of more than 2 billion housing units. Bhutan's capital, Thimphu, the fastest-growing city in Asia with a current population of just over 100,000, will need to produce 1,000 units of housing every year until 2030. Colorado, where the Denver area is witness to growth well above national averages, anticipates an annual demand for 100,000 units. In Kenya, on a continent where the largest increases in population are expected, 250,000 dwellings will need to be constructed every year until regional growth flattens, a dim prospect in any demographic forecast. Comparing these statistics may be equivalent to measuring the relative travel speeds of a snail and a supersonic jet, but within their own political, economic, and social contexts, these demands will prove—indeed, have already proven—to be significant, if not traumatic, systemic stressors.

To put this volume of global construction into perspective, by 2050 we will need to double the entirety of the existing global building stock. If we continue to build with the sprawling footprints that characterize the current morphology of most of our built environment, we will consume three times the land area currently occupied by urban buildings and infrastructure. As a matter of material dimension that would equate to a building (not a city, but a one-story building) the size of the entire state of New York—or, for our European readers, a building that covers a land area equal to two Irelands. This is great news for builders since it represents an estimated $97 trillion of construction value. To realize that value, the sector would have to overcome its chronic shortage of skilled workers, the methodological inefficiencies that drive construction costs ever higher, and a historically glacial adaptation to change.

This glut of global building, which considered from an environmental standpoint is simply a massive form of resource consumption, has truly tragic implications for our terrestrial systems. The forests, peat- and wetlands, marine environments, and atmosphere that provide natural capital and ecosystem services—the fresh air, clean water, and stable and biodiverse ecosystems that are essential to the creation of healthy living environments, if not human survival—are the increasingly finite sources of the material and energy we extract and the ultimate repositories of the waste we generate over the full building life cycle. These are the sites and systems of initial and consequential environmental injury, where the unseen or *embodied* impacts incurred in the extraction, transport, and processing of raw material and the production of the buildings themselves—greenhouse gas emissions, land conversion, biodiversity loss, waste generation—contribute significantly to the aggregate impacts of the global building sector.

So What Does All This Have to Do with Affordable Housing?
Unfortunately, the means by which we deliver affordable housing in the United States—the economic instruments of its finance, the materials and methods of its delivery, and the land- and infrastructure-intensiveness of our conventional, relatively low-density typologies of building and distributions of urban space—all fail to acknowledge or assign meaningful value to a growing array of environmental externalities. These long-term, systemic drivers of cost will likely ultimately determine where on the planet resource scarcity will have the most profound effects, when the resulting socioeconomic inequities will be most strongly felt, when and where populations will be forced to move, and where new demographic, social, and economic pressures will throw into disarray our current definitions of affordability and our ability to deliver sufficiently durable and decent housing. Put plainly, our inability to address the global, systemic implications of the way we currently materialize and monetize housing will ultimately rebound at home. Despite the inexorable consumption of global raw material and energy (some of which is applied to meet the ever-increasing demand for housing) and the steady degradation of the natural environment that has accompanied recent building cycles, we have failed to effectively and securely (let alone affordably) house vast swaths of humanity.

Rather than simply asking how to create housing that is affordable, perhaps we should ask what we can and cannot afford as a society. Can we afford to provide insufficient housing for our neighbors and community? Can we afford to rely on conventional construction practices that have proven incapable of producing reliably affordable, livable, and durable housing? Can we afford to remain agnostic to the sourcing and provenance of building materials? Can we afford to utilize global industrial supply chains reliant on extractive practices that impact remote communities and bioregions for the worse? Can we afford to produce buildings and infrastructure responsible for a significant portion of global carbon and greenhouse gas emissions?

Redefining "Affordable" Here at Home

In light of this transscalar and profoundly interwoven set of costs, causalities, and consequences, it seems essential that we clearly define affordability, whether as professional practitioners, policymakers, or just inhabitants of the planet. At a local level, the most simplistic calculation of the relative affordability of housing requires that we establish a direct correlation between the cost to rent or own a particular residence and the average income of a particular demographic. This conventional assessment, however, doesn't fully account for the costs of housing that residents must ultimately bear, never mind broader systemic impacts. An expanded view would consider many factors in assessing an individual or family's capacity to truly afford housing: recurring monthly utility costs, longer cycles of maintenance and repair, proximity to mobility services such as mass transit and meaningful and sustaining employment opportunities, availability of quality public education and public services, and a neighborhood's cohesion, safety, and inclusiveness. These broader questions of cost and access speak to the need for affordable housing not only to meet quantitative, calculated metrics driven primarily by development costs or the availability of financial subsidies but also to address critical qualitative conditions more difficult to calculate or neatly define.

The challenge in identifying a singular definition of affordable housing speaks both to the inherent difficulty of providing affordable housing and to the complex matrix of stakeholders involved in the regulation, development, design, delivery, management, and—most important—inhabitation of housing. Each stakeholder has a significantly different perspective from which to evaluate the affordability of housing: How many units of affordable housing are required in a particular municipality or neighborhood? Does the construction of new affordable housing provide a net benefit to the surrounding community? What are the development and construction costs for building new residential units or converting existing structures? Are tax credits and public subsidies available to offset financial obligations? Can residents afford the monthly mortgage or rent payments? Does the building require costly maintenance and refurbishment? These questions all represent critical issues for assessing and advancing the development of new affordable housing through the lens of conventional economic frameworks, but just as residents must evaluate a wide range of qualitative criteria in determining the real affordability of housing, we should consider an expanded analysis of how we understand what is truly affordable.

Examining affordable housing through this prism of externalities reveals a persistent misalignment between the aspiration to provide desirable, convivial, secure, and sustainable living environments and a current set of circumstances that is heavily constrained by the immediate expense of constructing and operating new buildings. The latter embodies the proverbial "race to the bottom," that is, trying to produce a minimum viable product at the lowest cost possible in order to lower rents to a level where housing is both affordable to tenants and provides an acceptable return to investors. The onus of achieving required financial returns is only exacerbated considering that the degradation of housing's initial capital investment places the burden on the developer to reduce costs and increase revenues. In this approach to affordable housing, a project's perceived up-front costs are limited to land acquisition, professional services, and construction materials and labor. This narrow framing of the problem reduces the number of levers available to make homeownership or rental truly affordable, leaving only a few conventional options: acquire low-value land (either outside of desirable neighborhoods or encumbered by existing conditions), negotiate for lower professional service fees, and minimize the expense of materials and labor by downgrading construction quality. Public subsidies or land grants may help offset some of a project's up-front expenses or assist future residents in affording their monthly obligations, but the most obvious means to reduce cost is to cheapen the materials and methods of building.

However, an expanded view of "project cost" offers more options for decreasing the true cost of a project and potentially even increasing the net benefits produced by affordable housing. Rather than harming remote landscapes and ecosystems, building materials drawn from rapidly renewable sources could improve ecosystem health and biodiversity benefits while storing carbon within durable construction systems. Developing housing as a set of flexible, modular, and replicable systems could amortize the soft costs of design and development over a number of projects instead of only a single project. Designing for prefabrication could replace costly, on-site labor with off-site production and just-in-time delivery. Incorporating new structural typologies could offer opportunities for underrepresented groups in the construction sector to gain footholds in valuable trades. Developing systems that can be easily disassembled and reused at the end of a building's serviceable life could convert an otherwise depreciated structure into a valuable bank of future assets. Building high-performing housing with minimal operational emissions could reduce recurring utility costs to residents and avoid future carbon emissions. Ultimately, the expanded value proposition of what constitutes affordable housing creates more agency and capacity to address a range of issues beyond the reductive cost-per-square-foot calculations that drive conventional affordable housing development.

Biomaterial Building: An Alternative Pathway to Systemic Affordability

As noted at the outset of this essay, no discussion of building costs and affordability can ignore the most pressing impacts of contemporary construction, for both the present and the immediate future. The built environment is a significant contributor to global greenhouse gas emissions, and the materials, resources, and energy required to create, renovate, and demolish buildings consume vast quantities of nonrenewable resources. Pivoting to rapidly renewable, bio-based construction systems is one strategy that could reduce the embodied emissions of construction and thereby mitigate their negative effects on the climate.

A survey of the current landscape of affordable housing development and contemporary construction highlights the recent emergence of mass timber and other bio-based materials, components, and systems and their ability to offer an alternative pathway to conventional development, design, and building practices. With their rapid renewability and low embodied emissions, these bio-based materials—wood fiber and cellulose insulation in an array of formats; thermally or chemically modified exterior cladding and decking; and a host of more typical wood flake and strand panel products and interior finishes—have steadily gained traction in the marketplace as alternatives to conventional mineral-based material systems, fossil-energy-intensive manufacturing methods, and large carbon footprints.

Buildings as Carbon Banks

Another critical component of housing affordability lies in the type and amount of potential subsidy that is available to building developers and their investors. As industrial greenhouse emissions are more reliably assessed, more accurately quantified, and more effectively regulated, the "cost" of emitting greenhouse gases will become an ever-greater liability to the producers of goods and the owners of property. The recent and ongoing development of economic incentives to limit such emissions—carbon credits to renewable energy producers and forest landowners, the refinement of regulatory programs that penalize excess emissions through instruments such as carbon taxation—has begun to assign a premium to the benefits of biomaterials that are photosynthetically derived and therefore literally *made* of carbon. The carbon storage capacity of trees and the transfer of their woody material into building products mean that buildings, the largest and most durable of consumer "goods," and the cities they might one day constitute, can become significant material storage banks of carbon that would otherwise have been emitted into the atmosphere as carbon dioxide. This quality in turn suggests that a carbon credit program that rewards the sustainable management of forest land could be conferred as well on sustainably sourced wood products and the buildings that use them. Large buildings could be awarded credits for their capacity to store carbon. As the global climate emergency deepens and the associated costs of emitting carbon rise, the potential of construction-stored carbon as a form of subsidy to builders and building owners may become a decisive factor in the adoption of alternative biomaterials. Among the wood-based building products capable of creating the primary structural system of multistory buildings—the heaviest portion of the construction assembly and also the densest form of bio-based carbon storage other than trees—is a class of engineered-timber structural components commonly known as "mass timber."

The earliest manifestation of mass timber—glue-laminated timber, or "glulam"—was developed in Europe in the early 20th century as a way of finger-jointing and adhesive-laminating smaller sections of softwood lumber into larger, longer-span, engineered structural members with a predictable primary axis of strength. An ancillary benefit of this system was the incorporation of "low-value" softwoods into the inner lamella of the glulam; since tension and compression are weakest here, manufacturers were able to source a wider range of forest stocks as well as waste by-products undesired by other industries. By the mid-20th century, glulam products were commonly specified as alternatives to long-span steel or concrete beams and columns for institutional, commercial, residential, and even infrastructural projects. The late 20th century heralded an expansion of engineered-timber products in the construction sector: laminated veneer lumber, parallel-strand lumber, laminated strand lumber, and cross-laminated timber. Of these products, CLT has demonstrated the highest potential for replacing structural materials drawn from nonrenewable resources and simultaneously transforming the process of design and construction.

Unlike glulam, which is limited in dimension by the width of its lamella and limited in structural application by the parallel orientation of its fibers, CLT elements are produced from alternating perpendicular laminations of lumber, which allows manufacturers to fabricate panels up to 11 feet wide and 55 feet long. Thanks to the size of these panels, the high strength-to-weight ratio, and the capacity to span in two directions, CLT panels can be utilized for entire building systems: walls, floors, roofs, and even shafts. This invention marks a significant evolution in construction practice, as conventional building approaches rely either on the aggregation of many individual components (such as structural steel or traditional timber framing, both of which require significant on-site coordination and finishes to "dry-in" a building) or on monolithic systems (such as in situ concrete, which is limited by weight and inflexibility). In contrast, cross-laminated timber systems offer "one-stop shopping" for the primary structure, enclosure, and even some interior finishes of a building.

Short- and Long-Term "Costs"

Mass timber conveys a number of expanded cost benefits at the construction site. A streamlined palette of construction materials can dramatically simplify the bidding and pricing process, while a need for fewer subcontractors and suppliers offers an opportunity to shorten on-site construction timelines. Expedited on-site installation lowers holding costs borne by affordable housing developers and, when applied to a sequence of development projects, reduces the construction time required, compounding the net benefit of bringing more housing to the market more quickly than is possible with conventional building systems. Even the construction site itself can benefit from mass timber systems: prefabricated panels reduce on-site construction waste, just-in-time delivery of materials minimizes the need for additional lay-down space (typically unavailable for urban infill sites), and simplified installation—mass timber requires only mobile cranes and screwdrivers, not the ongoing cacophony of trades, equipment, and materials characterizing most projects—limits disturbances to the surrounding community during the course of construction.

Other benefits stemming from the use of mass timber in affordable housing include potential increases in the building's operational energy performance. Unlike construction systems that rely on the on-site aggregation of myriad products to create dried-in enclosures, a technique based on large-format CLT panels dramatically reduces the number of joints that need to be sealed to create the kind of air-tight enclosure that is required for high-performance HVAC systems. Additionally, the hygrothermal properties of exposed timber surfaces passively absorb and desorb interior humidity, effectively turning building interiors into "lungs." Affordable housing, a class of buildings with a track record of poor interior air quality and sick building syndrome, would benefit from the moisture-buffering effects of wood-lined interior surfaces: a contribution to the general well-being of the inhabitants.

The novel materials and techniques entailed in mass timber construction will inevitably transform construction delivery methods (and the business models and workforces associated with them). This shift will in turn confer employment opportunities on both urban and rural communities all along the building value chain. Groups currently underrepresented in the construction sector will gain new access to the kinds of trades uncommon in conventional affordable housing but well poised for future growth. In this way, housing is made more affordable by providing meaningful jobs that pay living wages to its inhabitants.

CLT and other mass timber systems offer advantages in comparison to conventional construction methods in an expanded cost analysis as well. Though mass timber is still an emerging technology in many global markets, affordable social housing projects in Europe and North America have demonstrated that mass timber can be cost-competitive for mid-rise construction. Beyond its streamlined sourcing, mass timber as a value-added manufactured system typically experiences less price volatility than commodity materials such as dimensional lumber. Furthermore, thanks in part to recent advances in fire safety testing, manufacturing certification protocols, and international building codes, mass timber structures are allowed to exceed the 6-story height that typically limits combustible, light-frame construction. While these regulatory changes have not yet been adopted universally, some countries and jurisdictions permit mass timber buildings to be as high as 18 stories. At this scale, mass timber is no longer competing with low-cost, low-rise construction systems but with more advanced building systems such as steel and reinforced concrete. And unlike steel and concrete, mass timber components store atmospheric carbon for the life of the building, turning these structures into valuable carbon futures rather than future environmental liabilities.

Systemic Interventions

Significant evolutions to any industry are not without their challenges, a fact that is especially true of the construction sector. In spite of transformations in the ways we use, insulate, condition, power, and finance buildings in contemporary society, the structural systems at the heart of construction have remained largely unchanged for nearly a century. Though contemporary steel, concrete, and light wood framing have become more efficient, resilient, and structurally capable than their 20th-century predecessors, the fundamental processes and protocols informing their design and construction have been remarkably static. In contrast, mass timber has not only undergone industrial evolutions that have created a diverse range of engineered product types and scales, but these innovations have spurred international regulatory bodies to codify mass timber construction as fundamentally unique from other structural systems. For example, in the 2021 International Building Code, the recent expansion of Type IV Heavy Timber construction illustrates how the use of mass timber affects a building's structure, fire safety, resistance to seismic activity, and—perhaps most critically—thermal and energy performance.

Our layering of arguments in favor of mass timber as a potential means to produce affordable housing comes with an important caveat: the question of how we define affordability in an age of increasing social inequity and impending environmental crisis (if not climate catastrophe). Deep and broad affordability in housing cannot be created through point interventions alone. Neither a well-crafted tax incentive nor the efficient organization of dwelling space, utilization of a novel building material, or optimization of a construction system will answer the demand for accessible, safe, secure, and durable homes situated in vibrant, stable communities sharing convivial urban spaces that function in symbiosis with well-balanced and biologically diverse regional ecosystems. A program of mass timber construction will prove to be affordable and environmentally sustainable only if its source forests are carefully and sustainably managed, disturbed forestlands are restored, and new forests are allowed to flourish. Upstream environmental health and stability can confer downstream public health and well-being, but only when a regenerative symbiosis is the framing principle that guides us as we remake and maintain our homes, our cities, and, ultimately, our planet.

Portfolio

Affordable housing can be beautiful, dignified, and well-designed, as demonstrated by the projects featured here. The development of efficient housing was central to the mission of the modern architectural movement begun in Europe in the early 20th century, when distinguished architects such as Le Corbusier, Bruno Taut, and Moisei Ginzburg created innovative mass housing for the citizens of their war-ravaged countries.

Unfortunately, most housing in the United States has suffered from a lack of commitment, by both government and private developers, to good design under the false premise that it costs more. The result was bland, repetitive, badly scaled, and disconnected projects, such as Pruitt-Igoe, in St. Louis, and Cabrini-Green, in Chicago. Such places became hotbeds of crime and suffered deterioration, leading to their eventual demolition. Thousands of residents were displaced, their former communities erased.

Design has again become an important part of the criteria for affordable housing. Talented architects have proven that better-designed housing does not need to cost more. The examples here range from residential architecture in the South by Rural Studio to housing in the dense inner cities of Chicago, New York, and Los Angeles. All have a sensitive yet bold relationship to the immediate context, whether an elevated highway, a train, or a street in the South Bronx. All are memorable places that use economical means—such as bold colors, patterns, and materials—to enliven the architecture, producing extremely livable environments with a certain magic that might summon a sense of community among the residents.

These projects are the optimistic result of the forces analyzed in the first four sections of *Housing the Nation*, the end goal of the essays. Although they are not sufficient to make more than a dent in the need, they are an auspicious beginning. **— AG**

New Carver Apartments

Michael Maltzan Architecture

Location
Los Angeles, California

Date
2006–2009

Client
Skid Row Housing Trust

Program
97 units for formerly homeless seniors and residents with disabilities

Building area
53,000 square feet

Project cost
$34 million (total); $18.4 million (construction)

Funding sources
Undisclosed

Just south of Los Angeles's fast-growing downtown and immediately north of the I-10 freeway, New Carver Apartments provides permanent housing for formerly homeless senior and disabled residents along with opportunities for solace, support, and personal growth. The faceted exterior of the building articulates the scale of the individual units within, expressing a dynamic relationship between the building, the neighborhood, and the freeway infrastructure. Communal spaces—kitchens, dining areas, gathering spaces, and gardens—are incorporated into the building's raised form. Medical and social service support facilities are integrated into the plinth below, encouraging residents to reconnect with one another and with the world outside.

New Carver Apartments

Previous pages
View of New Carver Apartments next to the I-10 in Los Angeles.

Opposite, from top
Faceted, six-story circular volume adjacent to the Santa Monica Freeway. Facets creating a sound buffer by minimizing the portion of the building close to the freeway.

This page, from top
Perspective showing communal spaces, medical facilities, and social services in yellow. Site plan showing natural light and views in all directions.

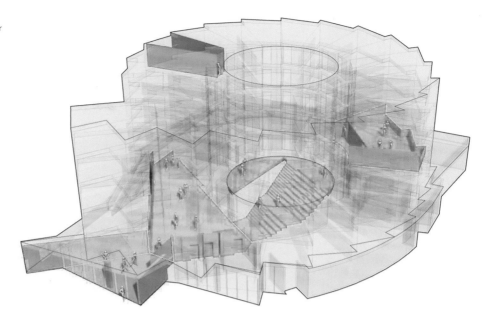

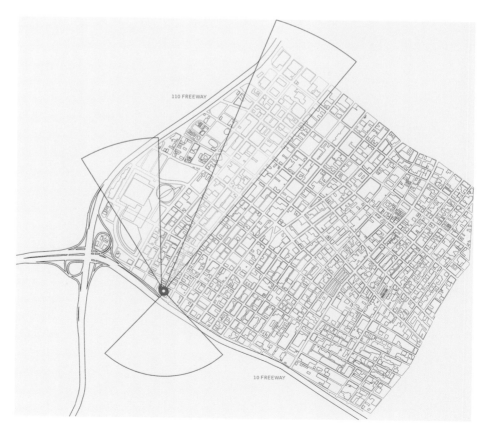

This page, from top

Vertical circulation punctuated by open views to Los Angeles. Fins creating a rhythm of light and shadow across central gathering space.

Opposite, from top

Tapering perspective view through the interior to the streetscape beyond. Exterior facets echoed on the interior at unit entrances. Central courtyard offering flow-through ventilation to each unit and views in all directions. Community network of kitchens, dining areas, common spaces, and support spaces connecting individual units and the city as a whole. Private central courtyard defined by spiraling form of building with ascending staircase that can be used as seating.

13604

Crest Apartments

Michael Maltzan Architecture

Location
Van Nuys, California

Date
2013–2016

Client
Skid Row Housing Trust

Program
64 units for formerly homeless veterans

Building area
45,000 square feet

Project cost
$23.6 million (total); $14.2 million (construction)

Funding sources
Undisclosed

Crest Apartments transforms an open site in suburban Los Angeles into an apartment complex for formerly homeless veterans. Located on a busy thoroughfare near two freeways, the project has easy connections to public transportation and area resources. The permanent supportive housing model includes individual efficiency apartments, on-site social services, and community spaces. These combined programs support the highly vulnerable residents in an effort to reduce chronic homelessness. The building's form, an arc in plan, stretches the length of the site, creating a sheltered courtyard with tiered terraces above that includes open-air corridors and a ground-level landscape zone; it also introduces a new density to the neighborhood. Shared spaces and community resources include residents' lounge, community kitchen, laundry room, conference room, social service offices, health clinic, and outdoor community garden.

Previous pages
Low massing at front and back creating a relationship between Crest Apartments and the smaller-scale single-family residences behind the property.

This page
Stepped forms reducing apparent scale of building.

Opposite, from top
Second floor plan. Fifth floor plan. North elevation.

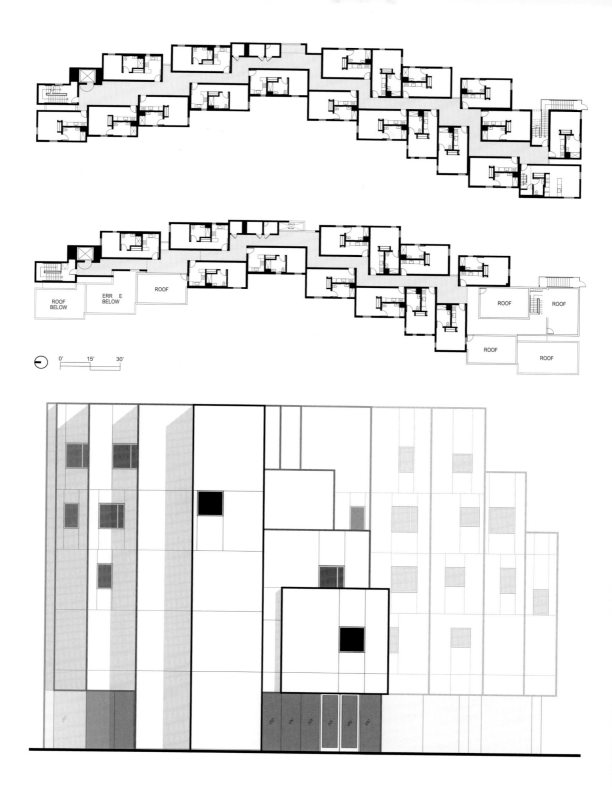

ROOF
BELOW

ERR E
BELOW

ROOF

ROOF

ROOF

ROOF

ROOF

0'   15'   30'

163   Crest Apartments

**Opposite,
from top**

Open-air corridor connecting units. View of Crest Apartments and surrounding neighborhood.

**This page,
from top**

Bedroom area with windows for natural light and air. Kitchen area with energy-efficient refrigerator and range hood, biobased marmoleum composition floor, and tile made from recycled content. Landscape zone with drought-resistant plantings.

The Arroyo

Koning Eizenberg Architecture

Location
Santa Monica, California

Date
2017–2018

Client
Community Corporation of Santa Monica

Program
64 units for families

Building area
50,259 square feet

Project cost
$44 million (total)

Funding sources
Permanent mortgage, DK gap loan, Investor Equity tax credit, DK equity (land)

Located at the edge of transit- and job-rich downtown Santa Monica, the Arroyo provides housing for families earning between 30 and 60 percent of AMI. The mid-rise structure is anchored by a green space that converts a site constraint—a nine-foot-diameter concrete storm drain—into a landscaped social hub for residents. The project name and rippling facade hark back to a long-gone arroyo, a seasonal creek carrying water to the ocean, that once passed through the site. Activity spaces include job training facilities and after-school programs, and a courtyard spills onto a basketball half-court and homework/picnic zone that extends below an undercroft to create a weather-protected gathering space.

Photographs: Eric Staudenmaier

Previous pages
View of the Arroyo with ground-floor courtyard and community spaces connecting to the street.

Opposite, from top
Central courtyard along the path of a former arroyo. Exterior bridges for promoting informal interaction, minimizing number of exit stairs, and reducing costs.

This page, from top
Typical floor plan. Ground floor plan. Juliet balconies and sunshades for facade ornament and function.

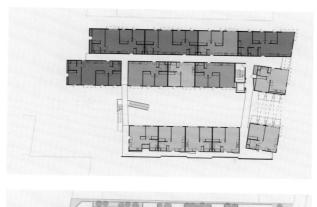

Hunters View
Blocks 5 and 6

Paulett Taggart Architects

Location
San Francisco, California

Date
2007–2013

Client
John Stewart Company

Program
53 units for families

Building area
67,800 square feet

Project cost
$22 million (construction)

Funding sources
San Francisco Mayor's Office of Housing and Community Development, HUD funds and grants, CTCAC LIHTC, CDLAC Tax-Exempt Bond Allocation, San Francisco Redevelopment Agency loan, Federal Home Loan Bank AHP, private grants

Two new blocks of family housing are the first components of a master plan conceived to transform a decaying, crime-ridden housing project into a safe, inviting new neighborhood. Stepping, stacked units—a modern interpretation of traditional residential patterns for this particular site and neighborhood—take advantage of a steeply sloping site. Each block consists of two L-shaped buildings that form continuous street frontages and surround common, secure courtyards. Shared laundries and mailrooms are located off the courtyards as are entries to the one-to-four-bedroom units, creating gathering spaces that help build a sense of community.

Previous pages
Street facade
stepping down
the slope.

**Opposite,
from top**
Public-private
transition at entry
stoop. Mid-
block courtyard.
Generating com-
munity in a court-
yard. Layering
functions to foster
new relationships.
Visibility and secu-
rity at courtyard
entrance.

**This page,
from top**
View of Hunters
View Blocks 5 and
6 on steep site.
Section. Site plan.

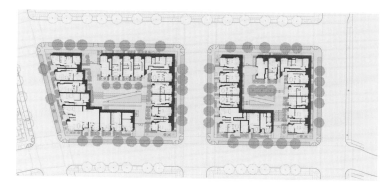

Pico Place

Brooks+Scarpa

Location
Santa Monica, California

Date
2010–2013

Client
Community Corporation of
Santa Monica

Program
32 units for families

Building area
41,000 square feet, not
including 19,100 square feet
for garage

Project cost
$10.1 million (construction)

Funding sources
Santa Monica Housing Trust
Fund loan, CTCAC

Pico Place incorporates two-
and three-bedroom family
units along with a common
courtyard, patios and balconies, a below-grade parking
garage, bike racks, common
rooms, laundries, and mailbox
areas. Strips of fabric floating
above the courtyard shade the
outdoor space and provide
privacy and at the same time
encourage a sense of place. A
"frame" on the Pico Boulevard
facade unifies the project,
allowing views of the interior
courtyard from the street but
also protecting its private
nature. Shading, natural light
and ventilation, and exacting
building orientation induce
buoyancy and natural breezes.
A small green roof takes advantage of and contributes to the
pedestrian nature of the street.
The major exterior material is
recycled cementboard siding in
different colors, textures, and
patterns, which creates an ele-
gant facade that is contextual
and varied and complements
the surrounding buildings.

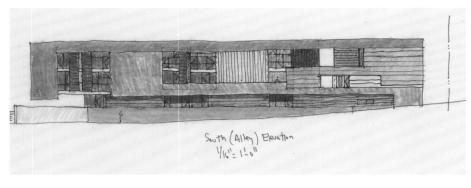

South (Alley) Elevation
1/16" = 1'-0"

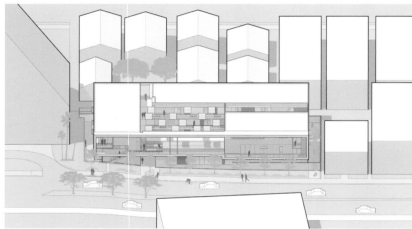

Previous pages
Main entry along
Pico Boulevard
with green roof
above a one-story
community room
and sunshades
above the court-
yard beyond.

**This page,
from top**
Early design
drawing of the
south elevation.
Overview of the
building in its
urban context.
Second floor plan.

**Opposite,
from top**
View of Pico Place
from east. Building
"frame" along Pico
Boulevard.

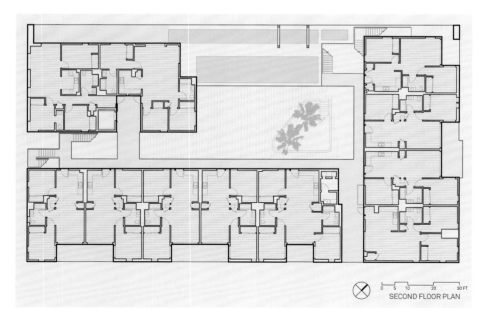

0   5   10   20   30 FT
SECOND FLOOR PLAN

Pico Place

This page
Building courtyard
with direct, light-
filled connection
to the parking
area below.

**Opposite,
from top**
Facade detail at
the community
room and unit
above. Typical
two-bedroom unit.
Common court-
yard providing pri-
mary public open
space for the build-
ing. Evening view
of Pico Boulevard
facade.

Pico Place

Blue Water

DPZ CoDesign

Location
Tavernier Key, Florida

Date
2010–2011

Client
Gorman & Company

Program
36 units

Building area
38,818 square feet

Project cost
$5.1 million (construction)

Funding sources
LIHTC

Blue Water consists of a series of interlocking courtyard residences. The plans dovetail for efficiency and privacy and generate units of one, two, and four bedrooms. Skylights augment the courtyards to maximize daylight and cross-ventilation. Among the cost-saving strategies are single-story construction; unified floor slab on grade; standardized roof trusses, windows, and doors; and a single kitchen layout. Green building components include energy-efficient appliances, low-VOC paints, an on-site recycling center, xeriscaping, and stormwater retention and filtering. Fifty-four required parking spaces are accommodated on two internal streets. Included on the site are a community building/library and recycling pavilions. In 2017, Blue Water successfully weathered Irma, a category 5 hurricane that devastated the Florida Keys.

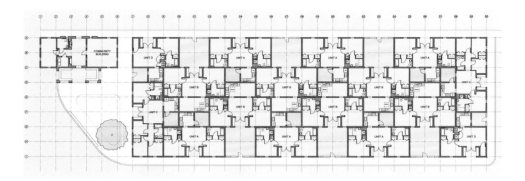

El Borinquen Residence

Alexander Gorlin Architects

Location
Bronx, New York

Date
2017–2022

Client
Comunilife

Program
148 units for teens aging out
of foster care, low-income
seniors, working families, and
formerly homeless individuals

Building area
90,000 square feet

Project cost
$62.3 million (construction)

Funding sources
NYS Housing Finance Agency
first mortgage, NYS Homes
and Community Renewal
programs, NYC HPD, LIHTC,
deferred accrued interest

El Borinquen Residence was
built for the neighboring Latino
community. Art as an integral
aspect of the healing process
is a central part of the design,
from the colorful facade
(inspired by the flags of Latin
America and the logo of client
Comunilife filtered through the
paintings of Paul Klee) to the
art gallery and studio spaces
for local artists and residents
on the main floor. The entry
facade is elevated on columns
to allow light and views to pass
through to the gallery spaces
and two courtyards beyond.
Built-in sunshades and deeply
recessed windows shield the
interior. The courtyards provide outdoor spaces for gathering and enhancing the sense
of community. Services in the
facility include the program
Life Is Precious, which helps
prevent at-risk young women
from committing suicide.

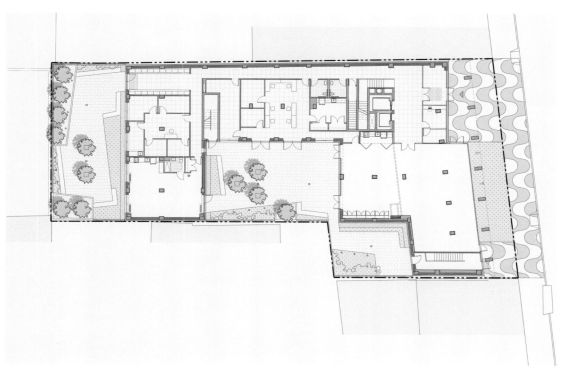

Previous pages
Gridded concrete facade with colorful painted-steel panels.

Opposite, from top
Entrance with concrete sidewalk pattern derived from the sidewalks of Rio de Janeiro. Art gallery and multipurpose space on the ground floor. One-bedroom apartment. Studio apartment with window looking to Franklin Avenue Armory. First floor plan.

This page, from top
Concrete facade with sunshades and painted-steel panels. Hallway with multicolored vinyl flooring. Colored tile pattern, derived from the flags of Latin American countries, on elevator core; mural painted by Aurelio del Muro and Marta Blair.

El Borinquen Residence

Assemble Chicago

Studio Gang

Location
Chicago, Illinois

Date
2021 (competition design)

Client
City of Chicago

Program
207 units

Building area
225,800 square feet

Project cost
Undisclosed

Funding sources
Undisclosed

The winning competition design for Assemble Chicago proposed a carbon-neutral residential community in downtown Chicago, designed to give rise to a more resilient, equitable, and vibrant city. Created for Chicago's C40 Reinventing Cities competition in 2020, the proposed design comprised apartments for downtown workers earning as little as minimum wage; dedicated space for community development and cultural programing on the first three floors; and an inviting public realm featuring a generous tribune stair overlooking a revitalized Pritzker Park. Employing a modern interpretation of the classic Chicago window, the design included an articulated brick facade and operable side windows providing natural light, fresh air, and a window garden to every apartment. Leveraging community partnerships and innovative building technologies, the design also proposed a large terrace on level three with a vegetable garden and species native to Chicago to promote urban biodiversity.

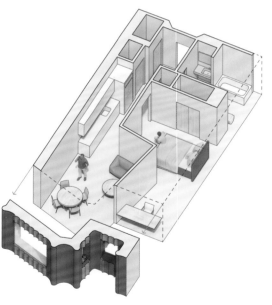

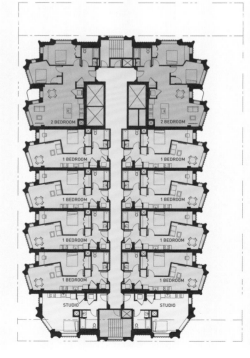

Previous pages
Rendering of east
facade with Harold
Washington
Library Center.

**Opposite,
from top**
Rendering of
east facade from
Pritzker Park.
Interior axono-
metric of a typical
apartment.
Typical residential
floor plan.

**This page,
from top**
First floor plan.
Second floor plan.

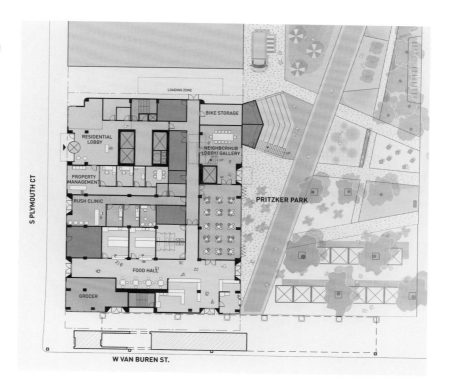

Rev. Walker's Home

Rural Studio

Location
Newbern, Alabama

Date
2020–2021

Client
Reginald Walker

Program
One-bedroom, one-bathroom residence

Building area
498 square feet (enclosures combined); 1,700 square feet (total slab foundation footprint)

Project cost
Undisclosed

Funding sources
University support, foundations, competitions, grants, research contracts, in kind, speaking fees

Students
Addie Harchelroad, Becca Wiggs, George Slaughter, Paul Fallin

Faculty
Andrew Freear, Steve Long

Rev. Walker's Home is one of the more than 200 houses built by Rural Studio in Hale County, Alabama. A large roof overhangs a concrete slab, providing shelter for a conditioned enclosure, which occupies only part of the space. The covered space celebrates outdoor living; it also reduced weather delays during construction. The conditioned enclosure—intended for one or two occupants—can adapt to changing lifestyle and household needs. The design allows for expansion so that future additions will not undermine the original home. The design encourages the client to make a place that is distinctly his own.

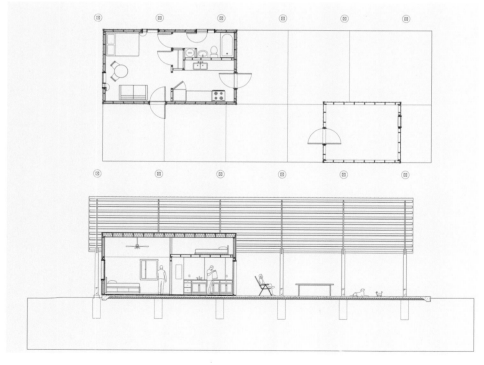

Previous pages
View from north.

**Opposite,
from top**
Patio. Plan and
section.

**This page,
from top**
Interior view. Site
plan with floor plan.

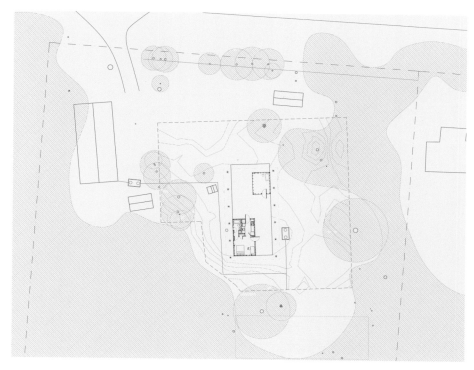

The Aya

Studio Twenty Seven Architecture + Leo A. Daly

Location
Washington, DC

Date
2016–2020

Client
District of Columbia Department of Human Services

Program
50 units for emergency family housing

Building area
53,005 square feet

Project cost
$24.8 million (total)

Funding sources
District of Columbia Capital Budget

In order to satisfy the requirements of its "right to shelter" law and other legislation, the District of Columbia sponsors development initiatives to provide affordable and emergency housing to all residents. The Aya supplies short-term housing to families in need of emergency shelter. Wraparound services for residents and a nonprofit clinic for residents and the neighborhood are included in the project. The design of the Aya responds to program needs, input from neighbors, and the site, which is situated on one of the wide diagonal avenues Pierre Charles L'Enfant developed in his 1791 plan for Washington. Each floor accommodates seven to ten housing units, community rooms, laundry facilities, private and family baths, and outdoor play areas. On the ground floor are a dining area, computer room, and administrative areas.

Previous pages
South facade.

**Opposite,
from top**
Reception
area. Corridor.
Community room
with view of the
US Capitol.
Family room.
Terrace play area.

**This page,
from top**
West facade.
Section showing
the theme color
for each floor.

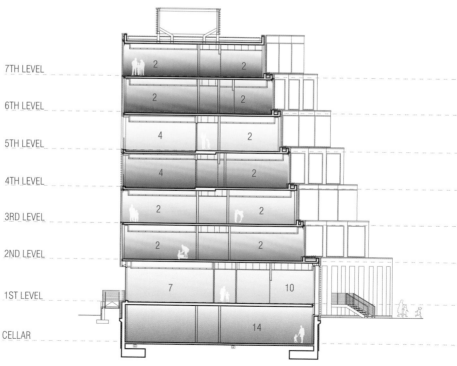

7TH LEVEL

6TH LEVEL

5TH LEVEL

4TH LEVEL

3RD LEVEL

2ND LEVEL

1ST LEVEL

CELLAR

Home Street Residences

Body Lawson Associates

Location
Bronx, New York

Date
2018–2020

Client
Home Street Partners

Program
63 units for low-income individuals, families, seniors, and formerly homeless seniors

Building area
75,000 square feet

Project cost
$35.9 million (construction)

Funding sources
Bank loan first mortgage, HPD City Capital second mortgage, HPD HOME third mortgage, fourth mortgage (accrued interest), deferred reserves, LIHTC, deferred developer's fee

Home Street Residences delivers a safe, state-of-the-art residence and senior facility for low-income individuals and families in a setting that enlivens a transitional area of the Bronx. The prominent site and importance of community support in this location drove many of the design decisions, including community amenities and minimized construction and operating costs. A long-standing church once occupied the corner lot. The building integrates elements from the demolished church, includes multigenerational community uses, and offers large units with lasting finishes. The structure employs highly insulating, prefabricated six- to eight-inch steel studs; passive design principles reduce energy and operating costs.

Home Street Residences

Photographs: Erik Rank /erik@erikrank.com

Nehemiah Spring Creek

Alexander Gorlin Architects

Location
East New York, New York

Date
2002–2015

Client
Nehemiah Housing
Development Fund

Program
578 town houses for first-time
home buyers

Building area
44 acres

Project cost
$257 million (total)

Funding sources
Community Preservation
Corporation loan, Lutheran
Church–Missouri Synod
loan, St. Paul Community
Baptist Church of Brooklyn
loan, NYC HPD, LIHTC

Built on the site of a former
landfill, Nehemiah Spring
Creek is part of an initiative that
creates housing for first-time
home buyers. Modern inter-
pretations of the 19th-century
Brooklyn brownstone, the town
houses maintain the street wall
and feature a front stoop. But
the similarities to traditional
brownstones end there. Twelve
different facade types in twelve
different colors introduce indi-
viduality to the area and create
a modulating rhythm on the
street. Modular construction
gave rise to reduced construction costs and time, greater
quality control, and waste
reduction (through panelizing
the exterior wall cladding).
"Boxes" for floors, ceilings, and
walls were constructed in the
Brooklyn Navy Yard by Capsys
Corporation, then trucked to
the site and lifted onto the
foundation by crane.

Previous pages
Multicolored street facades in a new urban setting.

This page, from top
Crane lifting modular unit into place. Master plan showing shopping center to the south.

Opposite, from top
First, second, and third floor plans. Block plan with row houses defining the street and interior courtyard with rear alley parking.

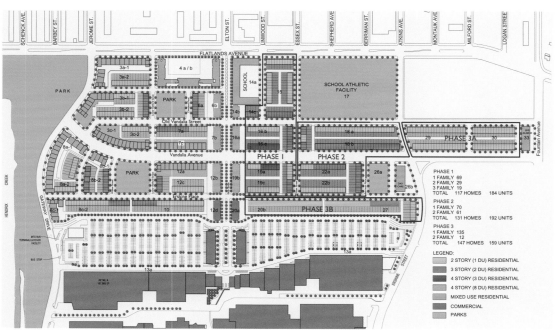

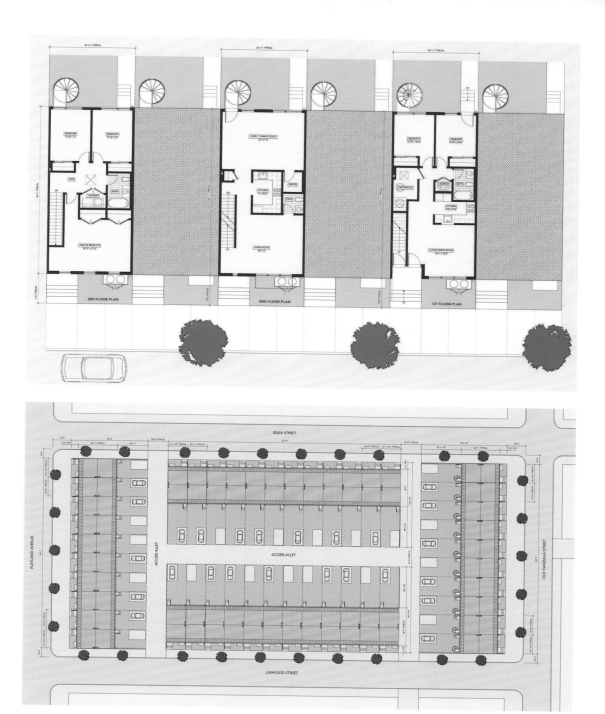

Nehemiah Spring Creek

Opposite
Jane Jacobs's
"eyes on the street"
concept fostering
a safe urban
neighborhood.

**This page,
from top**
Town house
facades with differ-
ent colors and bay
windows. Modern
interpretation of
traditional brown-
stone stoops and
bay windows.

1490 Southern Boulevard

Bernheimer Architecture

Location
Bronx, New York

Date
2017–2021

Client
Type A Projects

Program
114 units for seniors

Building area
75,000 square feet

Project cost
$59.1 million (construction)

Funding sources
Tax-exempt bonds, LIHTC, NYC HPD Senior Affordable Rental Apartment Subsidy, NYC HDC Extremely Low and Low-Income Affordable Subsidy, NYC Council and Bronx Borough President Resolution A Funds

1490 Southern Boulevard provides dignified, affordable housing for the elderly population of New York City and the South Bronx. At street level, materials are colorful and bright. Yellow-painted metal cladding gives way to large glass openings that offer views into the first-floor spaces. Above street level, dark-enameled brick cladding has a reflective character that provides an ever-changing play of light. Recessed accent panels of glazed yellow brick contrast with the dark brick. Thirty-two of the studio and one-bedroom units in the building have been reserved for individuals who were previously precariously housed, and on the ground floor is community space for the Jewish Association Serving the Aging.

1490 Southern Boulevard

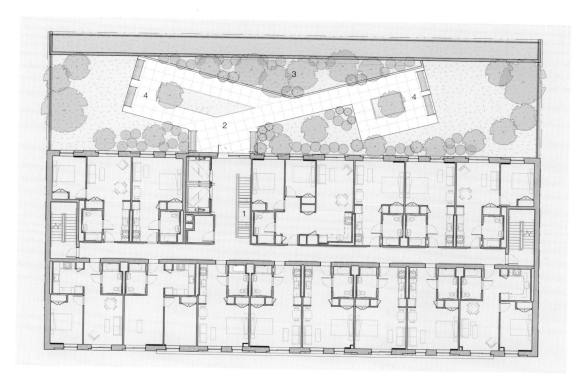

Previous pages
Glazed gray and black brick and metal panels differentiating pieces of the building.

Opposite, from top
Southern Boulevard facade. Color-coded social welfare nook. Communal gathering space off the main lobby. Canopy structure and seating at primary setback. Furnished apartment for a formerly housing-challenged occupant.

This page, from top
Plan. Section.

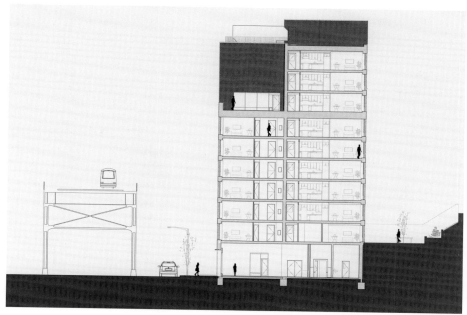

Mueller Row Homes

**Michael Hsu Office
of Architecture**

Location
Austin, Texas

Date
2018–2021

Client
Austin Habitat for Humanity

Program
11 units

Building area
15,110 square feet

Project cost
$2.4 million (total)

Funding sources
Austin Housing Finance
Corporation General Obligation
Bond forgivable loan, private
banking institution grants,
Austin Community Foundation
line of credit

Mueller Row Homes provides
affordable family residences
in a mixed-use neighborhood
in central Austin. The block
offers the density of a condominium grouping without the
condo model. Each of the
attached, single-family
residences has an individual
identity; the overall design narrative fits easily into the district.
Three facades repeat across
the units: one is brown brick
laid in vertical and horizontal
courses; another is white
fiber-cement soffit panels; and
the third is gray board-and-
batten fiber-cement panels.
Inset walls at each front porch
are laid with colorful tiles
selected by the homeowners.
Additional design elements
include decorative steel
awnings, window surrounds,
and address plates that play
directly with light and shadow.

Previous pages
Pieces in a whole.

**Opposite,
from top**
Building elements—custom tiles and steel members—repurposed from other Austin projects. First-floor interior with ten-foot ceiling. Second-floor interior with large window and skylight.

**This page,
from top**
Tiled feature wall. Decorative steel design components. Site plan.

Portfolio

Artisan Court

Christine Pierron and Mark Weinke

Location
Santa Barbara, California

Date
2008–2011

Client
Housing Authority of the City of Santa Barbara

Program
55 units for teens aging out of foster care, special-needs individuals including those formerly experiencing home-lessness, and low-income downtown workers

Building area
42,678 square feet

Project cost
$10.2 million (construction)

Funding sources
LIHTC, CTCAC, City of Santa Barbara deferred loan

Artisan Court provides housing and support services to three different groups. The name celebrates the residents by focusing on their backgrounds as skilled workers, or artisans. Modern-day artisans would include the barista making that perfect cup of coffee or the gardener creating that beautiful landscape. Artisan Court also refers to the inhabitants' own lives and the art that they bring into the facility, whether by painting, music, good deeds, or a life well lived. The unique design style has been dubbed "Eco-Span-Deco." This name evolved from a emphasis on ecological building practices (eco) and a synthesis of Spanish Colonial (span) and Art Deco (deco).

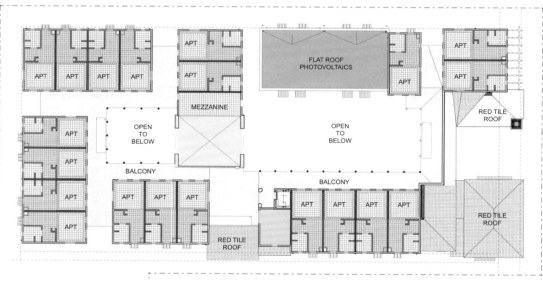

Previous pages
Entry court with tower and zigzag design elements.

Opposite, from top
View through main courtyard toward community room. Third floor plan with open-air courtyards.

This page, from top
Site plan. Studio apartments clustered around a courtyard.

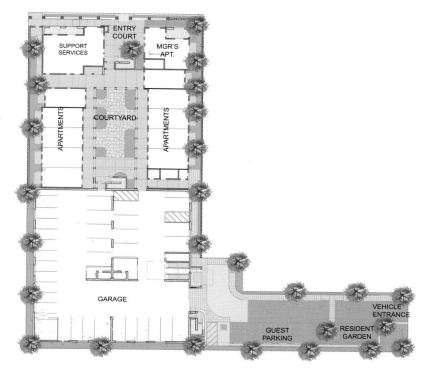

The Jennings

Alexander Gorlin Architects

Location
Bronx, New York

Date
2015–2019

Client
New Destiny Housing

Program
42 units

Building area
54,000 square feet

Project cost
$26 million (construction)

Funding sources
Bank loan, HPD second mortgage, HHAP, NYSERDA, LIHTC, deferred developer's fee, deferred reserves

At the head of Charlotte Street in the South Bronx, where President Jimmy Carter stood in 1979 on a visit to the "devastated, abandoned neighborhood," now stands the Jennings, a development providing secure housing for women who are survivors of domestic violence and the formerly homeless. The building is divided into two blocks—a tower with a facade of textured brick symbolizing a protective shield and a connection between the facility and its surroundings. Pastel colors derived from Andy Warhol's *Flower* prints enliven the perforated screens in front of the air conditioning and heating units. Occupying two floors are services and amenities, including social support services; play areas; multipurpose room; and computer, laundry, and bicycle rooms. Active design elements, such as the open lobby stair, encourage residents to walk when possible, and a walk-out garden is located at the rear of the building.

The Jennings

Previous pages
Facade with textured brick and pastel metal panels.

This page, from top
Site plan. Open stair in entry lobby.

Opposite, from top
View along Charlotte Street to the Jennings.

The Jennings

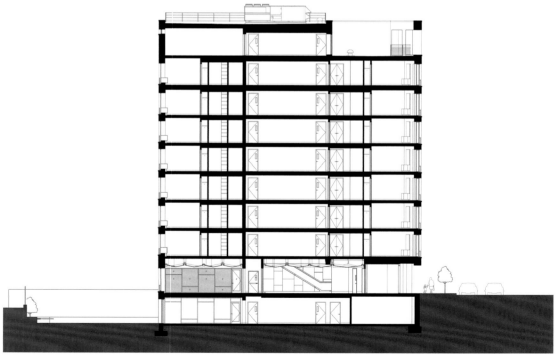

**Opposite,
from top**
Living room with a
view of the Bronx.
Section.

**This page,
from top**
Seventh floor
plan showing
one-, two-, and
three-bedroom
apartments. Floor-
to-ceiling windows
in bedroom.

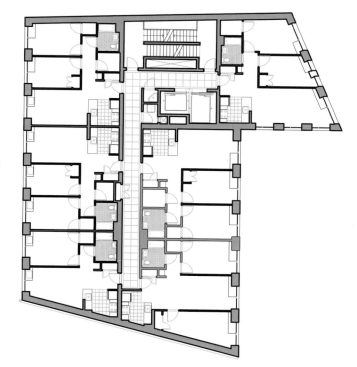

The Jennings

Edwin M. Lee Apartments

Leddy Maytum Stacy Architects

Location
San Francisco, California

Date
2015–2020

Client
Chinatown Community Development Center, Swords to Plowshares

Program
119 units for families and formerly homeless veterans

Building area
123,701 square feet

Project cost
$59.6 million (total)

Funding sources
Wells Fargo Bank, Federal Home Loan Bank AHP, California Community and Reinvestment Corporation, California Department of Housing and Community Development–Veterans Housing and Homelessness Prevention Program, CDLAC, CTCAC

Edwin M. Lee Apartments balances a civic scale and a feeling of home, responding to the wide and busy Third Street corridor with a colorful serrated rainscreen facade and providing an oasislike restorative landscape within. A dramatic solar canopy utilizes low-carbon design. Family apartments are available to families earning between 50 and 60 percent of AMI. Counseling and career services are available to veteran residents. One of the two nonprofit clients, Swords to Plowshares, operates a kitchen that offers free meals in the community room at the center of the building, adjacent to the courtyard garden.

Photography: Bruce Damonte

Previous pages
Third Street facade with communal activity spaces, a three-dimensional cyanometer graphic ribbon at upper floors, and a continuous rooftop solar canopy.

This page, from top
Garden breezeway between the veteran and family wings, the community room, and the garden court. Community room.

Opposite, from top
Solar canopy cascading from the roof to the entry lobby. Site plan showing native plantings.

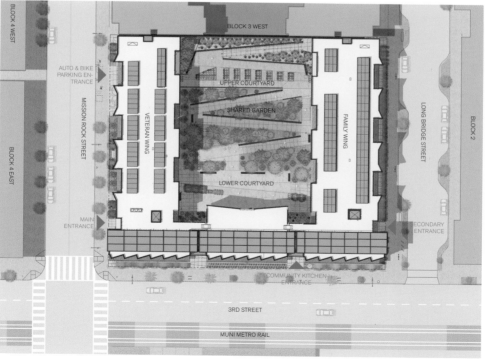

Sister Lillian Murphy Community

**Paulett Taggart Architects
with Studio Vara**

Location
San Francisco, California

Date
2017–2021

Client
Mercy Housing of California

Program
152 units for families

Building area
185,150 square feet

Project cost
$97 million (construction)

Funding sources
San Francisco Mayor's Office of Housing and Community Development, CDLAC, Affordable Housing Program, HUD Section 8, Affordable Housing and Sustainable Communities Program, San Francisco Office of Community Investment and Infrastructure

This new development fosters community, encourages a healthy lifestyle, creates a sense of place, and facilitates connections between neighbors. The design takes the typology of the perimeter block and breaks it into four articulated wings around a central courtyard; the wings are connected by outdoor circulation and multilevel landscapes. Open-air bridges allow residents a visual connection to the surrounding neighborhood. Outdoor spaces offer seating and lush landscaping. The community room spills out into the ground-floor courtyard, extending its program space. Other amenities are a teen room, offices for management and resident services, and tenant space for a childcare center and music school.

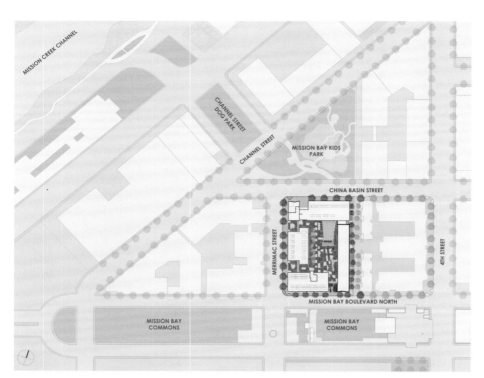

Previous pages
Articulated facade looking to Mission Bay Commons park.

This page, from top
Site plan. First floor plan. Second floor plan.

Opposite, from top
View into community room. Entry.

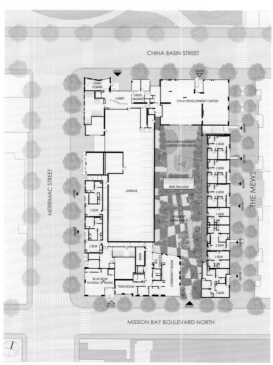

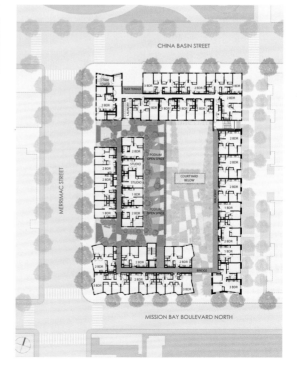

Sister Lillian Murphy Community

**Opposite,
from top**
Open-air bridges
to connect
building wings,
admit sunlight
to the courtyard,
and furnish visual
connections to
the neighborhood.
Lobby with natural
light, warm mate-
rials, and human-
scaled details.
Central courtyard.
Courtyard on
second floor look-
ing over central
courtyard.

**This page,
from top**
Light-filled
stairwell.

Acknowledgments

In the two years of preparing this book, we talked with dozens of people who are involved with affordable housing.

Among the many we thank for their invaluable help are Eric Anderson, Carol Ross Barney, Richard Baron, Xavier Briggs, Angela Brooks, Adrienne Brown, Carlton Brown, Amanda Burden, Nancy Cantor, Jeff Davies, Annette L. DeLara, Ingrid Gould Ellen, Rosalie Genevro, Rosanne Haggerty, Molly Heintz, Richard Kahan, Jessica Katz, Jonathan Kirschenfeld, Ted Liebman, Marie Lopez, Donald Newhouse, James Polshek, Mario Procida, Jonathan Rose, Linda Samuels, Avery Seavey, Allison Silver, Suzanne Stephens, Joseph Stiglitz, Darren Walker, Adam Weinstein, Clifton Wharton, and Kathy Wylde.

Alex is grateful to Richard Roberts for helping show the path to building affordable housing; Dr. Rosa Gil for her inspiration; and Mike Gecan for his guidance, generosity, and wisdom. He also thanks Joan Beck, David Beer, Sharon Browne, Carol Corden, Paola Duran, Josef Goodman, Kirk Goodrich, Richard Hayes, Olga Jobe, Nadine Maleh, Lucille McEwen, Joel Mounty, Michael O'Donnell, George Poulon, Brenda Rosen, David Rowe, Jeff Scheuer, Sharmi Sobhan, RuthAnne Visnauskas, David Walsh, and Elissa Winzelberg. Alex especially acknowledges Quncie Williams for his help in realizing the affordable housing of Alexander Gorlin Architects, Vincent Linarello for his work on Nehemiah homes, and Justine Buchanan for her valiant efforts in promoting affordable housing.

We recognize Chris Barker, Théadora Williams, and Parker Limón, who played essential roles in obtaining the essays for this book and in organizing different aspects of this complex project. Andrea Monfried's brilliant text editing perfected our writers' expression. Douglas Curran guided us through the labyrinthine process of book preparation and production. Michael Bierut and Laitsz Ho of Pentagram expertly captured our concept for this book: a practical guide to addressing the current housing crisis. Donald Newhouse has provided invaluable help in promoting the book, as has Ken Frydman of Source Communications. We appreciate Charles Miers's unfailing support of our vision. — **AG and VN**

Editors

Alexander Gorlin is principal of Alexander Gorlin Architects, based in New York. He is a leader in the design of affordable housing and has built more than 1,000 units in New York City. Gorlin is also a scholar and critic; has won the Rome Prize in Architecture from the American Academy in Rome; and has taught at Yale, Cooper Union, and the University of Miami. He is the author of five books including *Tomorrow's Houses: New England Modernism*, *Kabbalah in Art and Architecture*, *The New American Town House*, and *Creating the New American Town House*.

Architectural historian **Victoria Newhouse** has written extensively on the architecture of cultural facilities. Among her books are *Parks of the 21st Century: Reinvented Landscapes, Reclaimed Territories*; *Site and Sound: The Architecture and Acoustics of New Opera Houses and Concert Halls*; and *Towards a New Museum*.

First published in the United
States of America in 2024 by
**Rizzoli International
Publications, Inc.**
300 Park Avenue South
New York, NY 10010
www.rizzoliusa.com

FSC
www.fsc.org
MIX
Paper | Supporting
responsible forestry
FSC® C008047

Publisher Charles Miers
Acquiring Editor
Douglas Curran
Production Manager
Kaija Markoe
Managing Editor
Lynn Scrabis
Design Manager
Olivia Russin
Proofreader Richard Slovak

Editor Andrea Monfried

Design Michael Bierut and
Laitsz Ho, Pentagram

Printed and bound in China
2024 2025 2026 2027 2028 /
10 9 8 7 6 5 4 3 2 1

ISBN-13: 978-0-8478-7398-2
Library of Congress
Cataloging-in-Publication
Control Number: 2023945881

Visit us online
Facebook.com/
RizzoliNewYork
Twitter: @Rizzoli_Books
Instagram.com/RizzoliBooks
Pinterest.com/RizzoliBooks
Youtube.com/user/RizzoliNY
Issuu.com/Rizzoli

Image Credits
Numbers refer to page numbers.
2–3: Nehemiah Spring Creek, photo © Michael Moran; 18: New
Carver Apartments, photo by Iwan Baan; 58: El Borinquen
Residence, photo © Michael Moran; 94: Sister Lillian Murphy
Community, photo © Bruce Damonte; 130: Marcus Garvey Village,
photos courtesy Curtis + Ginsberg Architects; 131: Marcus Garvey
Village, photos courtesy GDSNY; 134: New Carver Apartments,
photo by Iwan Baan; 138: Modern House, images courtesy © DPZ
CoDesign. Photography for the portfolio projects (beginning on p.
154) is credited with each project. Back cover (top to bottom): Pico
Place (p. 174), photo by Tara Wujcik, courtesy Brooks + Scarpa;
Rev. Walker's Home (p. 192), photo by Tim Hursley; Aya (p. 196),
photo by Anice Hoachlander.